WHAT LISA KNEW

ALSO BY JOYCE JOHNSON

Come and Join the Dance
Bad Connections
Minor Characters
In the Night Café

What Lisa Knew

The Truths and Lies of the Steinberg Case

JOYCE JOHNSON

G. P. PUTNAM'S SONS/New York

For Susan Brownmiller,
my friend throughout the Steinberg trial,
whose writings have done so much to help
women lead independent lives

Published by G. P. Putnam's Sons,
200 Madison Avenue, New York, NY 10016.
Published simultaneously in Canada

The text of this book is set in Gael.

Library of Congress Cataloging-in-Publication Data

Johnson, Joyce, date.
    What Lisa knew : the truth and lies of the Steinberg case / Joyce Johnson.
        p.   cm.
    ISBN 0-399-13474-3
    1. Steinberg, Joel.   2. Nussbaum, Hedda, 1942– .   3. Murderers—
New York (N.Y.)—Biography.   4. Steinberg, Lisa, 1981–1987.
5. Abused children—New York (N.Y.)—Biography.   I. Title.
HV6248.S6282J64   1990   89-48171 CIP
364.1′524′097471—dc20

Printed in the United States of America
1   2   3   4   5   6   7   8   9   10

This book has been printed on acid-free paper.

Hate is not the opposite of love, apathy is.
The opposite of will is not indecision—which
actually may represent the struggle of the
effort to decide, as in William James—but
being uninvolved, detached, unrelated to the
significant events. Then the issue of will
never can arise.

—ROLLO MAY
Love and Will, 1969

ACKNOWLEDGMENTS

I am deeply grateful to many people for their help and encouragement.

I would first of all like to thank Tina Brown and Wayne Lawson of *Vanity Fair* for bravely sending a novelist on the journalistic assignments that led to the writing of this book.

A large group of writers, reporters and observers converged on Centre Street in the fall and winter of 1988 to cover the Steinberg trial. Although views differed sharply, it became a true and remarkably warm community, freely sharing information and materials. No one could have been more generous to me than Maury Terry and Susan Brownmiller. I would also especially like to thank Timothy Clifford, Linda Gordon, Ken Gross, Elizabeth Hardwick, Jeanne King, Erika Munk, Mary Murphy, Mike Pearl, Jody Adams Weisbrot, Barbara Whitaker, and Marie Winn.

I feel indebted to the following people for agreeing to be interviewed at length and giving me so much of their time: Sherry Burger, Adrian DiLuzio, Ivan Fisher, Renee Gordon, Allen Jared, Romany Kramoris, Michelle Launders, Albert Krieger, Ira London, Sharon Rupert, Mel Sirkin, Shirley Unger and Marilyn Walton.

Judy Cochran's work with endangered children in Children's Rights Northeast has been an inspiration to me, and the knowledge she has shared in our many conversations has been invaluable. Seth Friedland of the LISA Organization to Stop Child Abuse has also helped me to understand how little protection children have under the existing laws.

A special thanks to Fred Schiafanda for lending me his videotapes of the Steinberg trial.

I am profoundly grateful to Robert F. Tannenbaum for his acute insights into some of the unique problems of writing this book. My literary agent, Berenice Hoffman, as always, unfailingly gave me emotional support and sound advice. I would also like to thank Phyllis Grann and Faith Sale of G. P. Putnam's Sons for their excellent editorial input; my original sponsoring editor, Christine Schillig; and my wonderfully patient copy editor, Margaret Wolf.

NOVEMBER 1987

THERE WAS an absence of light, although the electrical current was on in that one-bedroom brownstone apartment in Greenwich Village, where Hedda Nussbaum, a former writer and editor of children's books, had lived for twelve years with Joel Steinberg, a criminal lawyer. It was a place that would later be described by the police and the press as a cave. And a cave it was—dark, littered, reeking; bloodstains on the bedclothes, the walls. There was a pet brown-and-white rabbit; there were two tanks of tropical fish, ironically in excellent condition. The fish swam round and round, warm in their clean water, in the pale glow of their artificial universes. There was also a witness present, unimplicated in whatever had occurred the night before—a baby without language, sixteen months old. He was awake, lying quietly in his playpen on a mat that stank of urine, staring up at the ceiling. Police officer James Botte discovered him there when he walked around the living room to look for a table lamp—anything that worked. Boxes of old clothes were lying all about. There seemed to be a lot of dismantled electronic equipment.

There should have been light, a great deal of light. Every bulb in the apartment should have been burning. In a normal household, there would have been no need for Botte to grope around like that, looking for a lamp to turn on.

It was 6:45 A.M., Monday, November 2. On a normal Monday, six-year-old Elizabeth Steinberg would have been waking up soon on the living-room couch, getting herself ready, without much help from either of her parents, for her father to take her to school. Or maybe she wouldn't get to school because there was no one to take her. There were more and more mornings like that lately. In fact, nothing about Elizabeth Steinberg's life had ever really been normal.

On this particular Monday morning, Elizabeth Steinberg was lying naked on the floor, her head resting on the edge of the dirty living-room rug, her bare feet protruding into the little foyer. It was the only uncluttered area the paramedics had been able to find. They were working on her, trying to get her to breathe, looking for signs of life with their pocket flashlights.

The mother had called 911 around 6:32. She spoke to the operator rather slowly, without much inflection—sounding calm or numb, however you wanted to interpret it. She seemed quite collected as she gave the particulars of the family's address. When the operator said, "And what's going on there?" the woman got mixed up and said, "Um . . . my daughter doesn't seem to have stopped breathing."

"What is it?" the operator asked sharply.

"My daughter, she was congested and she's stopped breathing. She's six years old."

"Okay, she's having difficulty breathing."

"She's not breathing. We're giving her mouth-to-mouth."

The operator rang an EMS ambulance and recited the address. She told the mother she was sending it through right away. Did the child have asthma or heart problems? she asked the mother. "Does she have a high fever or anything?"

"Uh . . . no."

"Was she eating something? I'm just trying to find out why she would just stop breathing."

The woman hesitated. "Um—I think . . . well . . . I don't really know exactly why." She sounded like a schoolgirl, stumbling over a science question.

"You don't really know? Okay," the operator said.

"Food's coming up," the woman said helpfully. "She's throwing up a lot of food and water."

"Water?"

"And food, yeah."

The operator told her how to give mouth-to-mouth. To tilt the child's head back and pinch off her nose and turn her head to the side if she started vomiting and clean her mouth out. It was important to keep doing that until the ambulance arrived. Dutifully, the woman repeated each instruction aloud.

"Where are they now?" the woman asked.

"They should be there in two minutes."

"They'll be here in two minutes?" She repeated that, too, as if she couldn't believe they'd get there so quickly. She said her husband was doing the mouth-to-mouth.

"You hear me? The ambulance will be there in two minutes. Okay?"

"Yes," said the mother.

"Okay. Thanks."

The radio car from the Sixth Precinct, driven by Officer Botte, had arrived at 6:35, followed almost simultaneously by the ambulance from St. Vincent's. Botte and his partner, Vincent DaLuise, rushed into the small downstairs vestibule of 14 West Tenth Street. As Botte later remembered it, they had trouble getting into the building. Apartment 3W didn't answer. They had to ring a number of buzzers before anyone buzzed back. It could have been the Steinbergs, it could have been someone else. It was a delay of only a minute or two, but if there was a child dying up there, every second counted. When they reached the third floor, they knocked on both doors. A neighbor silently pointed to the apartment across the landing—the door with a large, ugly brass eagle on it. The Steinbergs' door shouldn't have been closed; someone should have been standing there to let them in right away. All this was taking another thirty to forty-five seconds. Then a woman opened the door—only a few inches at first. She didn't say a word.

Brian Gearity and John Filangeri, the paramedics from St. Vincent's, heard someone call out, "I've found the apartment!" and ran up the stairs. Gearity, too, remembers the strange slowness with which the door to 3W seemed to open. "All I could see was a face . . . I couldn't tell how old she was. She looked like an old person in a young body. She looked like the lion in the 'Beauty and the Beast' television show." Gearity asked her, "Did you call for an ambulance?" The woman's Yes was preceded by silence and was barely audible. "It ran through my mind, when you have a six-year-old in cardiac arrest, it's Let's *go!*" Gearity recalled in 1988.

"I ran to answer the door," Hedda Nussbaum would say a year later when she was testifying against Joel Steinberg. "I opened the door and let the men in."

The four of them—Botte, DaLuise, Filangeri, and Gearity—crowded into the small dark foyer. They would never forget what they saw next. From a room in the rear, a man emerged, tall, bespectacled, wild-haired, his arms stretched out in front of him.

He was walking a naked child toward them, walking her backward, holding her up under the armpits like a life-size puppet. Gearity and Filangeri took her from him and carefully stretched her out on the floor. The child was limp, blue, unmoving. Through his stethoscope, Brian Gearity heard diminished breath sounds on her left side that seemed to indicate an obstruction.

Steinberg was hovering over her, but the strange-looking woman had vanished. According to Nussbaum, Steinberg had ordered her to get back into the bedroom. She hid behind the bedroom door, peeping out into the hall.

Gearity and Filangeri were finding it very hard to see the patient; there was only a little bit of illumination that came in from the outside landing; there seemed to be no way of getting more. Wires were dangling out of a switch near the buzzer. The two paramedics were frantically working on the kid and asking Steinberg what had happened.

The man was a rapid talker—rambling sentences poured out of him. Filangeri kept thinking he didn't sound concerned enough—not when you compared him to other parents. Apparently his daughter had just eaten something that had caused her to vomit and then lose consciousness. But why was the child eating at 6 A.M.? Filangeri asked Steinberg. No, no, it was the night before; she had been throwing up since 8 P.M. and had choked on her vomit about an hour ago and her breathing had stopped. He and his wife hadn't called 911 right away because they thought Lisa would be all right. They had taken her into their bed with them. The child had eaten Chinese vegetables, since the family was vegetarian. The vegetables were fresh, freshly cooked.

Finally Filangeri had to interrupt. Wasn't there any way to get some light? In response, Steinberg asked him an absurdist's question: Was it important?

Filangeri used the resuscitator on the child. Then he tried the Heimlich maneuver. She did bring up a small amount of undigested food.

In the midst of all this, someone came up with a portable fluorescent trouble light. Filangeri had no idea who had provided it; he just saw it when Botte had it in his hand. It was then he noticed the bruises on the child's thin chest, the reddish marks just below her nipples. He asked Steinberg if the child had been beaten. Steinberg said he'd been pounding on his daughter's chest in order to revive her. "I know CPR."

Later, during the trial, one of Steinberg's lawyers said it was Steinberg himself who had produced the fluorescent light, yanked it out of the hall closet, scratching his hand in the process. Botte remembered it as a table lamp he must have managed to find. "Everything was being done very quickly," he said, "in an excited atmosphere." Gearity couldn't remember any light at all.

THE PRIVACY of American families is sacrosanct. It has far more legal protection than the lives of children. With each hour, new infant citizens are born, and there's no way of knowing, of really determining, what fates they're born into. The birth is recorded, the mother and baby leave the hospital; the child drops out of public view, vanishes behind the locked door of the home. As Dr. Richard Krugman, a child-abuse expert, points out, the state doesn't officially hear of the majority of these children again until five or six years later, at the time they start school. Then it becomes possible to track them to a certain extent.

Birth, then, is like a lottery. Babies win, babies lose. In this country, we do not even question this awesome randomness. We accept it as the inescapable order of things. At the same time, we speak loudly about the value of human life, even the life of the fetus. There is far more activism in America on behalf of the unborn than there is on behalf of living children. They have relatively few lobbyists. On the night of January 30, 1989, after the jury delivered its verdict, finding Joel Steinberg guilty of first degree manslaughter in the death of Elizabeth Steinberg, Juror Helen Barthell came to the microphone during the press conference and said she had a special message for Michelle Launders, Lisa Steinberg's natural mother: "Michelle, you did the right thing having that baby. You decided against abortion. That was the right decision." This juror just wanted to make very sure people were reminded that even for the Elizabeth Steinbergs, adoption was preferable to abortion.

In this case, adoption had failed, disastrously and tragically. In fact, neither Elizabeth Steinberg nor her baby brother, Mitchell, had ever been adopted legally. They were big losers in the lottery, born into limbo and mortal peril. It would be more accurate to call them stolen children than adoptees.

The man who had taken them had a profound understanding of the loopholes in the law, an expert's knowledge of how easy it was for children to fall through the cracks in the system, how little their rights counted, compared to his own as an adult. Both Steinberg and Nussbaum apparently understood that their particular chosen life-style made them totally ineligible for a legal adoption. Like many, though, they viewed children as an entitlement; if they were biologically unable to produce their own, they'd just have to get them some other way.

Lisa Steinberg had lived with Joel and Hedda since she was seven days old. Her identity and existence were dependent upon their exercise of will. They told her that she had been "chosen." Children themselves have no such choices.

At the age of six, Lisa Steinberg weighed forty-three pounds. She was a little thinner than most other first-graders. She had big hazel eyes and red hair. If she had ever grown up, people would have called her an Irish beauty. The fine shoulder-length hair hadn't been shampooed for a long time, it was terribly tangled and matted. It hid a large red bruise on the right temple that would be discovered in the emergency room at the hospital, along with two other large fresh bruises on her jaw and the back of her head.

Filangeri had noticed a very ominous sign right after the stretcher was carried into St. Vincent's. Gearity saw it, too: The child's pupils were not equal; the right was larger than the left, an indication of a problem with the brain. The two men looked at each other, and Filangeri shook his head and said in a low voice, "It just happened now."

When the blanket was lifted off the child under the white lights of the pediatric emergency room, the cops and the medics saw all the other bruises. Elizabeth Steinberg's small body was a map of pain. The marks were different colors, different vintages. Red, purple, yellowish-brown. It seemed as if she had been hit just about everywhere—on her arms and the calves of her legs, on her chest, her buttocks. One of the biggest bruises was in the center of her lower back—not a place where a child would be likely to injure herself. There were fresh scratches on her elbows, as if someone had grabbed her there. Her parents had just let her go dirty—her feet and ankles had a crust of black grime. The hair and the feet shocked everyone almost as much as the bruises.

Botte went out to the waiting area to talk to Steinberg, who had accompanied Elizabeth to the hospital. He found him smoking, pacing up and down. But somehow the man didn't seem frantic enough.

"How's my daughter?" Steinberg asked Botte, following this brief inquiry with, "I'm a lawyer. I represent Tommy Morrow and George Mourlot." Botte recognized one of the names, a detective at the Sixth Precinct. Steinberg reached into his jacket for his wallet and pulled out a card to further establish his upper-middle-class credentials. Botte may have looked to him like the kind of young guy he could easily impress. Even after four and a half years as a police officer, Botte still had the slightly diffident manner of a nice kid. He hadn't lost his rosy, cherubic face.

But Botte wasn't so impressed. He had become extremely interested in Steinberg's right hand. There were two small red cuts on the knuckles. When Botte asked Steinberg how he had cut himself, Steinberg said, "I didn't know I had this," and started nervously rubbing his hands together.

In the pediatric emergency room, the little girl with the red hair slept on, unable to move, unable to wake up, unable to tell anyone who had beaten her.

Botte left Steinberg and went back to the apartment with Vincent DaLuise to pick up a sample of the food the child was said to have choked on. The woman didn't want to let them in right away. She called out to them to wait—she had to put something on. When she opened the door, she had a bandanna tied around her curly gray hair. Botte had never seen a woman who looked as bad as she did. Hedda Nussbaum resembled a pugilist who had just lost the last of a long series of fights. Two black eyes, a split lip, a nose that no longer had a bridge. "She spoke very slow," Botte remembered in court. "She was kind of withdrawn, very slow responding." When they told her what they'd come for, she limped away from them toward the kitchen, hunched over like an old person. She wasn't crying. Botte had evidently had the sentimental expectation that she would be crying over the little girl. It was like Steinberg all over again: the emotions didn't match up with the situation.

Hedda Nussbaum took a plastic container out of the refrigerator and handed it to Botte. There were soggy vegetables inside. They're rotten, Botte thought to himself. The woman asked DaLuise a weird thing. "Do you have to take all the vegetables?"

Botte went to check out the baby he had seen earlier in the living room. The baby was still in his old, broken-down playpen.

In fact, he was tethered to it by a rope that went around his waist. The baby, the mat he was sitting on, the dirty sweatshirt he was wearing, had an awful stench of urine. Even the milk in the bottle the baby was clutching looked curdled to Botte, though he didn't think to take the bottle away to have the contents tested. Maybe there was nothing really the matter with either the vegetables or the milk, it was just that Botte was reacting viscerally and everything he saw seemed rotten, wrong. Nothing about the way these people lived or acted was the way things were supposed to be. He heard the woman say something to the effect that she was just about to change the baby. He wanted to remove him from her and from the premises, but procedurally, all he could do for the moment was fill out a report on suspected abuse and neglect.

He and DaLuise drove back to St. Vincent's with the food sample, then went to the Sixth Precinct, where they notified Special Services for Children and the Sex Crimes Unit. They were both feeling shaken, "a little confused." By the time they returned to St. Vincent's, Steinberg was gone from the waiting room; no one had stopped him. He had just decided to go home.

Before the morning of November 2, 1987, it is probable that if you happened to observe Joel Steinberg as he passed you on the street, you would have accepted him as the man he purported to be. A lawyer, therefore a relatively solid citizen—though he wore his black hair too long for the 1980s and his expensive suit may have needed pressing and his dark eyes may have glittered a bit too restlessly behind the thick lenses of his glasses and his loud nasal voice, carried back to you in a fragment of conversation, may have jarred you for a moment. But in a city like New York, you would not have looked at such a man too long, or reflected much upon his strangeness. Encountering him around Greenwich Village, you might have thought "Villagey" or quickly assessed Steinberg as someone who derived his style from the wilder days of the 1970s.

At St. Vincent's, though, the long hair became suspect, the black mustache criminal, the eyes guilty. According to Nancy Dodenhoff, a nurse on duty in the emergency room when Lisa was brought in, the eyes of Steinberg were "glazed. His visual field kept darting back and forth." She observed that he was nervous. "He was wringing his hands. It was not concern for the child." Officer Botte would later testify that Steinberg "looked messy—like a person who had been out all night." Also, his hair was uncombed. "I say they were dirty clothes," Botte said in an accusatory voice. "They weren't well kept." Steinberg's poor grooming would be one more thing to count against him. Yet, in a normal household where a small child had been ill through the night—say, with food poisoning—no one would have thought there was anything suspect about finding a parent with a disheveled appearance.

In less than two hours, however, an image of Joel Steinberg formed in the minds of all those who had dealings with him, even before the battered condition of Hedda Nussbaum was discovered. Shortly this image would be summed up in a word that will probably adhere to Steinberg for the rest of his days. *Monster.* Steinberg had taken on the lurid colors of a dying child's bruises. These bruises that everyone else could very plainly see were bypassed in all of Steinberg's stories about what had happened to his daughter. Even though he was a lawyer, he seemed unaware of his desperate need for a more convincing alibi.

Brian Gearity listened in when a police officer questioned Steinberg in the waiting room. The time frame had been adjusted. Now Steinberg was saying his daughter had trouble breathing only fifteen minutes before the ambulance was summoned, though the vomiting had gone on all through the preceding night. When Gearity heard him say it was his wife who had stayed with the child, he interpolated a question of his own: "Were *you* there?" There was a pause, and a correction was made: "My wife and I took turns with her during the night."

When Steinberg was ushered into the pediatric emergency room, others joined in on the interrogation as Mary Joan Marron, a pediatric specialist, and Patrick Kilhenny, a medical resident, examined Lisa and performed neurological tests. Over half a dozen people fired questions at Steinberg, trying to get as much information as they could. Nurse Dodenhoff called out his answers to the physicians.

Kilhenny had been the first to notice the reddish, right frontal bruise at the hairline. When he examined the child's eyes, the lack of pupillary response indicated there might be brain damage. He found blood in the back of the eyes, gross damage to the retinas. When water was injected into the child's ears, there was no reaction. There was no response to verbal stimuli or to pressure on her sternum. Everything indicated a deep level of coma.

After performing the tests, Kilhenny asked Steinberg whether Lisa had sustained a head injury. Had she fallen or tripped or been in a car accident? Steinberg stuck to his story about the upset stomach, about the vomiting that had begun when Lisa woke up around midnight: "We took her out of bed and she vomited. Later I heard her vomiting in the next room. I let her alone because I thought she was okay."

A child who is vomiting is not okay, Kilhenny thought to himself.

When Steinberg demonstrated how he had performed the Heimlich maneuver on Lisa around 6 A.M., Kilhenny asked him coldly whether that was how she had sustained so many bruises.

"What do you feel about this prognosis?" Steinberg demanded of Kilhenny.

The young doctor's first response was measured, professionally tactful, although he was not trying to spare Steinberg's feelings. Elizabeth would have what he called "neurological deficits."

Steinberg pressed harder. "Will she survive?"

Kilhenny's next answer was much blunter. "Yes, but with permanent damage. The damage will be severe."

"Well, what you're saying is that she's not going to be an Olympic athlete, but she will survive." There seemed to be a smile on the man's face. When Kilhenny testified a year later, he was very sure he had seen that bizarre smile, and he could remember his own "facial expression of disbelief."

Dodenhoff, who had heard Steinberg's remark, had become enraged. She walked up to him and said, brutally, "Your daughter's brain-dead," even though no doctor had yet voiced that opinion. To which he responded, "Is there anything else wrong with her?"

Right in front of him, Dodenhoff made a call to Special Services for Children on the emergency-room telephone, reporting a case of child abuse. She made sure she spoke loud enough for Steinberg to hear every word.

It was shortly after this that Steinberg said he had to be going. A CAT scan was going to be done on Elizabeth, but he evidently didn't want to wait around for the results. He went over to his daughter's bedside for a few moments. Dodenhoff saw him stoop down and kiss her on the forehead, then glance around the room as if to make sure people had observed this fatherly gesture. The kiss was very quick, so quick that Kilhenny didn't remember it. In Dodenhoff's mind, it didn't have a thing to do with affection.

It was four blocks from the hospital to the Steinberg apartment. Around 8:30 A.M., David Stiffler, an acquaintance of Steinberg's, was sitting on his stoop on Tenth Street drinking coffee. At this hour, he had often seen Steinberg walking his daughter to P.S. 41. This morning Steinberg was alone, going past him in the wrong direction, carrying what seemed to be an article of Lisa's clothing. Usually Steinberg would call out, "Hey, hey, Dave!" But today he didn't even turn his head. "I didn't observe him crying," Stiffler later told the court.

THERE ARE still a few parts of Greenwich Village that Henry James might recognize. Tenth Street, just west of Fifth Avenue, is one of them. It's a block of gracefully proportioned three- and four-story townhouses, built for the large families well-to-do New Yorkers used to have. The tall front windows one flight up are where parlors used to be; the children's nurseries were upstairs. Families are much smaller now, and the houses have long since been divided into apartments, many of them large enough only for a couple or a single person. But Tenth Street is still lined with trees; ivy and wisteria cling to brick and brownstone walls; and you can even see the old brass door knockers or some of the original cast-iron railings. If you're taking a stroll in the Village, it's a block you might deliberately seek out, especially after Eighth Street with its seedy shoe stores and fast-food joints, or the Avenue of the Americas with its unending streams of taxis and buses. On Tenth Street, everything becomes quieter; change no longer assaults you.

It's a street that has its landmarks. The house where Lisa Steinberg was dealt her fatal blows has become one of them for the time being. As they pass number 14, people tend to pause for a moment with an air of embarrassment, as if there's something unseemly about their curiosity. "Isn't this the house where—?" Guiltily they glance up at the third-story windows. "Does anybody live there now?" In past summers when those windows were wide open, people would sometimes hear very loud voices coming from the Steinberg apartment; shadows would move behind the dirty blinds. At the height of his fame, Mark Twain lived at this very address. The bronze plaque on the building was once a source of considerable pride for Hedda Nussbaum—a sign that she had moved up in the world as well as an auspicious omen for her own aspirations as a writer of juvenile books and perhaps even more ambitious works.

Ironically, Mark Twain's most successful book was a novel for children about a victim of child abuse. In *The Adventures of Huckleberry Finn,* fourteen-year-old Huck is extraordinarily resilient and resourceful. Neglected, exploited, held captive and beaten black and blue by Pap, his alcoholic reprobate of a father, Huck knows that his only safety in the world is to be responsible for his own fate and to live with the freedom of a grown man. He has been through so much that it is too late for him to become the ward of even a well-intentioned adult. In a fit of paranoia brought on by the delirium tremens, Huck's father sees his son as the Angel of Death and chases him with a clasp knife. Huck can only run away and find community with another escaped slave, the Nigger Jim. As for Pap, Twain holds out no hope of redemption or rehabilitation. There is only one thing Pap can do for his son, and that is to die. When Jim announces with all due solemnity, "He ain't a-comin back no mo', Huck," the boy receives the news with no emotion except curiosity about the circumstances of Pap's demise and profound relief. The relationship between Pap and Huck is insoluble. In fiction, Twain was allowed to kill the abusive parent. In life, few children escape as unscathed as Huck. A six-year-old has no hope of escape—cannot even conceive of such a possibility.

Even the statutes of penal law offer the Huck Finns and the Lisa Steinbergs little protection. On the books, the abuse and neglect of a child are only misdemeanors.

Two women who lived in the Steinbergs' building had a long-standing pact. They would keep an eye out for Lisa Steinberg. This did not mean they would get involved with the child. But if they saw a "hair out of place," as one of them put it, they would certainly *do* something. For years, they didn't really see a hair out of place, nothing you could put your finger on. But who can keep watch all the time? Most people lack the dedication of the amateur detectives in *Rear Window.* These two women happened to have demanding careers—one was a playwright, the other a television producer. They had odd schedules that did not necessarily coincide with the comings and goings of a small girl. The playwright lived right across the hall from 3W. Occasionally she'd ride down in the building's tiny elevator with Lisa. "Hi, Karen," the child would say, a little too chirpily, a little too *on.* There was something hyper about her whole performance, Karen Snyder thought. Almost invariably, the child would be accompanied by Steinberg. One day around Easter 1987, Lisa was very excited because she'd just been given a brown-and-white rabbit. Steinberg told Karen Snyder she had to come by and see it. She didn't take him up on that invitation, and no doubt Steinberg didn't imagine for one minute that she would. Everyone in the building knew he was a violent man. People were really afraid of him. They thought Joel Steinberg had underworld connections.

Karen Snyder always worried that Steinberg would figure out that she had been the source of the anonymous calls that had been made over the years to the police and the Bureau of Child Welfare. After all, she was a woman who lived alone. Perhaps he knew and was playing a little game with her of not mentioning it, and that was precisely why he had amused himself by daring her to come and see Lisa's rabbit.

The playwright shared a bedroom wall with Joel Steinberg and Hedda Nussbaum. At times this wall would transmit strange reverberations, a little like shock waves. Opera or folk music would be turned up deafeningly, then turned down to normal. If you'd ever seen Hedda Nussbaum, it was all too easy to imagine the scenes this music masked.

On the morning of November 2, Karen Snyder had opened her door just as the paramedics were carrying Lisa into the elevator. She caught a glimpse of something terrible and pitiful: the small, limp arm that dangled from the stretcher. "I saw her, I saw Lisa," she told me when I interviewed her a few weeks after Lisa's death. "I always thought it would be Hedda who'd be carried out of there."

When Hedda Nussbaum was on the witness stand in 1988 she had little to say about the morning she had waited for Steinberg to return from the hospital, or about how the two of them spent their final hours together. There are some who think they were busy destroying papers or getting rid of stashes of cocaine and other drugs. On the other hand, a strange peace may have descended upon them. They may really have managed to convince themselves that they were in no danger of arrest, that the story about Lisa's upset stomach would be believed. There was no blood, no weapon, no fingerprints. Only the two of them knew what had actually happened. Or maybe only one of them did. Joel or Hedda? Take your pick. Even after Steinberg's conviction, a shadow of doubt still hangs over the case.

I can imagine Steinberg insisting that morning that what happened to Lisa was no one's fault, just a terrible accident. "Listen, Hedda, we can beat this." And Nussbaum feeling boundless faith that Joel, the genius lawyer, could take on the cops, the legal system, the whole world. Or that if she had done anything wrong herself, Joel would think of a way to save her. Or maybe they didn't at that point believe Lisa would really die. After all, hadn't Dr. Kilhenny told Joel the child would just be a little brain damaged? That would be horrible, but maybe Lisa would recover. Certainly for Hedda, the most important consideration, the primary life-and-death thing, was her relationship with Joel. Above all, that had to go on and on. It would have been inconceivable to her that she could ever testify against him. Hadn't she always protected Joel? Even that morning by not going with him to the hospital because she didn't want anyone to see her bruises, she had protected him. She didn't even phone St. Vincent's herself. She heard about Lisa from Joel when he called to say her condition hadn't changed at all.

Naturally, she was extremely upset as she'd told that cop, Botte, when he had the nerve to accuse her of not changing Mitchell: "I knew he was wet earlier and I was so upset after they had taken Lisa out that for the first time *ever* I didn't change his diaper." But then Botte had left her alone, removing the container of vegetables that had absolutely nothing wrong with them, and Joel had come back to her and taken off his shoes and socks, and they both lay down on the bed, not having slept at all, and talked and talked until the telephone rang around 9:30 and some woman doctor asked if she were speaking to Lisa Steinberg's mother.

The caller was Dr. Marron, who needed some basic information: whether Lisa had been ill recently; whether she had allergies or had been exposed to poisons or toxins. Dr. Marron wanted to know all about Lisa's immunizations. Hedda said she was not currently familiar with them.

Dr. Marron also wondered whether Hedda knew about some bruises on Lisa's head. Hedda said Lisa had recently been hit on the head by a classmate, very, very hard. This was something that had actually happened a couple of weeks ago. She was able to think pretty quickly, really. She told Marron that Lisa rollerskated and fell down a lot when the doctor wanted to know how Lisa got the bruises on her legs—even though Lisa didn't fall anymore; she'd turned into a pretty good skater. Lisa is a healthy child, she told Dr. Marron. Then she came up with the name of a Dr. Eiger, whose office was only two blocks away. He was a pediatrician Joel had taken Lisa to a few years before. She didn't take the kids to doctors anymore herself.

Dr. Mary E. Lell, the head of Pediatric Neurology at St. Vincent's, was now in charge of Elizabeth Steinberg. She arrived at the hospital around the time Marron was speaking to Hedda and was surprised to find neither of the parents there. When Lell phoned the apartment and asked, "Is this Mrs. Steinberg?" she found herself talking to a woman who showed very little emotional response even when Lell told her how grave Elizabeth's condition was. The doctor was calling because the hospital needed permission to insert an intercranial monitor.

Lell seemed to be talking into an echo chamber. In her slow voice, Mrs. Steinberg would repeat whatever the doctor had just said, after which a male voice could be heard in the background. Then the man's words would slowly be relayed back to the doctor by the woman.

When Lell asked if there was any history of the child having head trauma, this question, too, was processed through the echo chamber. She heard the male voice say, "No trauma." "There was no trauma," said the female voice expressionlessly. (For some reason, Hedda Nussbaum did not volunteer to this doctor the story about her daughter's fight with a classmate.)

Hedda Nussbaum and Dr. Lell were still on the phone when the doorbell began to ring. Neither Nussbaum nor Steinberg went to answer it. The new visitors went away for a while, then came back and started ringing the bell again and knocking very persistently.

Finally Steinberg went to the door. Robert Columbia and Irma Rivera, two plainclothes detectives from the Manhattan Sex Crimes Unit, were standing in the hall. They had just been upstairs to Rita Blum's apartment, where they had tried the Steinbergs' number and found the line busy. They informed Steinberg they were police officers. When they stepped into his foyer, he walked away from them and disappeared into the bedroom. "Come back out!" Columbia shouted. "We're here to talk about your daughter's condition." When Steinberg reappeared, Columbia noticed that he wasn't fully dressed. Steinberg said the doctors had told him to go home and that he happened to be on the phone with the hospital right now. Columbia didn't believe any of this. He had the idea the bastard had been sleeping.

"I want you and your wife to come with us to the precinct," Columbia said. He didn't even have a search warrant with him.

Steinberg acted as if this was a complete surprise. "Right now?

Am I in trouble? Am I under arrest? Why do we have to go to the precinct?"

"Well, conditions would be better there."

Of course Steinberg saw through this. "Listen, I know how the police operate. I know Tommy Morrow and George Mourlot. George is the godfather of my son."

The apartment was still very dark. Evidently no one had run out to buy light bulbs since DaLuise and Botte had been there. Irma Rivera peered into the living room and caught sight of the baby boy they'd been told about. There he was in a makeshift playpen with a blanket over him. She and Columbia went over to Mitchell and he woke up and stared at them. When Rivera removed his blanket, they saw the rope around his waist. The kid was tied up like some kind of house pet. It upset Steinberg when Rivera took the rope off him. "Wait a minute! My wife will do that!" Ignoring him, Rivera picked Mitchell up and put him on the couch. Then she left the apartment for a few minutes and went upstairs to use Rita Blum's phone again. She had to get her patrol supervisor's permission in order to remove the baby from the apartment. Columbia held on to the rope.

Steinberg said in an aggrieved voice, "Can I take a shower? Can I have a shave? Can I have a cup of coffee?" He headed for the kitchen and asked Columbia why he was following him.

"I'm not following you," Columbia said. He asked Steinberg why he was so nervous.

"I'm not nervous. We've just been through a traumatic experience."

"What kind of attorney are you? Why is this place such a mess?"

Steinberg said he had been practicing law in the apartment, but that he was getting ready to move to Westchester.

Columbia kept the questions coming. "Where does the girl sleep?"

"On the couch," was the answer to that one. The baby, Steinberg explained, slept in the playpen because his crib had broken and they'd thrown it out. Anyway, he was about to move them all to his mother's house. "I'm a good father," he told Columbia proudly.

Columbia wanted to see the bedroom. Mrs. Steinberg had to be in there. He particularly wanted to get a good look at her.

"What are you doing?" Steinberg shouted. "Why are you going back there? She's getting dressed."

Hedda had been hiding herself, listening from behind the bed-

room door. When Columbia had said it would be more convenient to talk to them at the precinct, she knew that was just an
excuse. Then she heard them say they were going to take Mitchell. That was after the social worker showed up.

Joseph Petrizzo was an earnest, disarmingly gentle young man
who had been working for Special Services for Children for the
past six months, investigating child-abuse cases. He was thinking
of leaving social work and becoming a Franciscan monk.

When Irma Rivera let him in, he immediately went over to
examine Mitchell. The baby was very dirty; the living room was
filthy and terribly disordered. He felt he was drowning in Steinberg's body odor. The wet, dirty baby was very outgoing and
smiled a lot. He held out his little arms to Petrizzo right away.
Petrizzo noted that he seemed too sociable. That was one of the
signs he'd been trained to look for—small children from good
homes usually weren't so ready to cling to strangers. It was as if
babies like this one somehow knew they needed help.

He told Steinberg that he really needed to see the rest of the
apartment now to make sure there weren't any other children.
Steinberg looked at him and shrugged. "There are no working
lights." But he seemed resigned to having to show Petrizzo
around. As they were going into the bedroom, Steinberg's wife
slipped past them and went into the bathroom. Petrizzo saw a
caved-in nose, a face that seemed black and blue. The bedroom
was very disturbing—no one should have to see stains on other
people's filthy sheets or the clothes they had taken off and
dropped. Papers were pulled out all over the place—on the floor,
even on the bed.

Rivera needed clothes for Mitchell now. Steinberg didn't know
where they were kept, but Hedda did. After Joel and Petrizzo had
left the bedroom, she ducked in there again and called out to
Rivera, telling her where to find the baby's shoes, jacket, and
sweater. Finally, since she could no longer postpone making her
appearance, Hedda walked into the living room bringing some
socks for Mitchell. Everyone fell silent. Hedda kept her head
down, but now Rivera, Columbia, and Petrizzo could see her very
well. She was wearing jeans, a black turtleneck with an old plaid
shirt over it, and a black jacket. In the bathroom, she'd put on
heavy makeup and stuck a bandage over her nose to cover the
place where bone was protruding through the skin.

"We've gotta go," Columbia said loudly. At which point Steinberg asked him again if he was under arrest. "No. But you will be if you keep it up."

Brazenly, right in front of them, Steinberg leaned over to Hedda and said, "Go back inside and cover your head." When she hesitated, he insisted. "Go on. You have some bald spots. Cover them up." She obeyed him and went to the bedroom and returned with a bandanna tied around her head.

This was too much for Rivera. She couldn't contain herself. "What's the matter? You don't want us to see the cuts?"

Steinberg didn't seem to hear her. He'd noticed that Columbia still was holding Mitchell's rope. "Look Hedda, they've got the rope. Why are they taking the rope out of the apartment?"

As Hedda Nussbaum later remembered it, at the last minute she ran into the kitchen to get some fresh milk for Mitchell's bottle—her final act as a mother. Then she and Joel left, escorted by the police. They closed the door and Steinberg locked up the apartment, locked up a whole world in which they had lived for twelve years, a world ruled by Steinberg's obsessions and Hedda Nussbaum's strange acquiescence, where some of the history was incredible but real and some was only delusionary—and where a small girl, the prisoner of adult madness, had met up with the Angel of Death.

A neighbor on the ground floor was watching at her front window as Joel and Hedda walked out of the building. She didn't see the expressions on their faces, just their backs. They had their arms around each other.

They walked to the curb, where two squad cars were waiting by now. Detective William Lackenmeyer had just driven up in the second one. He told Steinberg to get into his car; Hedda was to ride with Columbia and Rivera. Hedda just kept staring at the ground, but Steinberg made a plea. "We can't be separated." It was almost as if he were saying he and Hedda were Siamese twins. "We've had a traumatic experience. We have to be together."

IN THE Steinberg case, it was the camera that would turn out to be the most potent witness. Words would come to seem increasingly unsatisfactory—too unreliable, too much the product of the prejudice or hidden agenda of the speaker. We tend to believe what we see before our own eyes; it sinks into the memory and remains there, long after complicated explanations have been forgotten.

By 12:45 P.M., Hedda Nussbaum was standing in a viewing room at the Sixth Precinct in front of a video unit sent over from the D.A.'s office at the request of Detective Lackenmeyer. There was a stark white wall behind her. The first shots were closeups of her face, the color of the bruises leached out by the lights.

The impression is one of terrible pallor; the skin seems only a shade less gray than the hair. The nose with its bandage stripped away is pulverized and scabrous. The lips are thickened, distorted. It's as if a roller has passed over the face, crushing and flattening it. In Hedda Nussbaum's eyes, there is no agony, but something worse—a look of utter indifference.

Detective Columbia is in that room as well as Irma Rivera and the cameraman. Rivera had examined Nussbaum previously and taken Polaroids. At Rivera's command, Hedda Nussbaum bends her head and a long wooden ruler appears, pointing out lacerations on her scalp and the places where hair has been torn away. There is something relentless about this moving ruler, shockingly dispassionate. It makes Nussbaum seem less than human. For the moment we are to look at her purely for her body's value to the investigators as evidence. You wish that she would protest, be upset by this awful violation of her privacy, try to put a stop to it. But she complies without a word, as if she has stood before a hundred such cameras—what difference does this one make? She pulls the black turtleneck over her head and then revolves like a model to show the bruises on her back, nine ribs with old fractures. She is standing surprisingly straight through all this. The viewer has no sense that she may collapse at any moment. With unchanging indifference, she pulls down her jeans. She is wearing bright red bikini underpants. There is an enormous circular black-and-blue mark on one of her buttocks. Her thin thighs have a slight curdling of cellulite—otherwise her slender body seems twenty years younger than her face. The pointer has descended to her legs. They're like the legs you sometimes see on winos or people who have lived out in the street too long. The skin is terribly cracked and abraded, oozing with pus.

At that point, the flow of images abruptly shuts off, and you're left feeling—what? For some, it's the legs that are the worst thing. How did she get sores like that? How could she stand the pain for so long without going to see a doctor? For others, it's the void in the eyes. They think of the little girl and remember the void in Hedda Nussbaum's eyes. Some say, of course there would be a void. What do you expect of a woman in that condition?

The Hedda tape has an awful power—far beyond any still photos of Hedda Nussbaum. The camerawork is so absolutely frontal, so raw and devoid of the mitigations of art. This is the whole truth about this woman, it tells you. How can you not trust it? This is all you need to know.

It was going to be one of William Lackenmeyer's last cases. He had been on the police force twenty-three years—maybe a little too long. Retirement loomed ahead for him in the coming months. The investigation of Lisa Steinberg's death required imagination, brilliance, at the very outset. Lackenmeyer was a literalist who'd run out of energy. The eyes behind the brown-tinted glasses he wore had a burnt-out look.

Lackenmeyer had mentally convicted Steinberg before he met him, after talking to DaLuise, Botte, and the doctors at the hospital. Since the couple was not yet under arrest, he had permitted them to ride together in the back of Columbia's car, but sent Nussbaum into a private office as soon as they reached the precinct. Steinberg kept pestering Lackenmeyer, "I want to be with my wife." He didn't know when to quit. As a lawyer, he should have known two suspects could not be interviewed together. He'd sit down and get up, sit down and get up, as if guilt was making him hyperactive. When Lackenmeyer, Columbia, and

Rivera were questioning Nussbaum, Steinberg actually came and stood alongside the closed door of the office. Maybe he thought she was making charges against him, which she should have done, but instead she was telling them what a wonderful guy Steinberg was, what a good father, and giving them the story about how the little girl had just been throwing up. Rivera was still in shock. She couldn't get over it that a woman as beaten up as that would have anything good to say about a monster like Steinberg.

Some of the things Lackenmeyer observed about Steinberg indicated substance abuse: his glazed eyes, his rapid speech, the sweat that kept running off him. His eyes would lock with Lackenmeyer's for a moment, then jerk away. It was the same with the voice, rising and falling abruptly, as if someone were fiddling with the volume dial on a radio.

When Lackenmeyer was through with Nussbaum, he told Steinberg to come into the same office and sit in the same seat right in front of the desk. For the moment, Lackenmeyer held off on saying any accusing words: "I'm investigating the injuries to your daughter."

"What injuries?" Steinberg said. "She was only throwing up."

Lackenmeyer asked Steinberg to put his hands on the desk. He would later testify that all of Steinberg's fingers looked red and swollen, that he saw fresh scratches on them. He took several Polaroids of the hands, but technology failed him. When the pictures were later shown in court, no one was able to see the scratches.

At three o'clock, Steinberg was finally arrested and put into a cell on the second floor. Nussbaum was arrested as well. But evidently Lackenmeyer had not a shadow of doubt about which one of them was the perpetrator. He was a man who believed in doggedly following through on procedures. Three weeks later, when one of his superiors directed him to interview Mitchell Steinberg, Lackenmeyer would comply despite the absurdity of such a request. He would report back that Mitchell was "unable to testify." That afternoon, however, Lackenmeyer was much less thorough. He ordered that fingernail scrapings be taken from Steinberg and even arranged to have a videotape made of the procedure. But he saw no need to do the same with Nussbaum. Later that night, he would confiscate the clothes Steinberg was wearing, even his shoes and socks, so that they could be subjected to laboratory examination. Each hair found on Steinberg's shirt would eventually be analyzed by an expert from the FBI. But none of Nussbaum's clothing would ever be taken and processed.

After his arrest, Steinberg made a call to Robert Kalina, a lawyer he knew, not a friend exactly, more of a long-term Centre Street acquaintance. Drug dealers constituted a good part of their respective clienteles. The prosecutions generated by the wholesale traffic of drugs had created a steady supply of cases for criminal lawyers, though Steinberg's own court appearances had become markedly infrequent. In fact, he had a lot of time on his hands, and he would while away some of it by turning up in people's offices unexpectedly. Kalina was one of the people Steinberg had felt free to visit, if he happened to be uptown on Madison Avenue. He'd have a case to refer to Kalina, or he'd want advice, or he'd just walk in off the street to use the phone for a few minutes. Now and then Kalina had picked Joel up at Tenth Street. He'd ring the buzzer in the vestibule and Joel would come right downstairs. He'd never been taken upstairs to meet Hedda or Joel's children.

When Kalina got Steinberg's call that afternoon, he thought at first it was business as usual.

"Hi," Joel said. "I'm down at the Sixth Precinct."

Kalina asked if he had a new client for him.

"Yeah, me," Joel said. "Lisa's injured. You gotta come down here."

In one day the tables had turned on Steinberg. He would soon be spending more time on Centre Street than he had in years. The following October he would find himself appearing as a defendant down there in a courtroom where he had argued some of his cases.

Joel Steinberg had a way of zeroing in on people he thought might be useful to him and trying to impress them by his largesse, as long as it did not involve an outlay of cash. A few did gain admittance to his apartment—one Greenwich Village cocaine dealer was reportedly almost a member of the household. Respectable people, like Elliott Koreman, the principal of P.S. 41, would be more likely to get invitations to go sailing on the *Aqua Viva*. "My boat," was how Steinberg would proudly refer to it. If the apartment on Tenth Street no longer symbolized the good life, the ownership of the thirty-two-foot racing boat, docked at the Five Points Marina in Patchogue, testified to the place Steinberg had purportedly arrived at in the world. Few people knew he wasn't the sole owner of the *Aqua Viva*. In fact, the major shareholder was a Greenwich Village gynecologist named Peter Sarosi, who allowed Joel to use the boat as much as he wanted. Sarosi's generosity to Steinberg went beyond that—it was he who had bestowed Mitchell upon Joel and Hedda after he had delivered him at Beth Israel Hospital.

Sarosi was another person Steinberg liked to drop in on. The doctor's office was on Tenth Street and University Place, only a couple of blocks from Steinberg's home. Karen Snyder had an office in the same building. She would often see Steinberg and Lisa going up in the elevator and think, My God, even here I'm not free of Joel Steinberg! It seemed to her as if Steinberg had tentacles stretching everywhere.

Joel Steinberg was Sarosi's attorney and financial adviser; recently he had inveigled the doctor into becoming the principal investor in a small corporation that was one of his latest ventures, the Greenwich Petroleum Company. Sometimes Sarosi visited Steinberg and Nussbaum at the apartment.

That afternoon at the Sixth Precinct, the person Hedda Nussbaum asked to see was Dr. Sarosi. He came and spent two hours with her and told the police she had the bad habit of falling down a lot.

The news about what had happened on Tenth Street trickled out into the world. Among the first to hear about it were Elliott Koreman and Lisa's teacher, Sylvia Haron, both of whom received phone calls from the police. As the day wore on, it became apparent to the doctors at St. Vincent's that there would never be any improvement in Lisa's condition. The damage to her brain was far too massive. Only artificial means could keep her alive. "Our sleeping beauty," one of the nurses called her.

Someone at the precinct got the word out to the press. At nine o'clock Steinberg and Nussbaum were to be brought down from the second floor to be booked at the front desk on charges of attempted murder, assault, and endangering the welfare of children. Irma Rivera apparently had some inkling of what awaited them there. She changed into a more becoming outfit before she took her place beside Hedda Nussbaum. In one of the news photographs, Rivera is smiling at the camera as she grips Hedda's arm; Hedda, staring straight ahead into a wall of white light, is wide-eyed, tearful, and dazzled like a child.

Television cameramen were standing behind the booking desk in defiance of regulations. The lobby was jammed with reporters holding up microphones.

In the past, one of Joel Steinberg's foolish, self-aggrandizing boasts was that he'd once taught a course at Columbia University on journalism and the law. Now he and Hedda were the stars of a sensational case that would have provided a perfect example for Steinberg's imaginary students of how the media and the legal system really do interact, how even the very first images broadcast far and wide can have the weight of verdicts.

"Did you do it?" one reporter yelled at him. "What about the bruises?"

It would have been Steinberg's privilege to say "No comment," but for a moment the lawyer in him took over, the combative, crafty lawyer who advised his client: Just keep denying everything.

"There isn't a mark on her. You can check the hospital records," he shouted back.

Kalina told him to shut up.

An hour later, a lone car appeared on a street in Queens, moving very slowly so its driver could make out the numbers over the doors of the identical two-story red brick houses.

Sherry and Mitchell Burger had been waiting for it since five o'clock when a social worker from a Jewish agency had phoned them, looking for a home for a one-year-old boy who had been taken away from his family because of abuse—"That's all I can tell you right now, Sherry."

At six she phoned back. This time she sounded distraught. The baby was okay, he hadn't been beaten too badly. All at once she was in tears. The boy had a sister who wasn't going to make it; her cranium had been crushed. An hour later, sounding more professional, the social worker came up with the baby's birthday and his name.

The Burgers started calling around the neighborhood to see if they could borrow clothes. They also let their in-laws know they were taking in a white, Jewish baby boy. Maybe this one they'd be able to keep. Sherry and Mitchell, who were Orthodox Jews, often sheltered foster children referred to them by the Ohel Agency; each time they were assigned a baby, they got their hopes up.

Sherry Burger can still recall every detail of Mitchell Steinberg's arrival. How their golden retriever Dudley had begun barking immediately. They'd put Dudley in the basement so he wouldn't scare the baby, but he'd started up the moment Mitchell was carried into the house. Two men from Special Services for

Children (formerly the Bureau of Child Welfare) had brought him straight from St. Vincent's. Mitchell was wrapped in a hospital blanket; he was wearing only an undershirt, a diaper, and a pair of oversized shoes. All his other worldly possessions were in a paper bag. The smell coming from that bag was something awful. "Phew! Get it out of the house. Throw it in the garbage, will you?" Sherry told the men. But the SSC workers decided they'd better take it back with them; maybe it could be used as evidence. They gave Sherry and her husband some of the details of what had happened to Lisa Steinberg.

Meanwhile, the wonderful, smiling baby had jumped into Sherry's arms and was already communicating with her. He was one of the brightest, sweetest babies she had ever met—really exceptional. Sherry was sure he wanted to see Dudley, so she let the dog come bounding up from the basement. Sure enough, Mitchell was all set to play with him, even though you could tell he was a little scared.

Sherry carried him upstairs and put him in the tub and started washing Tenth Street away. "I must have washed his hair three times before I knew it was blond," she remembers. "It was green when he came in." There were bad cuts on the top of his foot and by his knee, a small scar over one eyebrow. "I put him in pajamas and brought him into our bedroom to play. Then my father called and said, 'Turn on channel five quick!' " The Burgers caught the first segment of the eleven o'clock news. "That's how we found out who he was."

They never did call him Mitchell, not even that first night. For one thing, there already was an adult Mitchell in the house. But of course, the real reason was that you couldn't let a baby keep a name that had such terrible associations. You had to throw it out like those filthy clothes, start all over again from nothing. For now the Burgers decided to just call him Boomer. Boomer was his name the whole time he was with them.

Boomer knew three words. Mommy, Daddy, and bye-bye. Not enough to tell what he had seen. The Burgers taught him a fourth word. Nice. Make *nice,* Boomer, they'd say if he got a little too rough with the dog. Boomer couldn't bear to sleep in a crib. He kept having nightmares, but of course he couldn't tell anyone what they were. During the daytimes he was always happy.

Once Sherry took him over to her mother's house. Her mother had a visitor that day who looked, in certain ways, very much like Hedda—the same age, the same size and shape, the same curly gray hair. When the baby saw her, he started screaming; he held on to Sherry's legs and wouldn't let go. Sherry just picked him up and took him out of there, and finally he calmed down. Soon it was forgotten, and he went back to being his regular self.

IN 1987, an estimated four thousand children died in America as a direct result of abuse. Most of these were children of the poor and most of their deaths received very little media coverage, with an occasional exception. Three weeks after Lisa Steinberg's death, there were headlines in the New York papers about a three-year-old Puerto Rican child who had lived with her mother and stepfather in a Manhattan welfare hotel. The stepfather had been charged with giving the little girl a fatal beating, putting her corpse into a stroller and going out into the street with it to beg for money to buy drugs. But the small victim soon vanished into the statistics. In fact, the case was reported with comparative restraint. The way the welfare-hotel child had died was not interpreted as being totally against nature—there seemed an inevitability about it. Having essentially abdicated responsibility for its poor, America has come to expect the worst of them. All society can do is to uselessly and guiltily wring its hands.

But the Lisa Steinberg case was a different matter. Lisa was one of those children to whom we assign high value. On the face of it, the middle-aged criminal lawyer and the children's book editor could not have been more appropriate parents. "Why, the Steinbergs are people like us," we said, and we couldn't get over it or get past it. The case made Manhattan seem like a small town. You could start asking your friends, Did they know the Steinbergs? and they'd ask their friends, and if you kept boring down through enough layers of people, you'd eventually come up with a connection. But no one wanted to *know* Joel Steinberg, the "Svengali," the "Tyrant of Tenth Street," the despotic ruler of the "House of Horrors." The more we felt we knew him, the more we had to insist on the difference between him and us. He and Hedda Nussbaum, whom we desperately needed to believe was only a victim really, rather than a perpetrator, had willfully turned so many values of class and family upside down, ground them into the mud. It was as if all the darkest possibilities of family life, of the sacrosanct Home, had been glaringly illuminated.

The Latin root of *monster* is the verb *monere:* to warn. A monster carries the connotation of a warning, an omen, a premonition of evil. The discovery of a Steinberg reminded us of the potential for evil in human nature. According to Bruno Bettelheim, we do children a great disservice if we deprive them of the traditional fairy tales in which monsters appear. As he points out in *The Uses of Enchantment,* "the monster a child knows best, is most concerned with" is "the monster he feels himself to be." Therefore, if the child is not permitted to fantasize about monsters, "he fails to get to know his monster better, nor is he given suggestions as to how he may gain mastery over it. As a result, the child remains helpless with his worst anxieties."

On a rational level, of course, adults know very well that monsters do not exist. But our rationality is far from invulnerable. In response to certain kinds of horrific events, our old childish fantasies may overwhelm our thinking. To understand how a Steinberg could exist in our very midst requires us to look very deeply into ourselves and into our own experiences and histories as children and as parents. It is much less unsettling to decide that he is not like us at all.

When we call a man a monster, we are saying that he exists somewhere beyond the pale of humanity, and that if we encountered him out there, we would be overwhelmed by his force. A monster is totally remorseless. It devours and lays waste according to its insatiable needs and does so without guilt. A monster has no history other than the history of its heinous acts. It simply is what it does. It is what it is. Therefore, we do not need to understand it.

Nonetheless, the public did have a deep, inchoate understanding of Steinberg and, more reluctantly and belatedly in some quarters, of Nussbaum as well. This understanding explains why the two of them quickly became such archetypal figures—a Steinberg, a Nussbaum, we say now—and why the death of one particular middle-class child continues to grip the imagination. It is the blank affectlessness of Steinberg and Nussbaum that we recognize with a shudder. It is this that causes us fear and trembling even more than the blows that descended upon a six-year-old girl.

There is the sense that the blows were delivered with indifference rather than with any recognizable strong emotion and that with the same indifference the two "educated" adults in the apartment let the child slip toward death before their very eyes over the next twelve hours, while, as it was later discovered, they smoked cocaine. Even Hedda Nussbaum's eventual laconic phone call for an ambulance seems arbitrary, unconnected to any genuine maternal instinct. It was as if we had become aware that a new fully developed species had sprung from the earth—human beings without humanity, people whose narcissistic sensual gratification took precedence over life and death. Yet these are aliens we know all too well; they have been living in our midst for years.

The Steinberg case was like a smashed mirror; you'd look into its shards and find reflections of your own life. "Former children's book editor ... Random House ... Greenwich Village. ..." I, too, had edited books. I had been a working mother. Lived in and around the Village for many years. When my son was little, I had taken him to the playground in Washington Square where Lisa had later played. I'd pushed him on the baby swings, like Joel pushing Lisa in a photo I saw in one of the tabloids.

It's been years since I've lived downtown, but I still often visit friends in the Village. For about ten minutes on Halloween night, 1987, I was caught in the dense, immovable crowd that had gathered on the sidewalk at Tenth Street and Avenue of the Americas to await the start of the annual costume parade. It's possible I caught a glimpse of a tall, dark middle-aged man, making free with his elbows to clear a path to the curb, and of a small red-haired girl dressed as Roadrunner clutching the man's hand, and that I forgot them the next instant; your mind seldom stores those snapshots of strangers. I would have stared a bit longer and harder had I noticed bruises on the face of the little Roadrunner. But I can't say I would have done more than that. And anyway, most likely, Elizabeth Steinberg would have been smiling up at her daddy, shiny-eyed. She knew all about the importance of looking happy for him, of never being less than a delightful little girl. A strawberry-blond doll "right out of one of those boxes," as the principal of her school later described her—as if it had almost been her function to brighten the world of adults by her presence.

The last picture even taken of Elizabeth Steinberg—the one I saw that covered the entire front page of *Newsday* on Wednesday, November 4—wasn't the least bit adorable. It showed a little girl with downcast brown eyes and matted unkempt hair. She sat, hands curled in front of her on the school desk, seemingly quite alone, although a mother was taking a picture of a class party. You can imagine the clamor of high-pitched voices, the movement, the energy of all those other little bodies around that quiet child. First-graders are almost constitutionally unable to sit still. But Lisa Steinberg seemed to be waiting—not waiting *for* anything, just waiting something out, something dreaded and inescapable. It will happen, the look seemed to say. Portrait of an adorable child at Halloween party, P.S. 41. Really, it was amazing it had been taken at all. It was as if the camera, with its cold intelligent eye, had caught something everyone else had somehow missed.

She was still technically alive the day the picture ran, though she had neither moved, uttered a word, nor opened her eyes. The child's heart had outlived her consciousness.

That fall, a pretty young woman named Renee Gordon was working for Robert Kalina and his associate Michael Guido. On Thursday morning, a spokeswoman from St. Vincent's called the office to say that the hospital had disconnected Elizabeth Steinberg's life-support system. The time of her official death was 8:40 A.M. "Please inform your client," she said curtly.

Kalina was out of the office that day. Guido gave the job to Renee: "You tell Joel."

It was an awful thing to have to be the messenger. Renee had come to know Joel a little from his impromptu visits to the office, though she'd always been careful to keep her distance. Renee had been married to a rock musician, and Steinberg reminded her uncomfortably of people she'd known in that world she'd left behind. The way he'd sweat even when it was cold outside, his rambling, speedy, disconnected speech—the telltale signs of addiction. Still, she didn't doubt that he'd really loved his daughter and at the time she was convinced that he was innocent. Guido thought so, too. Kalina, who for the time being was under the impression that he would also be defending Hedda, didn't know what to make of what Joel had told him. For the past three days he'd been pleading with Steinberg, "Well, just tell me what the real story is."

Joel had been put on suicide watch in the hospital wing at Rikers Island. Prisoners were allowed to make one call a day, but Joel somehow worked it so that he was on the phone all the time. If Kalina wasn't available, he'd latch on to Renee, just talk to her on and on. "Uh huh," she'd say. "Right. Okay, Joel. Excuse me," she'd say and take another call; when she got back to him the stream of words would just continue.

Of course it wasn't long before he dialed the phone that morning and started babbling to Renee as usual. But then in the midst of it, he said, "Have you heard anything about Lisa?"

"My heart stopped," Renee remembers, "and I didn't know what to say. I said, 'Joel, Lisa is dead.' He screamed '*What!* What are you talking about?' I almost started taking it back. I said, 'Listen, you've got to talk to Bob. I'll get him to call you as soon as possible.' "

For some reason that calmed Joel down; a moment later he'd veered off into another subject. It was the strangest thing, Renee thought. Just a few seconds ago he'd been hysterical. "I'm shell-shocked," he'd told her. And now only a few words from her had pacified him. In his place, she would have pressed on, asked questions. But maybe Joel just didn't want to believe Lisa was dead.

The rest of their conversation that morning was about Hedda. "Please try to get hold of Hedda. Leave a message for her to please call me. Tell her I love her." Hedda, Hedda, Hedda.

Renee tried Elmhurst Hospital, where Hedda was in a locked mental ward, recovering from an operation on her ulcerated right leg, but she couldn't get through.

Hedda Nussbaum was lying in bed when some members of Elmhurst's staff came to tell her that her daughter had died. One of them later told the press, "I heard her crying. It was kind of like a quick yelp, tears, and it was over."

When she was arrested with Steinberg, Hedda had also been charged with attempted murder. With Lisa's death, her legal status had changed. Now, like Joel, she was charged with an even graver crime: murder. That very afternoon a makeshift court-room was assembled on the fourth floor of the hospital, and Judge Randall T. Eng, from Manhattan Criminal Court, drove out to Elmhurst to preside over it. At 3:37, Hedda Nussbaum was wheeled in wearing a striped hospital gown, an IV dripping into a tube in her arm. Accompanying her were her aunt and uncle and her parents, William and Emma Nussbaum, two small, bewildered octogenarians who looked almost twinlike in their round thick glasses and their tan raincoats that were too light for the crisp November weather.

It had been years since the Nussbaums had seen their daughter,

Hedda. On Monday night they had sent a note to her Tenth Street
address. An investigator found it still in its envelope a few weeks
later. By then everyone knew that Steinberg had barred Nussbaum's family from visiting the apartment, but even so, the four-
line message struck him as amazingly muted and inadequate,
considering the circumstances. The Nussbaums' daughter had
been accused of a terrible crime; their grandchild lay near death
in St. Vincent's; Hedda herself had been permanently disfigured.
We heard the bad news on television, they wrote her, and from
Charlotte (Joel Steinberg's mother). They didn't believe it; they
knew she would never harm the children. Since we can't get in
touch with you, you get in touch with us, the note concluded, as
if the Nussbaums were writing to a traveling acquaintance.

It turned out to be one of the many instances in the tragedy of
Lisa Steinberg when no one seemed able to come up with the
right lines, when you had to wonder why all the players up there
on the stage acted with such a deficit of emotion. You'd hear a
quote or two that struck you the wrong way and discover that you
had standards of grief, deep feelings became a touchstone of sanity.

According to the newspapers, Hedda Nussbaum wept into a
pink Kleenex when a court officer read out the description of Lisa
Steinberg's injuries. But then her sorrow changed to anger when
she heard that Irma Rivera had described the apartment as filthy
and disordered. For the moment this critique of her housekeep-
ing was as important as death and a direct blow to her pride, and
she shook her head fiercely and glared at the speaker.

The attorney doing the talking for her was not Robert Kalina,
but a new name—Barry Scheck, who had gotten himself appointed by the court to defend her. He had wanted the case very
badly, not only feeling sympathy for Hedda's plight but also perhaps seeing an opportunity for himself to achieve some promi-
nence. Hedda's family had quickly decided to sever her case from
Joel's. From a group called STEPS to End Family Violence that
immediately rallied to Hedda's support, they had gotten the
name of Michael Dowd, an attorney with a reputation for the
successful defense of battered women accused of murdering their
husbands. Although this case was different, perhaps the same kind
of reasoning could be made to apply—that a woman had been
battered to a point where she was not responsible for her actions.
Dowd was out of town when Hedda Nussbaum's sister Judy had
called him, and she had been referred back to Scheck as a tempo-

rary measure. When Dow returned to his office, he found that
Barry Scheck had preempted him.

That day Barry Scheck announced to the judge that his client
was ready to testify against Steinberg before a grand jury. She had
not actually indicated any such readiness, but Scheck had taken
it upon himself to make the correct responses for her. In the
upcoming months, keeping his client totally shielded from the
press, he would issue bulletins about the progress of her emotions.
"Hedda is very angry with Joel," he would declare proudly from
time to time, like a parent whose child had just taken her first
steps.

Evidently, anger turned out to be a feeling more accessible to
Hedda than grief. Reportedly, the day Lisa died, Hedda Nussbaum said an odd thing about her daughter: "I'm very glad I got
to know her."

"Terror Girl," the tabloids called Elizabeth Steinberg. "Torture
Tot." Elizabeth Steinberg was no one at all. She had been forty-
three pounds of flesh and blood, but legally such a person had
never existed. Right after her birth, she had been severed from
her only real identity as "Baby Girl Launders," the name in the
records of the hospital where she was delivered. If Elizabeth
Steinberg had survived to grow up, she would have become
aware of her anomalous status when it came time for her to get
a passport or a driver's license.

When it became clear that Elizabeth Steinberg should not be
kept alive, the HRA had been thrown into a quandary. To whom
could St. Vincent's Hospital go for a valid consent "to pull the
plug," as the *Daily News* put it. Since apparently the child had
never been adopted, consent would have to come from her birth
mother, but at first no one was able to trace her. At 2:30 P.M. on
November 5, the HRA went to family court and became Elizabeth Steinberg's guardian; two hours later, when St. Vincent's
declared her brain dead, the HRA was properly able to transfer
the responsibility for Lisa to the hospital. On November 3, however, the child's death created a new problem. Again, it came
down to the question of who really owned Lisa? Who was entitled
to bury her? It seemed outrageous, unthinkable, for Steinberg
and Nussbaum to do so.

Hundreds of strangers contacted the HRA and offered to pay
for the funeral. Other New Yorkers sent checks to the *Daily
News*. The P.S. 41 principal, Elliott Koreman, who by then was

under considerable fire for the failure of his staff to react to the bruises Lisa came to school with, vowed to the press that P.S. 41 would not let her body be turned over to the city for burial: "The school has made a commitment that if no one else comes forward, we will have a funeral for that child."

On Friday, Steinberg finally reached Nussbaum from Rikers Island, and the two had a brief conversation and agreed that Hedda's family should take care of the burial. William Nussbaum couldn't understand why his daughter was taking any calls from Steinberg, whatsoever. "What do you mean?" she said to her father. "I *want* to talk to him."

All week long, twenty-six-year-old Michelle Launders had been following the case, watching it on TV, telling herself Lisa couldn't be her kid, it was just a coincidence—just as she had once told herself she couldn't be pregnant. On Wednesday night, after seeing the P.S. 41 photo of Lisa Steinberg, Michelle's mother, Anita, phoned her. Anita Launders had stared at the face of that little redheaded girl in the school in Greenwich Village, and seen something about the expression, the mouth, that unmistakably reminded her of Michelle. "There's no way!" Michelle told her angrily. "There's no way!" But Anita kept asking questions, reviving all the old doubts about the Manhattan lawyer who had arranged for the adoption of the baby girl born to Michelle on May 14, 1981.

Back then Joel Steinberg hadn't seemed crazy; no one could have imagined he would turn into a child killer. In fact, Michelle herself had been very impressed with him, even a little intimidated by the fast-talking professional in the three-piece suit. She hadn't wanted to listen then either when her mother expressed misgivings about the arrangements they'd made for the baby.

She couldn't bring herself to kill it by having an abortion, and she couldn't keep it, wasn't up to doing that. She was nineteen and in the worst trouble of her life. She was a serious girl and had been, and still was, very much in love. The baby's father was a college student. For weeks and weeks she fended off reality before she went to her boyfriend's campus and gave him the bad news about their predicament. The predicament turned out to be hers alone. He didn't want to get married and become a father. Michelle went to a local gynecologist. Dr. Michael Bergman had offices in both Hempstead, Long Island, and Greenwich Village on University Place—the same office that would later be taken over by Peter Sarosi, when Bergman was forced to retire for health reasons. He gave her a test and the results were positive. That was when she told her mother.

Michelle Launders knew from her own mother's experience how hard it was for a woman who had no financial resources to raise a child on her own. Anita Launders had left Michelle's father and struggled to make a life for herself and her daughter. Michelle hated the thought of adding to her burdens, but fortunately Dr. Bergman went out of his way to be kind. He was a big teddy bear of a man. He said he had a friend who was a lawyer who'd handled many adoptions. Dr. Bergman's receptionist, Virginia Liebrader, whom everyone called Jeannie, was also remarkably helpful and understanding. She invited Michelle to live with her during her last three months of pregnancy. Jeannie was a cheerful soul, sort of a hippie, Michelle thought. Whenever Michelle got depressed and thought about keeping the baby, Jeannie would turn her around again: "You're so young. How could you give the baby a proper life?"

Michelle never wondered why the doctor and his receptionist were going to so much trouble. She actually believed that people were basically good—a belief that would be severely shaken in the years to come. "Don't worry, Michelle. Everything will be taken care of," Bergman kept reassuring her. The only thing that seemed to worry him a little was her health. She had a prediabetic condition that he was watching very closely.

For a while Mr. Steinberg was just a voice on the telephone, calling up to ask her how she was. One day she and her mother took the train into the city to have lunch with him in Greenwich Village. They met him at One Fifth Avenue, a chic-looking place decorated with Deco fittings from the Italian ocean liner *Corona*. Mr. Steinberg was the only one who ate lunch. Everything on the menu was so pricey that Michelle and Anita just had coffee. Mr. Steinberg let Anita Launders pick up the entire check. For the forty-five minutes they were there, Michelle had the feeling he took up more than one seat at the table because of his superabundant personality. That day Anita also gave him five hundred dollars in cash, which he had requested as a token of good faith. The sum was her entire life savings. Mr. Steinberg acted as if it were customary for the birth mother to pay the lawyer something. There was a lot Michelle and her mother didn't know.

Actually, Michelle was feeling very grateful to Mr. Steinberg because he had gone out of his way to find the ideal couple to adopt the baby. A wealthy Roman Catholic lawyer and his wife, who lived uptown near Central Park and would send the child to private schools and college. So Michelle had been right to make this decision to give the baby up to people who could give it infinitely more than she could. What Steinberg told them that day would later become the basis of Michelle's comforting fantasies about her daughter. Now she's four, she'd tell herself, now she's five. And she could almost see that tiny girl fast asleep in an immaculate room, like a nursery in a magazine photograph, painted with pastel clouds and rainbows.

When the baby was born at Beekman Downtown Hospital, Michelle saw her for only a few seconds. She signed the relinquishment form when it was brought to her by Joel Steinberg. There was no time for her to reflect or change her mind. Of course Steinberg neglected to tell her that the relinquishment would not become a matter of record until there was an adoption hearing in Family Court. Or that by law the birth mother must be notified in writing about the date of such a hearing.

In the wake of Lisa Steinberg's death, New York State passed new legislation in 1988. The "Lisa Law" attempted to close off some of the loopholes in private adoption, making it mandatory for prospective parents to start adoption proceedings within ten days of taking a child into their home. Previously a couple could have waited indefinitely before notifying a Family Court judge of their intent and undergoing a review into their fitness as parents, including an investigation into whether they had ever been charged with abuse.

Yet even these new regulations wouldn't have thwarted a Joel Steinberg. "If you don't bring to the court's attention that you intend to adopt, there really isn't very much we can do," one Family Court clerk observed.

The police found Michelle Launders's name; they didn't get it from Steinberg or Nussbaum. They were ransacking the apartment, looking for drugs, weapons, pornography, equipment for sadomasochistic sex, financial records—tearing the place apart, dumping the contents of file cabinets onto the floor. Joel Steinberg had forgotten to throw out a pile of unpaid bills from Beekman Downtown Hospital, dating back to May 1981. Virginia Liebrader had checked Michelle in on May 13, telling the hospital that Michelle was her sister; on the forms Jeannie filled out, Michelle's address was listed as c/o Joel Steinberg, 14 West Tenth Street.

In November 1987, Michelle was working for an insurance company as a policy writer and sharing an apartment in Hempstead with a couple of friends. On Friday, November 6, she came home from her job and found Assistant District Attorney Nancy Palmer and a detective waiting to see her. Her roommates had let them into the apartment. "Don't go anyplace," Nancy Palmer had told them. "She's going to need you."

O N S A T U R D A Y, November 7, Joel Steinberg had two visitors at Rikers Island—Robert Kalina and his assistant Renee Gordon. Renee, who aspired to be a journalist, had begged to come along. As they drove there, Kalina confided to Renee that he wasn't sure he wanted this case. (In 1989, in fact, he would turn it over to Ira London.) Steinberg had been saying some very strange, disturbing things—he kept referring to people involved in what he called a "cult." These cult people were supposed to be dangerous—so dangerous and inimical to Steinberg that even a lawyer who represented him could also be at risk. "We could all die," Steinberg had warned Kalina, and he had actually given Kalina instances of suspicious, untimely deaths. One of the deceased was Dr. Michael Bergman, who had succumbed to a massive heart attack the previous year. It was the kind of talk that was very hard to believe, yet Steinberg did seem so obsessed with the threat posed by this cult, that the whole idea of it was making Kalina extremely uneasy—uneasy enough to want to find Steinberg another attorney. A woman from this cult, according to Steinberg, had called the house around four on Sunday, November 1. He was watching football, so Lisa had answered the phone, as she often did. The caller had said a "buzzword" to Lisa, and shortly after that, when she was eating Chinese vegetables, she had started feeling sick.

At Rikers Island, Renee waited alone for two hours while Kalina met with his client. Then a guard escorted her into the attorney conference room—an office with cinderblock walls, a tiny barred window, and steel desks. She perched on one of them. Joel seemed highly agitated, "nervous as hell." Renee noticed the way he was sweating and his greasy hair; she had the impression he was withdrawing from something. Already he had taken on the look of a ruined man. His clothes had been borrowed from other inmates—black nylon jogging pants, an acrylic cream-colored fisherman's sweater with fuzz balls all over it. He was clutching a can of Coca-Cola, which he would gulp from time to time, and smoking one cigarette after another. When his pack ran out, he begged the guard for more. It was true what Kalina had said. Joel did have a weird obsession with this cult. He got so wound up talking about it that at one point he suddenly climbed upon a bench and spoke to them as if from a platform.

The cult had gotten to Hedda, that was what concerned him most. In fact, he'd had to report injuries inflicted upon Hedda by members of this cult to the FBI. Kalina had to find Steinberg's friend Greg Malmoulka, because he knew all about it. "Bob," Steinberg said urgently, "you can't let Hedda go into a trance. You've gotta make sure you do this to her." He demonstrated his cure for trances on Renee, who was still sitting on the desk, slapping her lightly on the cheeks with the tips of his fingers, then putting his thumbs and forefingers at the corners of her eyes and moving her eyelids up and down, the way you would move the eyelids of a doll. "See this? See what I'm doing?"

A little later, when Renee was about to leave with Kalina, Joel Steinberg took her hand. "Thank you very much," he said fervently. Suddenly she felt his lips on the back of her hand, his mustache rasping across her knuckles.

"Listen," he said. "I want you to have the rabbit. You gotta get the keys. You gotta get in there and get the rabbit."

Michelle Launders spent the weekend overwhelmed with grief and guilt, totally unable to decide what to do. Should she come forward now to bury this child she had given to the man who had murdered her? Or should she be sensible and expedient and self-protective, and take the route of silence and retreat—the route Lisa's natural father was taking? No one was compelling her to do anything. She could make either choice, as long as she could live with it. She had rejected motherhood once. Now fate had dealt her a second chance—to become the mother of a child who had stopped breathing.

In half a dozen years, despite what she had gone through at nineteen, Michelle Launders had managed to assemble the components of a more or less acceptable life. She worked hard all week at a respectable job that didn't interest her a whole lot; she lived in a nice enough apartment and had a closetful of clothes, and she had ordinary worries about loneliness and keeping her weight down and wishing the job weren't so routine. Some weekends she got away from everything and went skiing or sailing and cleared out her mind. She was a forthright young woman with a good, ironic sense of humor and a plainspoken way of getting to the heart of things. She lacked confidence in herself. One of the things she hated most was having her picture taken.

In the hundreds of news photos of Michelle Launders, you can recognize bits of Lisa—the red in the hair, the small, heart-shaped mouth. Perhaps Lisa's complexion would eventually have been like hers—the kind of transparent skin that's always flushing and paling, changing with every unvoiced emotion. Lisa, though, at the age of six, was said to be remarkably free of shyness, never at a loss when it came to posing before a camera. She even had one of her own, which she used to take pictures of some of her daddy's friends, like Greg Malmoulka. Except for that last shot at her school party, she always remembered to smile.

I can imagine Michelle Launders staring and staring at that picture, the same one that had prompted her mother's phone call and her own denial, "There's no way!"

On Monday, Mayor Koch held a news conference and gave Lisa Steinberg her latest designation. "A new Kitty Genovese," he called her, comparing the child to the young woman who had been stabbed repeatedly on a street in Forest Hills, Long Island, in 1964, while thirty-eight neighbors ignored her cries for help. No one seemed to have informed the mayor about the complaints that had been made over the years by Karen Snyder and a few others to the police and the Bureau of Child Welfare. Koch made no mention of the ineptness of the city investigators who had followed up on calls or of the inexplicable blindness of Lisa's principal and teachers. Instead, he singled out Lisa's neighbors, denouncing them for turning their backs because they didn't want to become involved. It soon became an ordeal for Karen Snyder and other tenants to go in or out of the house, to confront the accusatory stares of the people gathered outside.

Meanwhile, since Lisa Steinberg's natural mother had still not surfaced publicly, the controversy about who had the right to bury the child intensified. Globe Monuments in North Arlington, New Jersey, offered a fifteen-hundred-dollar headstone and the owner of a chain of Jewish funeral homes volunteered to absorb the cost of all the arrangements. "I am losing track of all the calls

I am getting," said a weary official in the medical examiner's office. Each day the steps of 14 West Tenth Street became an impromptu shrine. Flowers, lighted candles, toys, poems, and notes addressed to Lisa accumulated on the steps of the building. "I feel your terror, sweet one, soft one, little one," read one scrap of paper. "I wish there was a way to hold your little body and cover you with gentleness." The dead child had become an object of worship. Death had made Lisa Steinberg both poignantly real, yet increasingly abstract—a vessel to hold a flood of sentiment. Yet much of the emotion was genuine. It was as if multitudes of strangers were subconsciously reacting to the inability of those who had constituted Lisa's "family" to express remorse or overwhelming grief; they felt compelled to somehow fill the gap.

Something indeed was missing from all the newspaper and television accounts of the unfolding events in the case, from all the quotes of what Hedda Nussbaum and even Lisa's grandparents had reportedly said. Charlotte Steinberg, for example, complained that she had bought Lisa and Mitchell Christmas presents. "Who am I going to give them to now?" The Nussbaums hardly mentioned the two children; their thoughts were all with their own daughter. As for Hedda, she was judged by some of the feminist supporters who had gathered around her to have passed to a stage beyond grief. Of course she can't feel much, is the way they interpreted her. At the same time, they held a rather idealized view of the circumstances surrounding Lisa's death. Taking for granted a close bond between mother and daughter, they believed that Lisa had been struck down while trying to protect Nussbaum from Steinberg's blows. But other women, trying to put themselves in Hedda's place, allowed themselves to imagine how they would feel if they lost their own children. Why, they would be totally devastated; they would not be able to go on. How could a mother survive the murder of her child?

Barry Scheck and Lawrence Vogelman, an associate, had asked to have a second autopsy performed over the weekend, which horrified Rabbi Dennis Math of the Village Temple. "It's like victimizing Lisa all over again," he told the press, since by Jewish law a body should be buried as soon as possible after death. Rabbi Math appealed to all the competing would-be buriers of Lisa to put their interests aside. In his own opinion, it would be most appropriate for the little girl to be buried by P.S. 41, because "in reality, the student body and the principal were her real family." Barry Scheck was quick to disagree: "Since the city has declared the adoption illegal and since there is no legal next of kin, the arrangements should be handled by friends of the deceased, in this case relatives of her adoptive parents and friends in the community." He indicated that Hedda wanted Lisa to be buried by her parents and Joel's mother and by P.S. 41. William Nussbaum told the press he was going to stand by Hedda. He would see to it that Lisa was put in the Nussbaum family plot.

One of Hedda Nussbaum's most important new supporters suddenly emerged—Sister Mary Nerney, head of STEPS to End Family Violence. She had dedicated herself to helping battered women and ran a shelter for women and children in East Harlem. Sister Nerney visited Hedda at Elmhurst over the weekend and was appalled to find her shackled to her bed by one leg. She brought with her a woman who had stood trial for murdering her husband and been acquitted. Sister Nerney told a reporter that although Hedda seemed unable to talk about Lisa at this point, she was "very sad" about her death and had even expressed the desire to attend her funeral. From time to time, Sister Nerney would continue to speak for Hedda, communicating, as Barry Scheck did, news about her appropriate feelings to the public.

Columnist Jimmy Breslin was among the journalists keeping vigil at Elmhurst Hospital, hungry for each meager scrap of news. On Monday, he talked to a group of women who had just seen Hedda and were leaving the hospital with color photos of her injured flesh. "From what I could see," he wrote in his Tuesday *Daily News* column, "the woman had been beaten from head to toe. Literally. In one picture, there was a hole in Nussbaum's head that was about as big as I have seen." He ran into a nurse who refused to give him any hard information but told him that apparently Joel Steinberg had taught Hedda Nussbaum "that she was nothing and that he could beat her as if she were some farm animal." Breslin was seething with righteous moral indignation over Lisa's death, Hedda's beatings, and the tangentially related fact that there were eighteen thousand black and Hispanic children in New York City who could not find adoptive homes. In the last third of his column, he would rage against Steinberg. But before doing that, he swung the weight of his anger down hard on Lisa Steinberg's natural parents. "They had handed her out," he wrote, "as if she were a loaf of bread." Why had they not been required to keep the child and raise it? "It's bad enough that there is a full complement of black and Hispanic babies without the selfish and greedy whites starting to hand out their own." Breslin could summon up empathy for Hedda, but none whatsoever for the desperation of a white, unwed, pregnant teenage girl. Strangely enough, not one question about the issue of Hedda Nussbaum's culpability in Lisa's death was raised in his column. Breslin's wife, Ronnie Eldridge, in fact, had quickly become one of Hedda's supporters.

If Michelle Launders was still reading the papers at this point, Breslin's line about the loaf of bread could only have sapped the courage she needed for what she was about to do. Breslin knew his audience—he was not the only one who would condemn her for giving birth to Lisa and then giving her away. REAL MOM IN TORMENT, the Tuesday morning papers said, REAL MOM WON'T ATTEND FUNERAL. Lisa's natural mother had "expressed no wish or desire to become involved in the burial," the general counsel for the HRA announced. He had written the Jewish Free Burial Association, informing them that her body could be released to them for burial by the Nussbaums. In her darkest hours over that long weekend, Michelle Launders had evidently been overwhelmed by the urge to just let go, not become involved.

On Monday, Michelle Launders changed her mind. With the support of her mother and grandmother, she had pulled herself together and come to the only decision she could live with. Her grandmother had terminal cancer. You can bury Lisa with me, she told Michelle. Michelle and her mother went to St. Patrick's Cathedral for a meeting with Cardinal O'Connor, who gave them a special dispensation to bury Lisa as a Catholic even though she was unbaptized, because the child had died before the age of seven.

On Tuesday evening, accompanied by Anita Launders and a lawyer, Joe Famighetti, Michelle walked into Manhattan Surrogates Court for an emergency hearing before Judge Marie Lambert. Wearing black slacks and a white turtleneck sweater, her eyes behind her round glasses swollen from weeping, the young woman who hated to have her picture taken moved blindly forward past a phalanx of cameras. A few hours earlier, she had given her lawyer a statement to be released to the press: "If I had wanted my child murdered, I would have had an abortion."

When she took the stand, Michelle Launders went bluntly, quietly, and bitterly to the point: "I don't feel it's right to have my child . . . buried near, close to, or by the people who did kill her."

When Famighetti gently asked her if that meant she wanted the court to release her daughter's body to her, she answered "Yes," flushing and quaking from head to foot.

In the silent courtroom, there was a palpable feeling of relief.

Lisa Steinberg's life had gone all wrong from the start. Finally someone was trying to do right by her.

The hearing that followed to determine Lisa's legal identity took eight hours. At one point, Lisa's unnamed natural father phoned the court and had a long conversation with the judge. At 1 A.M., Judge Lambert declared herself convinced "there never was an adoption in this case" and ruled that Michelle Launders "had the right of the body of Elizabeth Steinberg."

The following day, Lisa was buried in the Launders family plot at the Gate of Heaven Cemetery in Valhalla, New York. District Attorney Robert Morgenthau granted Michelle's request to have the death certificate read: "Baby Girl Launders, also known as Lisa."

The casket was white with a red trim and only four feet six inches long. The services were held in Redden's Funeral Parlor, a brownstone all the way west on Fourteenth Street, a wide, bleak block near the meat markets and river. The chapel looked like a flower shop, with gladioli banked around the coffin and sprays, bouquets, and wreaths in every available space. It was far too small to hold all the mourners, the nearly one thousand who lined up outside in the cold. Many of Lisa's mourners were black and Hispanic; even some of the homeless stood on that line. There were neighbors who had known her, parents and teachers from P.S. 41, others from Greenwich Village who hadn't known her at all. People kept coming up out of the subway, arriving in cabs. The people on the line talked about kids, wondered how many there were in danger of dying like Lisa Steinberg. "There's the mother," they whispered when they saw Michelle walk up the steps and go inside.

She entered the chapel and made a sharp, wordless sound when she first saw the casket. Maybe what ran through her mind was the terrible irony that now she would see her child at last—the child who had been real, not the happy little girl she had imagined. She managed to walk all the way forward; then her legs seemed to give way and she sank down suddenly on a chair.

At ten, Cardinal O'Connor arrived; he knelt by the casket, whispered a brief prayer, and left with his entourage. Next there was a joint Catholic-Jewish ceremony; Michelle had thought clearly enough to agree to that. After the services the mourners from the street were allowed to come up one by one. It took three hours before the last of them filed past Lisa's casket.

None of Hedda Nussbaum's family came to the funeral. Hedda

Nussbaum had composed a eulogy for Lisa the day before and given it to Barry Scheck to be delivered to Redden's. She was disappointed when Scheck told her he didn't think it would be welcome there, and that no one would read it aloud. Months later Hedda would complain to her psychiatrist, Samuel Klagsbrun, that she had wanted to join Michelle in mourning for Lisa, but that Michelle herself had rejected her. She would say angrily that Michelle Launders had gone around acting like "the real mother."

Renee Gordon remembers hearing Joel Steinberg "definitely crying uncontrollably" in the midst of one of their conversations a few days after the funeral. For the following week or so he'd keep suddenly breaking down during his numerous calls to her. "I'm sorry, I'm sorry," he'd say, then pull himself together. As the weeks passed, though, he started making jokes again. During the period when he seemed to be mourning Lisa, he told Renee he wanted to give her a present—a token of his appreciation for her understanding. If she could locate the wallet he'd left in the bedroom of the apartment, she'd find a one-hundred-dollar gift certificate in it from Hammacher Schlemmer. You take it and get yourself something, he urged her. Renee had no intention of accepting anything from Joel Steinberg, but she did find the wallet, which contained, among other things, an old press pass issued by Columbia University. There was also a dirty, much folded, tattered piece of paper; when she unfolded it, it proved to be the gift certificate he had mentioned to her. The weird thing was, it was dated 1977. Renee couldn't get over it—he'd been carrying that around with him for ten years!

HEDDA NUSSBAUM, Barry Scheck told reporters the day after Lisa's funeral, was "literally a wreck—mentally and physically. It's beyond ordinary imagination or understanding." Her attorney did not elaborate, but the statement was well timed to stimulate the mounting sympathy for Hedda—the public could fill in the blanks and imagine her prostrate with grief over Lisa's death. Scheck had just come from a hearing in which he won a thirty-day stay for his client before she would be required to make an appearance before a grand jury. In the upcoming months, quiet postponements of other appearances would become almost routine; in December 1988, when Hedda Nussbaum finally did testify against Steinberg at his trial, few would remember or ask themselves why she had never been required to appear before a grand jury.

Skillfully, brilliantly, brick by brick, Barry Scheck was building an image: Hedda Nussbaum as victim—even an almost "pure victim," as many advocates of battered women were coming to see her. Now, in the latest papers filed by the Department of Social Services, Hedda was charged merely with neglecting her children, not with abuse. In regard to Mitchell, for example, only the unsanitary conditions in which he had been found were cited.

The upcoming court hearings about Mitchell Steinberg's temporary custody were about to provide Hedda Nussbaum's defense team with an excellent opportunity to add a touch of pathos to Hedda's maternal image. Hedda was not only Joel Steinberg's victim, but a mother bereft of her blond, blue-eyed baby boy. She was so concerned about his welfare that attorney David Lansner went to court on November 13 to demand that Hedda be granted the right to visit him. He read aloud to Judge Jeffrey Gallet from the plea Hedda had written herself on a yellow legal pad: "It would cause great harm to the child to totally remove him from all contact with the only mother the child has ever known."

It's doubtful that Lansner actually hoped the judge would grant visitation rights. But if the plea was also made with an eye to improving Hedda's image, it certainly generated some dramatic headlines. LET ME SEE MY CHILD (the *New York Post*'s) was the most heartrending one.

Judge Gallet, however, was unmoved. "One of the real questions," he told Lansner with a touch of sarcasm, "is whether your client—I hate to make this seem like a property matter—has a claim to this child." If the exact quality of Hedda's care remained a gray issue; property rights were definitely in the realm of black and white. Mitchell Steinberg, as far as anyone could tell, had never been adopted. On that basis, Gallet denied Nussbaum the right to visit him in his foster home.

Even more avidly than millions of other New Yorkers, Sherry Burger and her husband had been following the Steinberg case from day to day, holding their breaths when there was news of any developments concerning Mitchell. No one at the SSC would tell them very much; basically, they knew what they read in the papers. One night they went out to dinner, taking Boomer to a restaurant on Queens Boulevard; when they walked in, everyone was holding the *Daily News* with a big picture of him sitting in Lisa's lap right on the cover. It gave the Burgers a strange feeling to think he was probably the most famous baby in America. The truth of the matter was, they were hoping Boomer's real family wouldn't want to claim him; they'd grown dangerously attached to him. They'd felt pain before when it came time to give up other foster children, but they knew Boomer's departure would be the hardest one of all. If Boomer goes, I can't go through this again, Mitchell Burger told Sherry. "It almost broke up our marriage," she remembered later.

At the beginning of the second week Mitchell stayed with them, the Burgers had reason to feel a little hopeful. Mitchell's natural mother and her family had been located and were said to be cooperating with the district attorney's investigation, but for a while they seemed to show no great eagerness to take him back. The name of the baby's family, Smigiel, had first appeared in the papers on November 8. When a *Daily News* reporter called the Smigiel house in Massapequa Park, Long Island, and asked Dennis Smigiel, the baby's grandfather, for a comment, the answer was a curt denial: "I don't know what you're talking about." Yet the following day, when Joel Steinberg was summoned to family court for a preliminary hearing to determine who should have custody of Mitchell, the Smigiel name certainly came up again.

According to what David Verplank, a Long Island attorney, had first told law-enforcement authorities, Mitchell's mother was a teenager, who, on June 21, 1986, walked in off the street in labor and delivered her baby a few hours later in Beth Israel Hospital. She had asked Peter Sarosi, her attending obstetrician, to arrange an immediate adoption. As luck would have it, the doctor had known of a wonderful couple, a Mr. and Mrs. Steinberg, who wanted very much to have a second child. After Joel Steinberg got in touch with him, David Verplank arranged to have papers drawn up by still another attorney, David Lowe. The baby by this time had already been delivered to Joel and Hedda.

Verplank said he had worked with Steinberg on a private adoption seven years before (he did not indicate whether or not he had been involved with Steinberg on a more extensive basis). He claimed he had no reason not to believe Steinberg when he promised he would marry Hedda Nussbaum as soon as possible and legalize the adoption of his newborn son. Verplank admitted he had later learned that neither of these steps had been taken, but at the time he just didn't see how he could possibly inform the natural mother. So he simply decided "to do nothing and keep my fingers crossed" in the naïve hope that Joel Steinberg would eventually be motivated to keep his promises.

There was the sense, however, that Steinberg's broken promises had not greatly concerned Verplank; nor had he felt enough responsibility for the welfare of the child he had placed with him to want to pursue the matter. As for the young mother who had walked in "off the street," why should he have extended himself for her? Girls had babies they didn't want all the time, and needed to get rid of them, and he just happened to be one of the middlemen. Or a Good Samaritan, as Dr. Sarosi had originally seen himself—you could look at it that way as well. In one baby-selling ring in Brooklyn, a white baby went for thirty-six thousand dollars. In a similar operation in Pennsylvania, the prices were in the same ballpark. Some made even greater profits. When the Manhattan district attorney's office conducted an investigation into private adoption in 1988, they found one group of six New York lawyers and several doctors (one of whom had placed 200 infants) that had been selling babies for as much as one hundred thousand dollars. Joel Steinberg, however, had gotten Mitchell from Sarosi for free—it had been an altruistic act of friendship.

Verplank swore that Mitchell's "adoption" was the first Peter Sarosi had ever been involved in. The distraught doctor had recently phoned him and asked if he was in trouble: "I told him I didn't think so." Now, of course, Verplank was greatly shocked by the revelations about conditions in the Steinberg household; in fact, if there had been a seismograph to measure human shock, his would have been of the same magnitude as Sarosi's. "The one thing you never have to worry about," he blandly assured *The New York Times*, "is the petition for adoption being filed in court."

Soon Verplank stopped giving interviews. Although Peter Sarosi became the *first* Manhattan doctor to be prosecuted in connection with the unauthorized placing out of a child for adoption, the Manhattan district attorney's office never went after the lawyer. Verplank is a quadriplegic, which may have discouraged the authorities from attempting to press charges, since a jury would be unlikely to convict a man in that condition.

At his trial before Judge John Stackhouse in December 1988, Sarosi would plead ignorance of the law and claim that Steinberg had duped him. In view of the fact that he was an "admired, highly respected, and beloved physician," with no previous offenses, Judge Stackhouse sentenced Sarosi to three years' probation, one hundred hours of community service and the surprisingly low maximum fine of one thousand dollars. But, of course, the doctor had only been found guilty of a misdemeanor; his role in turning Mitchell over to Steinberg would have been deemed a misdemeanor even if Steinberg had paid him.

Although Judge Stackhouse briefly acknowledged in his written opinion that Mitchell Steinberg might suffer psychological damage for the rest of his life, it was Sarosi's fall from grace that inspired his eloquence: "How ironic that one who has served so well for so long should find himself singled out as an object of public ridicule, hatred and scorn." Stackhouse then indulged in a quote from *Julius Caesar:* "The evil that men do / lives after them, / The good is oft interred / with their bones."

But the State Board of Regents took a far less compassionate view of Sarosi's "serious lapse of judgment." In June 1989, it revoked his license for one year, leaving reinstatement open to questions. Sarosi continued to practice, pending his appeal.

On November 18, Sherry Burger got an early morning phone call from a social worker at SSC. She was peremptorily told to bring Mitchell to the agency; that afternoon he was going to be taken to Family Court to meet his natural mother. The young woman now wanted temporary custody of him and would ultimately ask for permanent custody. "Is he going to go home with her?" Sherry asked tearfully, but the social worker wouldn't say. "Just pack him up and bring him here."

"Just pack him up!" The words made Sherry indignant. They were talking about a baby, a baby who had been through a terrible ordeal and was just beginning to adjust to his new life. He'd be frightened all over again when he was turned over to strangers. Besides, no one would tell her a thing about Nicole Smigiel. She'd had to give children back before to parents unfit to take care of them. One of these children had died. She called a lawyer to find out if the baby had any rights. The lawyer thought Mitchell might be able to stay with her until he and Nicole got to know each other.

Mitchell's mother was only eighteen years old. She showed up in court that day, hand in hand with her own weeping mother, Graceanne Smigiel. Their entrance into the drama provided an unexpected bonanza for the media. After so much grimness, the story needed an upbeat note. What could be better than a heroine in the ingenue role who looked the part? Nicole Smigiel was not a tragic, depressed figure like Michelle Launders; nor was she at all shy of the camera. She had the big-eyed, sensuous face of an Italian starlet, a perfect figure, and an irrepressible exuberance. (In 1989, she embarked on a modeling career.) Graceanne also proved to be youthful and photogenic—a volatile woman who looked a bit like Elizabeth Taylor, with a penchant for big earrings and expensive flashy clothes.

In fact, Verplank's rather disparaging description of Nicole as a girl who had walked in "off the street" now turned out to have been extremely misleading. Nicole Smigiel's street happened to be right on the waterfront in Massapequa Park; the brick ranch house she had grown up in with her younger brother and sister had five bedrooms and was assessed to be worth two hundred thousand dollars. Her father was an executive in a boat sales company. Nicole herself seemed a classic American archetype, practically a cliché—as if the scriptwriters had suddenly grown weary of constantly coming up with unusual characters.

She was the kind of girl born and groomed to succeed in high school. Had it not been for certain accidents of fate, she might have been able to define herself forever as one of the most popular girls at Massapequa High. To no one's surprise, Nicole had been a cheerleader, an activity that had her mother's support. Even though Nicole had gone on to college, Graceanne remained the adviser of the local pep team. Nicole was the apple of her mother's eye—there was the sense that Graceanne had relived her own adolescence by identifying with her daughter's teenage triumphs. Nicole was gorgeous and having a wonderful time. What else did a mother need to know? When Nicole was seventeen, Graceanne apparently had the illusion that her daughter told her everything, though even happy girls have their secrets. That summer Nicole perfected her tan on the local beaches and on the Smigiels' boat and broke up with a nice blond boy named Mark Urban, who was going away to college in the fall.

Parent-child relations, like love affairs, can fracture under the weight of absolute truth. The Smigiels were Catholic, and the parents of good Catholic girls, even today, do not talk to them openly about birth control. The fiction is that somehow nice girls remain virgins, despite the headiness of popularity, despite the raging hormones of adolescence, despite the trouble other people's daughters get into. Dennis Smigiel seems to have had impassioned, very old-fashioned ideas on the subject. "My husband will kill us if he finds out," Graceanne reportedly told Peter Sarosi a few hours before Mitchell's birth.

For the previous nine months, she had excluded from her awareness the possibility that her daughter might be pregnant, though everyone had noticed that Nicole was rapidly putting on weight. Graceanne had even enrolled her at the Jack La Lanne Health Spa so that she could work off those extra pounds. Nicole herself refused to believe she could be pregnant—such a terrible thing couldn't happen to a girl who'd led a charmed life. She worried instead about having a fatal disease—in a way, that must have seemed a preferable catastrophe. She had gotten over Mark Urban and had a new boyfriend who was taking her to the senior prom. Graceanne had bought her a strapless powder-blue formal for the occasion. One night during the third week in June, her mother came to her room to see how she looked in it. Nicole broke down because she couldn't get it on. She had to tell Graceanne how long it had been since she'd had her period.

Graceanne didn't waste time. Fiercely maternal, she came up with a rescue plan so fast there was no space for either of them to think beyond their panic—to think about the baby. Graceanne acted before the baby seemed at all real, before she was capable of imagining it as a person rather than a threat to Nicole's future, an accident that had somehow befallen them.

She knew what her priorities were—saving her daughter, saving her marriage. Somehow Nicole had to give birth to that baby and find a good home for it right away, without Dennis Smigiel's ever finding out. People were always looking for babies to adopt; people were desperate for babies. Graceanne made a phone call to her Massapequa health clinic and was referred to Dr. Ellen Miller, who was handling emergencies. Dr. Miller advised her to buy her daughter an Early Pregnancy Test at a drugstore. The following morning, June 21, Miller examined Nicole, found that she was ready to deliver, and made an appointment for her to meet Dr. Sarosi a few hours later. Sarosi, Dr. Miller assured them, would help them discreetly put the baby up for adoption.

Graceanne and Nicole packed overnight bags and hastily left town—ostensibly to visit a college Nicole was interested in attending. Dr. Sarosi examined Nicole in his University Place office, admitted her to Beth Israel Hospital under what Judge Stackhouse later called a "cloak of secrecy," and gave her a drug to induce labor. A few hours later, he was able to phone Joel Steinberg and announce, "I've got this beautiful little baby for you!" On June 23, Graceanne carried the baby out of the hospital and handed him over to Sarosi's partner, Dr. Mitchell Essig, who was entrusted with delivering him to the wonderful Greenwich Village couple Sarosi knew. Essig had met the "Steinbergs" himself. In fact, they named the baby after him.

Graceanne and Nicole Smigiel returned to the ranch house in Massapequa Park and for the next sixteen months successfully managed to act as if nothing out of the ordinary had happened. The baby would remain their secret, as if it had sunk into a lake of silence. Nicole never even told Mark Urban about it, although a year later she started seeing him again. The other boy took her to the prom in her blue strapless. In the fall, Nicole went off to LaSalle College in Baltimore, hoping to someday become a lawyer. So her life was just the way it was supposed to be, except there was this little baby she could talk about only to Graceanne.

A beguiled reporter dubbed Nicole "the princess of poise." Preceding her courtroom appearance with Graceanne, there may have been stormy confrontations with the head of the Smigiel household, days of painful indecision before the family decided to go public with the secret Nicole and her mother had kept for seventeen months. But now the Smigiels were able to say unequivocally that they wanted Mitchell. And maybe they also wanted fame—the most bankable kind of popularity. The fame and sympathy Graceanne and Nicole were about to get would make up for a lot of anguish and embarrassment, although it would never wipe away their feelings of guilt or the awful things they hoped Mitchell would never find out about his previous life.

Thanksgiving was just around the corner; in 1987, America would celebrate it with the Smigiel family, including Mr. Smigiel, who had metamorphosed quickly into a proud grandfather. Mitchell's televised homecoming, two days after his first meeting with his mother and grandmother, would seem the happy ending of the kind of soul-satisfying, wholesome, old-fashioned movie no longer made in Hollywood, like the finale of *Miracle on Thirty-fourth Street* or *It's a Wonderful Life.* In a deeper way, it was like a traditional fairy tale come true, or the enactment of the classic fantasy children have when they feel unloved or ill-treated—the foundling prince rescued from his evil surrogate parents and restored to his rightful kingdom and castle. Because we have no control over the circumstances of our births—because all we know about our beginnings is what we're told—we all identify a little with foundlings who come into the world stripped of their history and seem even more at the mercy of circumstances than the rest of us. We need to believe in happy endings—in the power of love to undo the harm done to us when we were small and helpless. In that sense, mistakenly, we put our faith in forgetfulness: If Lisa Steinberg had only been rescued, she would then have gone on to have a good life. Nicole Smigiel's kisses, a nursery full of toys and adorable outfits, would guarantee Mitchell a happy childhood, as if he had never been filthy, hungry, and untended, or frightened by the sights and sounds of the Steinberg household. Yet every manual on the care of infants tells new parents how much the child learns in the early months of life, how knowledge is transmitted to the infant with every touch.

"He's my baby. He's my baby," Nicole Smigiel kept mouthing during the hearing as the son she had last seen for minutes in Beth Israel Hospital dozed in a court officer's lap. Every reporter in the packed courtroom could read her lips.

Again David Lansner pressed Hedda's claim to the boy, this time casting aspersions on the character of Mitchell's natural mother. She had lied to her father and boyfriend about her pregnancy; she had abandoned her son. She had no right even to be in that courtroom. Again he pleaded for temporary visitation rights for "the only mother" the boy had ever known, as Nicole angrily shook her head and whispered, "No!"

The relinquishment and guardianship papers Nicole had signed now were made public. In language obviously framed by an attorney, Nicole described herself as "abandoned and deserted" by her child's father—though Mark Urban had only just learned to his astonishment that he had impregnated her. The papers also stated that she had not arrived at her decision to give up her baby hastily, "having given it careful thought, believing that my child should have both a mother and a father." This statement, of course, did not reflect the speed and impulsiveness with which she and Graceanne had acted. In seeking a "suitable home" for the child born to her, Nicole had been "satisfied"—purely on the basis of Sarosi's and Verplank's assurances—that the Steinbergs "could and would provide the minor . . . with the love and affection of devoted parents."

Mitchell's devoted "adoptive" mother was absent from this second hearing as well. The previous day Hedda had been transferred to the psychiatric ward of Columbia-Presbyterian, a private hospital. But Steinberg showed up to support Nussbaum's claim; his lawyer echoed Lansner's unconvincing arguments. Looking seedy in his Rikers Island hand-me-downs, Joel Steinberg sat at the defendant's table, scribbling incessantly on a yellow legal pad as he would later do all through his own trial. He may have had hopes of seeing Hedda in court that day and thus fortify his influence over her; it may not have quite dawned on him that Barry Scheck was determined to see to it that the two of them would have no further contact.

For the second time Judge Gallet ruled against Hedda Nussbaum. He granted temporary custody of Mitchell to Nicole Smigiel but stated that he would wait twenty-four hours before making his final decision in order to give Nussbaum and Steinberg a chance to appeal. "I'm not a big fan of foster care," he said. That night Mitchell went home to the Burgers for the last time. The following day Appellate Division Presiding Justice Francis Murphy denied the appeal of Gallet's decision, wasting no words in his written statement: "Joel Steinberg is in prison. Hedda Nussbaum is in a mental hospital. It does not lie in their mouths to question the custody of the child."

Triumphantly the Smigiels carried off Mitchell, mobbed by a pack of cameramen from the networks. Additional news crews had been dispatched to Massapequa Park to camp out on their lawn. Nicole looked radiant with her arms around her wide-eyed son, her cheek against his clean blond hair. She bestowed upon reporters a headline for the morning papers: "He called me Mommy!"

Sherry Burger saw Mitchell going away from her on TV. She got Nicole's number from information and called the house to tell her some things she thought she should know about the baby, his medical history, for one thing. The Smigiels seemed to be having a party. Someone took the message, but no one got back to her.

In her room at Columbia-Presbyterian, Hedda Nussbaum also watched the evening news. According to David Lansner, she broke down and cried when she saw Nicole holding Mitchell. Lansner told her that it would be unlikely that she would be able to get Mitchell back; that a battle for his custody would be a long, expensive, fruitless fight. Over the weekend, on another yellow legal pad, she wrote a three-page statement, surrendering all rights to the custody of the child, which her lawyers promptly released to the press.

Although Scheck had painted a dire picture of his client's mental condition, and would soon be intimating that she had suffered brain damage, the statement was remarkably cogent, eloquently expressed, and sane. It created the image of a woman capable of empathy and even of an unselfish act, prepared to do what was in the best interests of her son. Perhaps the woman Hedda Nussbaum had once been had surfaced for a while. On the other hand, she was giving up nothing by writing such a letter, since it was clear that the battle had already been lost, although Steinberg, with his combative zest for litigation, would continue for a while to claim his right to custody.

The Monday *New York Post* ran Hedda's "letter of heartbreak" on the same page as an interview with a friend of hers named Larry Weinberg, who gave some graphic details of her years of torture. A photo just below the letter showed Nicole Smigiel looking stunning in a white Mongolian lamb jacket returning from church with Mitchell, also in white, who had just been given the name of Travis Christian Smigiel.

"I have just made the most difficult decision of my life," Hedda began. "From behind my tears," she had seen Mitchell smiling and Nicole "beaming with joy. And I was now glad he is no longer in foster care but with his natural mother who, it seems, will give him plenty of love.

"I believe that it will be a long time before I completely recover from both my physical ailments and the psychological suffering

I've been going through. By the time I might be ready to care for him, he would have been in Nicole's custody for many months, and would have formed a strong love attachment to her . . . One painful separation is enough in a child's life."

In the entire text, there was only one passing reference to Lisa. In the sentence that preceded the one with Lisa's name, Hedda wrote about her son with what sounded like genuine passion: "I truly love Mitchell and have held him both in my arms for 16 months and in my heart for 17 now, and will continue to forever." Then the language cooled down, and become merely conventional: "Both he and Lisa will always be an important part of me, and I miss them both terribly."

In her last paragraph, Hedda, oddly enough, considering the horrific circumstances of her life with Steinberg, wrote about joy: "I know the joy Nicole has now and will have for years to come. I had that same joy for 16 months. I do not begrudge Nicole her newfound love; I do envy her. But I wish her the best for Mitchell . . . or Travis. I can only hope that one day Nicole will allow me to see him again."

Those were the last words, coming directly from Hedda Nussbaum, that the public would be able to read for the next twelve months.

ONLY A WEEK before, on the weekend of November 14-15, as Hedda Nussbaum awaited the first hearing on her right to visit Mitchell, she wrote a letter to Joel Steinberg, telling him that Barry Scheck had advised her not to appear in Family Court. She was disappointed at losing that chance to see Joel.

The letter was unreproachful and long—Hedda filled four and a half sheets of yellow legal paper with her large rounded handwriting. "I will choose my words carefully," she wrote, "because this will be seen by more eyes than yours." If Hedda had been in a daze when she was arrested, two weeks later she seemed to have a reasonably clear—even legalistic—understanding of the predicament she was in and the limits of what she could set down in a letter addressed to Joel. (Indeed, after she finished writing it, she showed those yellow sheets to Scheck like a dutiful student handing in a paper; when he advised her not to send it, she obediently followed his counsel.) She knew it would be unwise, for example, to proclaim her undying love for Joel, and so she took the precaution of expressing it in code. "And yes I do," she wrote cryptically a number of times. "And yes I do." In a way, the need for secrecy may have added a certain exhilaration to the writing—it gave Hedda an opportunity to play Joel and Barry off against each other, as if they were rivals for her favors, each to be kept slightly in the dark.

There was another thing she would only refer to in code—the name of Dr. Michael Green, a pulmonary specialist who had once been a friend of hers and Joel's and was now the person Joel hated and feared most in the entire world. Joel may have cautioned her during their last hours together at the apartment to use particular discretion in bringing up Michael Green (the doctor and his alleged involvement in the cult Steinberg had discussed with Kalina were going to be important elements in the story he was going to tell about what had happened to Lisa.) "Dr. G. is in Pennsylvania," Hedda wrote, "and will not be contacted except by private detectives—anonymously, of course." In another passage, she told Joel she had talked to one of Scheck's assistants about "many things, including green things" (she may have enjoyed this pun because Joel knew how much she loved plants), but she assured Joel that everything she told her doctors and her legal team was "privileged"; in fact, she had discovered that she was in control of what her lawyers and doctors told others. Barry had been surprised she hadn't realized that. She was going to remain in control of her secrets and Joel's even after she was transferred to Columbia-Presbyterian Hospital in the next few days.

There was no safer subject, of course, than her maternal feelings. She wrote a few lines about Mitchell similar to the visitation plea she had given to Lansner: "No one thinks of Mitchell. He's got to wonder what happened to me, you and Lisa. We just disappeared from his life." If the general public had the impression that Mitchell had been neglected by Hedda, she clung to the idea she had spoiled him. She was sure Mitchell missed her, just as she missed him. Nowhere in the letter did she specifically write that she missed Lisa, even though a line to that effect would have been legally advisable.

Hedda had evidently quickly assimilated the fact that Lisa was dead—no longer a living, breathing presence in her life, but the sentimental focus for memorial services. Hedda herself would have liked to be a visible mourner, craved that attention and sympathy. She fretted to Joel over the suppression of her eulogy, which she claimed Barry Scheck had praised for its beauty of expression. It must have angered her to think it could never be read under her name, even at the service for Lisa that her parents were planning. Still she was quite proud of her literary effort—so much so that she was hopeful some of the New York papers would quote it, as if its sheer eloquence would make it newsworthy.

Joel's mother was going to be invited to this second service, of course, but it was important to Hedda that certain others be present there as well. "Should we invite friends who loved Lisa— like Greg, Bobby, Chubby?" Hedda lamented that unfortunately Greg seemed unreachable, unaware that Malmoulka had vanished a day or two after Lisa's death, leaving no forwarding address (even by 1990 he remained among the missing). Chubby, one of Joel's clients, happened to be an exceedingly questionable and inappropriate mourner. Chubby was also known as the Fat Man. His real name was Andrew D'Apice, and he was reputedly involved with the Gambino mob. He ran a small company on Spring Street that produced and distributed pornographic films. By 1989, Chubby was serving a prison sentence.

There seem to have been a number of things Hedda was still not confiding to Scheck; if he had known about Chubby, he would have strongly advised his client not to attempt to contact him. Nonetheless, a transference was under way, even two weeks after Lisa's death when Hedda's loyalty to Joel was still unshaken (she still believed her attorney and Joel's would work in concert). Scheck must have winced when he read the line, "I pray your idea [probably referring to an alibi she and Joel had agreed upon] will be effective," after Hedda informed Joel that she and her attorneys would soon see the second autopsy report on Lisa. But perhaps the letter also made Scheck realize that Hedda would increasingly look to him for protection, approval, confirmation of her importance and worth, that it would be possible to mold her into the Hedda *he* wanted her to be—the Hedda who would someday testify against the very man to whom she wrote "And yes I do."

There are certain women for whom men serve as mirrors. Without them they cannot quite see themselves, or want to reject what they see. Separated from Joel at Elmhurst Hospital, Hedda had caught a glimpse of a reflection that momentarily horrified her. Watching "20/20," she had heard a neighbor describe her as "a beautiful woman" who had become "an old hag." "I looked in the mirror. She's right. I will change that," she vowed to Joel, "and be beautiful again." It was as if she had forgotten she was addressing the agent of her destruction. Quite the contrary. The mere act of writing to Joel magically empowered her. When you love, anything seems possible—even the restoration of youth and beauty.

When all was said and done, aside from that awful moment when she had dared to look at her face, it was a letter overflowing with what one might call "positive thinking." She enthused over the sympathetic Elmhurst staff. She was eating well, but was careful to promise Joel that she was remaining thin. Even the pain caused by the condition of her right leg had turned out to be of psychic value, although she had been told she could have lost the leg if it had gone much longer without treatment. Interestingly enough, Hedda reminded Joel that he too had warned her that it was potentially gangrenous. With a certain relish, she described her operation—how no anesthetic would work because one ulceration had gone straight down to the nerves.

The pain Hedda felt under the surgical knife may have given her the illusion that she was feeling what she could not truly feel, but knew she should have felt: "I must say it was a great release. I yelled and cried and talked about Lisa."

"Amazingly," she wrote in the last paragraph of her letter, "even though I miss some little people a lot, I'm feeling real fine. And yes, I do."

When an orderly came in with her breakfast tray, she added in a coy postscript: "It doesn't take much to make me happy."

Another postscript reflected on the fate of the brown and white rabbit and the tanks of fish: "The rabbit was rescued by the police when they searched. The fish have probably eaten each other alive. *C'est la vie.*"

II

THE "STEINBERGS"

IN THE SUMMER of 1989, the Romany Kramoris Gallery in Sag Harbor, Long Island, received a number of anonymous bomb threats because it was about to sponsor "Signs of Life," a show of twelve small black-and-white photographic prints by Hedda Nussbaum. Romany Kramoris abruptly canceled "Signs of Life," then defiantly rescheduled it.

At Kramoris's urging, Nussbaum had prepared a very brief statement of artistic purpose, explaining that the work had been done at Four Winds Hospital during an eighteen-month period while she was "coming back from emotional death." But the prints themselves reveal little about Hedda Nussbaum beyond her facility in using a camera and the conventionality of her imagination. The imagery is so predictable, you could almost describe the show without ever seeing it; black twisted branches against an ominous sky, bare tree trunks rising up along a snow-covered path, a calligraphic leafless shrub, pale budding blossoms symbolic of regeneration. A white rose with curling petals emerging from darkness was perhaps meant as a self-portrait.

Without the signature, there would be nothing arresting. Only the name forces you to stare at each shot. But Hedda Nussbaum remains impenetrable.

One closeup has some directly autobiographical subject matter. A dark rabbit with white markings crouches on frozen ground, one small round eye peering warily up at the viewer. As it happened, this rabbit was brown and white and looked just like the one Lisa had, Hedda Nussbaum told Romany Kramoris, except that "Lisa's bunny was a little dwarf."

Mister Bunny is the name Hedda Nussbaum has given this photograph. Even more than the eleven others, it presents a mystery. It is rather astounding that Hedda took this picture, that

the sight of that brown rabbit so much like the dead child's was
not so unbearably painful that all she could do was look away.
Instead Hedda Nussbaum reached for her camera. But there is
nothing in the picture that tells us why, and perhaps Hedda does
not know herself.

Nonetheless, in preparation for "Signs of Life," she made up a
number of prints of *Mister Bunny,* matting each one in quite a
professional way, so that it could hang framed on some stranger's
living-room wall, signed Hedda Nussbaum.

Each life is a story. People tell themselves or relate to others their
true lives or their false ones. But even if "true," any story takes
its form from the particular weight and order an individual as-
signs to remembered events. All that is forgotten also shapes this
version of reality. Events acquire meaning from their juxtaposi-
tions to each other. Omit one thing and the meaning changes.
The attempt, then, to remember everything, or at least as much
as humanly possible, becomes a moral exercise as well as a fierce
striving toward sanity.

Hedda Nussbaum's story is as amorphous as her photographic
work. The few things she has revealed about her history do not
seem to add up. Nothing really accounts for the degeneration of
the attractive, hard-working children's book editor into the
woman who opened the door of apartment 3W on the morning
of November 2, the woman who remained with a man like Steinberg for so many years.

No one could have been more determined than Joel Steinberg's
defense lawyer, Ira London, to extract some psychological logic
from Hedda Nussbaum's story. "Your life is the testimony, is it
not, Miss Nussbaum?" he remarked with some exasperation at
one point during Steinberg's trial in December 1988. By then,
London had discovered that much of Nussbaum's testimony con-
sisted of blanks and blind alleys.

On her third morning on the witness stand, he asked her: "Do
you consider yourself to have had an unhappy upbringing, Miss
Nussbaum?"

"Not especially. No," she said. Nothing in that impassive response created an opening for further inquiry along the same line.

London, however, would not back off. He repeated the question in more muted language:

"Do you consider it to have been uneventful?"

"I think," Hedda Nussbaum answered with the aplomb and
studied detachment of a social worker reporting on a case, "after

being in a hospital with people from dysfunctional homes, by comparison, my upbringing was rather normal and uneventful."

"By comparison to others?"

"Yes," Nussbaum insisted.

"By your own standards?"

"I think it was average."

At the time of the trial, one prevailing theory about Hedda Nussbaum was that she must have grown up in an unusually repressive household; outside experts and armchair psychologists went so far as to speculate that Nussbaum's helplessness as an adult, her inability to extricate herself from her tormentor, even her seeming lapses of memory, were consistent with having been physically or sexually abused as a child. Such a history would have been neatly in accordance with the profile of "the typical battered woman." For Ira London's purposes, it could have been used to create another hypothesis, also based on the findings of experts: that a woman who had been an abused child was likely to become an abusive parent.

Hedda Nussbaum was schooled enough to be aware how loaded that phrase "unhappy upbringing" was on Ira London's lips and how all that it might imply could be used against her.

"So at thirty, you entered into a therapy session, is that right?" he pressed on, leading her into what he knew would seem a more comfortable area.

Like so many in her generation, Hedda Nussbaum had believed she could become totally transformed if only she could connect with the right kind of treatment, the right doctor, some instantaneous zap of enlightenment. During the 1970s, Hedda had pursued a variety of cures for her troubled psyche. She volunteered to London that until she was thirty-two (the year she met Steinberg) she had gone to therapy sessions three times a week.

London took a deep breath and asked with exaggerated patience, "What put you into it?"

The answer to that was too self-evident to avoid. "I just felt I wasn't a happy person. Nothing specific."

"Did you think that your upbringing was uneventful? Or did you think something else about your own life, up to that point?"

"Well, I had discovered a lot of things about my upbringing when I was in therapy. I had also thought my upbringing was quite uneventful and normal, and I had discovered there were a lot of things that caused me problems, but I didn't think they were, you know, huge kinds of problems."

Then Ira London tried to ambush her: "Did you have friends?"

"As a child, I had few friends."

There was little doubt that this admission was truthful. Whether or not she considered her upbringing unhappy, Hedda Nussbaum had always thought of herself as an essentially friendless person—this was, in fact, a major motif in the story she had constructed about herself. Perhaps she had indeed been lonelier than most children. Certainly, by the time she testified, no one outside the Nussbaum family had ever come forward to fill in the earliest chapters of her life—the way childhood friends are apt to do when someone becomes a negative celebrity.

Still, lonely little girls do not necessarily have catastrophic adult lives.

Perhaps the key to Hedda Nussbaum's personality is something she has totally forgotten—some small but crucial clue, like "Rosebud" in *Citizen Kane.* But it's equally possible that there is no key, and that it's only the Freudian habit of mind that has made so many people look so hard for one. The most disturbing thing about Nussbaum is how ordinary and familiar she seems in her pre-Steinberg life, although desperate to be interesting, to be anything but a cliché. Clearly, this is still her quest. Now that the trial is behind her, she has convinced herself that suffering has turned her into the artist she was always meant to be, yet she is stuck with the triteness of her leafless trees and with *Mister Bunny,* to whom she cannot attach a valid emotion.

In a way it would be a relief to learn that Hedda Nussbaum had been beaten by her parents, that her relationship with her father had been incestuous. That would both explain her and distance her from those of us who consider ourselves more normal than she is. In fact, it appears she was not an abused child at all, that her upbringing was truly as average and uneventful as she said it was.

When Romany Kramoris first contacted Hedda in December 1988, she sent her a Mozart cassette and a long heart-to-heart letter, some of which was written under the assumption that Hedda had been an abused child. Although the two women have since spent a great deal of time together, Nussbaum has never given Kramoris such a confidence. Nor has Hedda's Four Winds psychiatrist, Samuel Klagsbrun, who has been extraordinarily vocal about his patient, ever indicated that Hedda was abused by either of her parents.

In the one interview Nussbaum has given to the press—an article published in *People* in 1989, written by her Hunter Col

lege classmate Naomi Weiss—Hedda herself seems to be casting
around for bits of autobiography that might conceivably account
for her disastrous failures of will, persuade the reader as well as
herself that they were inevitable. If psychological predestination
led her to Joel Steinberg, then choice would have been out of the
question.

Much of the article, however, focuses on Hedda Nussbaum's joy
at being reunited with her family, and the sorrows and disap-
pointments of her childhood sound no worse than yours or mine.
But it does become clear that Hedda Nussbaum grew up feeling
very angry with her mother. She was always much closer to William Nussbaum, according to what she has told Romany Kramoris.
This strong attachment to her father lasted until she became
involved with Steinberg. Even in her early thirties, while she was
working at Random House, Hedda would take the subway uptown and visit her father in his beauty shop on Fort Washington
Avenue in Washington Heights and have him cut her hair, just as
he had when she was a little girl.

A letter Hedda wrote in 1979 that her attorneys released to the
press states her belief that her mother had wanted to have her
aborted. Did Hedda actually find this out or did she make it up?
Or was it an idea suggested by Joel Steinberg that seemed to
validate the feeling she'd always had of being an unwanted child.

In 1942, when Hedda was born, her sister Judy was already
ensconced in the household. During the trial, when Hedda was
asked how much older her sister was, she replied, "Twenty-two
months," rather than saying two years. It seemed a child's answer.
Even in Nussbaum's middle age, each month of Judy's seniority
was still meaningful.

Resentment of Judy's status colors Hedda Nussbaum's recollections of her girlhood, although her sister did become her closest
friend. Her mother promoted this, turning Hedda over to Judy for
companionship, Nussbaum told Weiss, implying that it was all for
Mrs. Nussbaum's convenience. Emma Nussbaum dressed her two
daughters in matching outfits and they had the same friends,
Judy's friends. "It was always 'we' or 'us,' never 'I' or 'me,'"
Hedda said with residual bitterness. She is not the first younger
sister to feel she had been dragged along in the wake of her older
sibling, and that her own needs had been too often overlooked.
Yet perhaps Mrs. Nussbaum did go too far in forcing Hedda to
merge with a stronger personality. As an adult, Hedda lived the
life of a chameleon, adapting herself to whoever had influence

over her behavior at the moment. "Put her on red and she's red," observed Bellevue psychiatrist Michael Allen, who examined her in 1987. "Put her on green and she's green."

Although Mrs. Nussbaum presented her daughters to the world as if they were twins, there were striking physical differences between them. Judy was tiny and blond; today, she is elfin-looking, with her short neck and sharp, slightly wizened features. Hedda grew much taller than her sister. This may have contributed to Mrs. Nussbaum's unrealistic expectations that Hedda act as grown-up as Judy. As a young woman, Hedda made the most of her five feet six inches with the upward tilt of her head and her proud erect carriage. Her eyes were almond-shaped before the bone around them was broken. Her thick, curly hair was once black and glossy. Early on, the Nussbaums must have realized that Hedda would be the beauty of the family. But did Hedda herself feel beautiful? Did Hedda wish she could be Judy instead of Hedda, that she, too, could be tiny and blond and bossy and sure of her mother's love?

Yet Mrs. Nussbaum was hardly inattentive. In fact, Hedda felt her mother infantilized her by fussing over her far too much: "[she] insisted on doing everything for me—putting on my socks at age six, for example. . . . my father, on the other hand, was always saying, 'Listen to me. I'm older. I know better.' The combination made me feel like I couldn't do anything for myself and didn't know anything. I just went where I was taken," Hedda said plaintively, perhaps trying to drive home the point that in her life with Joel Steinberg she had also gone where she was taken.

Hedda also remembers herself as "always trying to be a good girl, so I wouldn't be left alone. I was very shy and timid. And I never showed any anger."

"So I wouldn't be left alone" suggests that Emma Nussbaum may have disciplined her small daughter by putting her in a room by herself on occasion. It's a fairly mild and common form of punishment, yet it can be as frightening as a blow. A small child lacks a sense of time, exists wholly in the present. A few hours in an empty room may seem a life sentence. As for the anger toward her exacting mother, which little Hedda was not permitted to express, it existed and was felt and became stored up inside her. But again, many of us carry within us deep anger caused by our parents' mistakes, and, like Hedda, later explore it in therapy.

From her entire childhood, Hedda Nussbaum can recall only one event that she can single out as "traumatic"—an event that

occurred when she was only two years old. Years ago, she told a
Random House colleague about this first trauma, and in 1989 she
seized upon it again as an experience that must have somehow
warped her personality.

All through her infancy, Hedda had evidently received much
affection and attention from her paternal grandmother, Rachel
Nussbaum. The old woman even slept in her room. But in 1944,
her beloved grandmother had been taken from her abruptly and
put into a mental hospital.

According to Nussbaum's personal mythology, the effect upon
her was devastating. She played up her grandmother's illness for
Naomi Weiss as if it had virtually made her an orphan, yet her real
mother, Emma Nussbaum, had remained firmly rooted in the
household, putting on Hedda's socks: "I didn't understand. I
thought I must have done something to make her leave. When
she came home a few months later, she stayed in her room with
the door shut. I hardly ever had any real emotional contact with
her again. She lived with us like that until her death twenty years
later, and," Hedda Nussbaum said histrionically, pulling out one
too many stops, perhaps some precooked insight from a therapy
session, "I lived with that rejection every single day."

It is hard to believe that as Hedda Nussbaum grew up and
acquired more understanding, her so-called rejection by her
grandmother would have continued to preoccupy her every single day.

"It's something I'll have to live with the rest of my life," Hedda
similarly said on the witness stand, when she was asked how she
felt about the failure of will that had prevented her from calling
for an ambulance for Lisa on November 1, 1987.

There is something studied and deliberate about the way Hedda
Nussbaum expresses herself. Although she was an editor and
wrote books, her spoken words lack cadence and fluidity. Sometimes they're coy and cloying, sometimes decidedly coarse. Sometimes she'll remind her listeners with an expression like
"dysfunctional homes" that she is an educated person. Or she may
seem disconcertingly blunt—but the bluntness, one suspects, has
more to do with literal-mindedness than honesty. Hedda's injuries
have damaged her vocal cords, but one wonders, Did that voice
ever have any real music in it? Even husky and flattened, the
voice of Hedda Nussbaum contains so much of her history—all
Hedda's aspirations and pretensions and her social uneasiness and

the immigrant background she tried so hard to leave behind. The crowded apartment in Washington Heights near her father's beauty shop, and his voice speaking Yiddish at home, more comfortable for him than the unfamiliar syllables of English, and her mother's Yiddish-inflected but American voice—a surer voice than that of her shy husband, the first cousin who had come over from Poland. And the grandmother's voice is lodged in Hedda's, too—the mad voice behind the closed door, babbling the language of the Old Country.

No wonder Hedda set herself to master English, to conquer its grammar and syntax, waging war upon language but believing she loved it in a sensitive way. She was never more powerful than in her editing days when she told other writers what to do and they bowed to her sensible advice. The voices of Washington Heights public-school teachers are in the books she wrote for children.

She worked hard for her teachers at P.S. 187, where practically the entire student body was Jewish. A number of Hedda's classmates came from refugee families. Thousands of German and Austrian Jews had poured into Washington Heights during the Second World War, giving the neighborhood a more European flavor than other parts of New York.

At George Washington High School on Audubon Avenue, Hedda first began noticing boys and they began noticing her. But there were rules regarding boys as immutable as the Ten Commandments, and Hedda—a good girl, not a rebellious one in the least—followed them because it was much too dangerous not to. Bad girls could get pregnant. Good girls got married soon after high school. Then they could have the sex reserved for married people. If they had to temporarily take jobs, they could look around for husbands in the places they worked—husbands who would rescue them from the struggle of making their independent way in the world and keep them safely at home. Logically, bright boys went to college but there was no need for girls to continue their studies. High school was enough for them, though it wasn't going to be enough for Hedda. It was unusual for a girl at George Washington High School to dream of having a career, but Hedda wanted one and also wanted a powerful and successful husband, who would confer his power and success upon her. A woman without a husband was a pitiful, failed creature who ate crumbs at the banquet table of life, no matter how smart she was or what she had accomplished in her work.

The Nussbaums looked forward to their daughters' weddings, to their marriages to nice Jewish boys with professions. But when the girls wanted to go to college, they did not stand in their way. Perhaps if they'd also had a son, the Nussbaums would have felt differently, but these two American girls were all they had. Emma Nussbaum, in particular, was proud of her younger daughter's good marks and was convinced she was very artistic. The paintings Hedda did in high school—rather stiffly executed still lifes of flowers and fruit—decorated the Nussbaum's rooms even after the bewildered elderly couple had lost touch with the daughter who created them. It was the real Hedda who had done those paintings, they thought. They did not believe the Hedda Joel Steinberg had brought into being could be equally real.

The summer she was eighteen, a year before she entered Hunter, Hedda Nussbaum was engulfed by a feeling of dread and despair, not necessarily more severe than the normal melancholy and pessimism of adolescence. She was working as a counselor at a day camp in her neighborhood, and it seemed to her that everyone there hated her, especially the other teenage counselors. Sometimes she wondered if she was going crazy, perhaps comparing herself to her grandmother. Was she paranoid? By then Hedda had learned a few such words. But then the awful feeling went away by itself. It was only a troubling memory by the time she started college.

On the Bronx campus of Hunter, only a few subway stops from Washington Heights, she finally did meet people on her own, friends who sought her out and really liked her, whom she didn't have to share with Judy. Naomi Weiss remembers Hedda Nussbaum as a loving, caring girl. The two classmates, both English majors, studied together and often double-dated; in class they amused themselves by scribbling comments in each other's notebooks about their sexy male teachers. Both aspired to be writers. Hedda formed a more complicated but closer alliance with a girl named Risa. Risa was sure of herself and adventurous. Risa led the way into new experiences and Hedda followed, almost the way she had followed Judy.

By 1960, when Hedda was a college freshman, America was in the throes of a vast sexual revolution. It was as if all the urges young people had been suppressing during the 1950s had suddenly become uncorked. There had been a previous sexual revolution in the 1920s, which had lost its meaning and energy during the anxious Depression years of the 1930s, when families huddled together. Mores loosened up again during the Second World War, but during the postwar period the ideal of the nuclear family became so firmly reinstated that the old "free love" idea seemed only a very subversive anachronism. Emma and William Nussbaum, products of the East European *shtetl* culture, probably had little awareness of the sexual revolution that had occurred during their own youth among more educated and affluent people, or the one that would confront their daughter as soon as she entered college, even though they hadn't sent her away from home. Young women like Hedda Nussbaum had the dizzying sensation of being time travelers, of having gone from a kind of Old World Victorianism straight into the libertarian sixties, skipping all the stages in between. The sexual revolution, moreover, was not in its beginnings, but had already been largely accomplished—all within the past four or five years. In the late 1950s, the writers of the Beat Generation—men twenty years older than Nussbaum—had drawn upon the experiences of a small group of bohemians and hipsters over the previous decade and made them emblematic of a widespread urge for sexual freedom, commitment-less relationships (a masculine need more than a feminine one), and consciousness-expanding experiments, having to do with Eastern mysticism and drugs. The revolution that ensued was not an evolvement but an explosion—with the new ideas instantaneously spread far and wide by the mass media, especially that powerful, relatively new invention, television. All the surface images were instantly made available for superficial imitation by children of conservative parents like the Nussbaums. Hedda Nussbaum's generation never had time to define their own rebellion or quest. They inherited a secondhand victory without having struggled for it, without feeling a sense of triumph in breaking new ground. For young people like Joel Steinberg and Hedda Nussbaum, freedom became a misunderstood and empty concept, synonymous with license—the license to enjoy unbounded sensual gratification, one thrill after another, anything to escape boredom.

With almost no preparation for the shock of the new, a girl like Hedda would abruptly discover that all the rules that had governed her life were absurd and even irrational, dangerous to her mental health. The chastity she had guarded during necking and petting sessions in her teens turned out to be valueless. Rather than fearing its loss, she should have been worrying about frigidity.

Meanwhile the old engrained prohibitions simultaneously exerted their grip. Many girls like Hedda, particularly those still under their parents' roofs, followed the rules a few years longer, even when they realized how naïve and backward they were, compared to some of their more daring friends.

If Hedda Nussbaum's mind was enflamed by the sexual longings she confessed to in her diary, she was still too scared to go all the way, though she did get a thrill out of being extremely flirtatious and seeing how various boyfriends responded. During her freshman and sophomore years at Hunter, Hedda filled her diary with entries about different men whom she believed found her attractive. Entries sometimes in the form of lists, as if list making imposed order on her chaotic feelings. After being rejected by one boyfriend, Hedda made up a kind of table, enumerating the parts of her body, rating each one, and recording the reactions of various males to it. It was as if she had internalized a masculine perspective and was seeing herself as an object. At one point she pulled back in embarrassment and took herself to task for acting just like a teenager.

When Joel Steinberg's two middle-aged male attorneys read Hedda Nussbaum's diaries, they were shocked by the extent of her obsession with men. But Hedda does not seem to have been more foolishly boy-crazy than many other girls of her age, and imagining sexual encounters can often be more exciting than experiencing them.

According to what she wrote at twenty-one, Hedda was quite swept away by her first experience of sexual intercourse, when it finally happened. She wondered in her diary whether now that she had tasted sex, she would ever be able to control her overwhelming desire for it. As with many things Hedda Nussbaum has said about herself, one should perhaps not take this statement at face value. It is such a stereotypical reaction—very much what a young woman with romantic notions in her head would have wanted to feel. Besides, the common wisdom about sex in those days was that once you started you couldn't stop, even if you wanted to. The boy who initiated Hedda was not a thrilling stranger, but someone she had known all her life. Hedda does not appear to have been in love with him, for soon she made a new list, this one of thirty or so prospective conquests.

Hedda Nussbaum's world had been expanding beyond the streets of Washington Heights and the Bronx. She explored Manhattan with her new friends and the men she dated. As she looked forward to graduation, however, she seems to have been more

timid than ambitious. Despite all her artistic and literary aspirations, she decided to become a schoolteacher. Perhaps she was
afraid to test herself in a more challenging line of work; or she was
still trying to be a good girl, intent on pleasing her parents, even
though she now secretly disobeyed them in the area of sex. In any
case, a teaching certificate practically guaranteed its holder a job.
She wouldn't have to compete in the marketplace with the
wealthy girls who lived on Central Park West or West End Avenue. In Washington Heights, a young woman who taught school
was considered to have made something of herself, to have used
her college training to take her as far as she could expect to
go—until the right husband came along. And what work could be
more feminine than to be involved with children?

Both Hedda and her best friend Risa graduated from Hunter in
1964, having qualified for their certificates in education, and celebrated by taking a trip to Puerto Rico—the greatest distance
Hedda had ever ventured from home. An automobile accident
there ruined their vacation. Risa went right through the windshield, permanently scarring her face. Hedda's injuries were less
serious. Twenty-five years later in an interview with Susan
Brownmiller, Risa was still bitter that Hedda had never come to
visit her in the Santurce hospital, where they had both been
taken. Instead, after her release, Hedda had run around with two
young men the girls had previously picked up. Long before she
met up with Joel Steinberg, as Risa saw it, Hedda was self-cen-
tered, incapable of feeling much for other people.

Stung by the interview, which she read in *Ms.* in May of 1989,
Hedda refuted her "ex-friend, Risa" in a letter to the same magazine, giving an extraordinarily detailed description of her own
injuries from the same accident: a fractured clavicle, a bruise on
her thigh "about a foot long and eight inches wide" and a
"severely sprained groin" which had confined her to a wheelchair
for several days and prevented her from climbing the stairs to
Risa's room (presumably the hospital lacked an elevator).

Only a few months earlier, Hedda had been claiming memory
loss on the witness stand in response to one question after another, but here was an instance in which she seemed to have total
recall. Still, after she had enumerated her injuries, an odd gap
appeared in Hedda's account of what happened following the
accident. For some reason, after Hedda had recovered enough to
walk out of the hospital, the two girls continued to remain out of
touch: "When I later called the municipal hospital in Santurce to

see how Risa was, I was told that she had been discharged. Her brother had moved Risa to a private hospital, the name of which neither he nor Risa bothered to tell me," Hedda wrote, as if it had been Hedda Nussbaum, not Risa, who had been slighted.

Nonetheless, Risa and Hedda made up before the ill-fated vacation ended. When they returned to New York together, Hedda didn't go home. She recuperated at Risa's house, hoping to keep the accident a secret from her parents. When her mother finally did find out, she descended upon Hedda and Risa. "My baby! My baby!" Emma Nussbaum cried, to Risa's disgust.

Risa remained Hedda's best friend for the next ten years. Perhaps *best* was not the right word, as Risa later saw it. One of Hedda Nussbaum's *only* friends was more accurate.

By September, Hedda was teaching third grade at a public school in Washington Heights. She took some graduate English courses at Hunter that year, but dropped out of the master's program before she earned her degree. Perhaps her flagging ambition was a sign that she was feeling depressed and discouraged about her future. She seemed to be trapped in Washington Heights, not only working there, but still living at home. Judy had escaped by getting married. Suddenly in 1965, Hedda, too, decided to escape. She flew out to California and was hired as a substitute teacher in the Oakland public schools. A wealthy uncle and aunt lived in the Bay Area. If her parents were opposed to her going so far away, Hedda may have been able to placate them by pointing out that even on the West Coast she would not be far from the protection of her family.

In California, there was no Risa to team up with and no young men fell in love with her and proposed marriage. She became filled with even more fear and self-hatred than she had felt the summer she was eighteen. But now she was twenty-three. She should have done much better at striking out on her own.

The Bay Area abounded in self-anointed gurus and therapeutic groups, forerunners of the human potential movement of the next decade. Thousands of Californians were into exploring their psyches. Hedda became involved in a "selective awareness" group run by a Dr. Muhkey, who saw Hedda's problem as difficulty in maintaining her alpha waves. Hedda evidently did not dispute his diagnosis. In the diary she was keeping while under Dr. Muhkey's influence, Hedda described herself as divided into four people: The Devil, the Primal Ooze, the fourteen-year-old

girl, and the loving, caring Hedda. On one page she drew two
stick figures. One of them said Yes to sickness; the one that said
No didn't seem to be functioning. Hedda turned to three of her
personas and begged them to kill the Devil. The Primal Ooze
tried to drown the Devil; the fourteen-year-old girl wanted to hit
her with a baseball bat; but the caring Hedda was useless and
would not fight her. Trying to summon up that weak but necessary Hedda, she wrote, "I'm desperate. I need your help."

In the end Hedda gave up on her West Coast adventure. She
was back in New York in time to be a guest at Naomi Weiss's
wedding. Hedda arrived in black—a cocktail dress with a daring
wide V-neck that bared her shoulders and showed quite a bit of
cleavage.

With Naomi married and absorbed in her new husband, just as
her sister Judy was, Hedda spent most of her free time with Risa,
who was now teaching school. The two decided to become roommates and soon found a bright, pleasant apartment with high
ceilings and a fireplace in a brownstone on West Seventy-fifth
Street. The Upper West Side hadn't become fashionable yet. West
of Broadway, it was a comfortable, still very Jewish, slightly melancholy neighborhood, filled with families and elderly people.
There were no boutiques on Broadway, no restaurants or bars
that attracted young singles. The streets east of Amsterdam Avenue, lined with tenements and rooming houses, were dangerous.
For a good time, young women like Hedda and Risa had to take
the subway to the Village or go to the new bars that were opening
on the Upper East Side.

Hedda had gone all the way to California to change her life,
only to wind up in a fourth-grade classroom in the Bronx. She told
everyone she loved teaching and adored kids, but she was too
ambitious to want to spend her life in front of a blackboard. In the
kind of job she set her sights on, however, Hedda still clung to her
schoolteacher role. Now she wanted to do educational writing
that would allow her to draw upon what she felt was her special
ability to communicate with children.

Secretarial work was still about the only way a woman could
enter a new field, especially if she was a Hunter graduate competing against polished, self-assured women from the Ivy League
schools. A young woman like Hedda, without helpful connections,
would have to inch her way up. She took a course at the Speed-
writing Institute, then landed a secretarial job at the Rockefeller

Foundation. Two years later she found a better position—executive assistant to the vice president of an educational company. It was a slow, no doubt frustrating advancement. When Hedda finally moved into publishing—editing and writing grade-school textbooks for Appleton Century Crofts—she was thirty years old.

Men came and went in Hedda's life and Risa's—nothing was as reliable and constant as their relationship with each other, despite their spats. Both were very attractive and there was no shortage of opportunities for casual affairs. By the 1970s there was carte blanche for almost any behavior in the sexual area—and a pervasive feeling of emotional exhaustion. People were still marrying each other, but some experimented with "open marriage." Others tried using narcotics as an accompaniment to sex; the experience was heightened but in a peculiar way—rather than "relating to" one another, each partner remained sealed up in the cellophane compartment of his or her intoxication. Technical experts on sex, such as Dr. David Reuben, author of *Everything You Always Wanted to Know about Sex but Were Afraid to Ask,* even suggested experimenting with a little bondage in order to enliven things—the use of ribbons, not tied so tightly as to cut off circulation. Stores that sold sexual aids cropped up in the East Fifties and in the Village. Your only obligation was the one you had to your own enjoyment—to do your own thing taking full advantage of limitless new freedom. Sex had become a kind of indoor sport, part hunt, part athletics.

The swinging single women of Hedda Nussbaum's generation learned through a succession of more and more predictable misadventures that because you were not responsible for anyone and no one was responsible for you, all that freedom could also bring pain. The man who was dying to climb into the bed of a woman he had just met was not necessarily planning to ever repeat the experience. Men still had the edge over women; in fact, they had never been freer to behave badly and with less guilt. The word *sociopath* became a common term of parlance; trusting women were always running into sociopaths. Manhattan singles bars institutionalized the one-night stand, and by the mid-seventies, sex clubs like Plato's Retreat on the Upper West Side objectified sex even more, making nude encounters totally anonymous. Every now and then a woman picked up the wrong stranger, took him home, and got murdered. The famous "Goodbar" killing took place in a furnished apartment in the West Seventies only a few blocks away from where Hedda and Risa were living.

The destructive potential in the new disengaged sexuality was defined by psychoanalyst Rollo May as early as 1969 in his widely read book *Love and Will*. Possibly Hedda Nussbaum, with her appetite for literature on sex and psychology, pored over Dr. May's text at some point during the years before she met Joel Steinberg. Even on the first page, there was a warning for her:

> It is always true that love and will become more difficult in a transitional age, and ours is an era of radical transition. The old myths and symbols by which we oriented ourselves are gone, anxiety is rampant; we cling to each other and try to persuade ourselves that what we feel is love. . . . The individual is forced to turn inward; he becomes obsessed with the new form of the problem of identity, namely, Even-if-I-know-who-I-am, I-have-no-significance. I am unable to influence others. The next step is apathy. And the step following that is violence. For no human being can stand the perpetually numbing experience of his own powerlessness.

Later, she would have come upon an astute description of Joel Steinberg's psychic disorder, for although Joel Steinberg no doubt considered himself an original, Dr. May and other therapists were discovering that the Steinbergs were legion:

> When inward life dries up, when feeling decreases and apathy increases, when one cannot affect or even genuinely *touch* another person, violence flares up as a daimonic necessity for contact, a mad drive forcing touch in the most direct way possible. This is one aspect of the well-known relationship between sexual feelings and crimes of violence. To inflict pain and torture at least proves that one can affect somebody.

Wilhelm Reich had called those who had lost the ability to feel "living machines." In Dr. May's opinion, psychoanalysis could only partially reclaim such a person. It could "prepare the way for the patient's working out values by means of which he can change. But it can never, in itself, carry the burdens for the value decisions which do change a person's life."

According to what Hedda Nussbaum believed about her value system, even as late as December 1988, all she had ever wanted out of life was a husband and a family. During the years that led her to Steinberg, however, she was hardly searching for mature responsibility, but for solution, rescue, a way of filling the gaping hole of Who am I? Unable to define herself, she yearned to be told who she was—but only by a man with a dominant personality. She had internalized the most limiting of the old rules, and the most dangerous and mindless of the new. Once she was no longer a good little girl, Hedda Nussbaum was unable to re-create herself as an adult woman.

Even in the singles life, Hedda was a follower, along the trails blazed by Risa. Their search for men was extensive and even took them abroad. They saved up and went on vacations together, flying to the Caribbean in the winter, touring Europe in the summer. They took risks and had occasional close calls. Once when they were hitchhiking in France, they stayed overnight at a farmhouse. When the farmer's son broke into their bedroom, Hedda drove him off. For once, Risa thought, Hedda had done something gutsy.

There were dangers enough closer to home. A woman who lived in their building had a boyfriend who beat her, and for a time, according to Hedda's *Ms.* letter, even Risa had an abusive boyfriend. It was up to Hedda to talk sense to her friend: "At the time I had no understanding of this kind of relationship, and I said to Risa, with love, 'You don't seem to want to get out of this relationship. You have to make him know that you mean it when you say, No more. Until you do that, don't come crying to me that he's hit you. Sympathy isn't what you need. You need to get out.'" (Only a few years later, no one could have made Hedda listen to the advice she claimed to have given Risa when they were roommates.)

In her twenties, Hedda modeled herself on her friend, just as she had once done with her older sister, stealing bits of Risa's personality and grafting them onto her own. In 1989, Risa was indignant about all the newspaper articles that referred to Hedda's great love for animals and plants. Animals and plants had been Risa's thing, something Hedda had appropriated. Risa even claimed to Susan Brownmiller that she had generated the ideas for two of the children's books Hedda had written. She seems to have been both gratified by and resentful of Hedda's dependence on her as a role model. When Hedda became notorious, resentment overwhelmed Risa's other feelings. She felt tremendous embarrassment that she had ever been Hedda Nussbaum's closest friend, and told Susan Brownmiller that she had refused to be a character witness for her.

Some of Risa's complaints about Hedda sounded like the classic ones made by roommates who have fallen out. Hedda did not do her share in contributing to their home: "Everything in that apartment was mine," Risa claimed bitterly. The words she used to describe the Hedda she had known were "narcissistic, selfish, passive, uptight, dependent, empty at the center," echoing what Bellevue and Elmhurst Hospital psychiatrists as well as Steinberg's attorneys were saying about her. The woman who looked into a mirror at Elmhurst and had been startled to see a hag had once infuriated her roommate by never passing up an opportunity to gaze at herself in a mirror and run her hands through her black curls. Still, their friendship had never sharply ruptured; Hedda had simply stopped seeing Risa during her thirteen years with Steinberg, just as she dropped away from everyone else she had once known.

One opinion of Risa's diverged rather sharply from Hedda's own view of her own history. Risa always thought Hedda, not Judy, was "her parents' darling, the favorite daughter." Had Hedda misperceived her relationship with the Nussbaums? In any case, even by her thirties, Hedda had not outgrown her jealousy of her sister and her feeling that she was the less favored child.

"PEOPLE GO to therapists to find substitutes for their lost will," wrote Rollo May. "Or to learn the latest method of 'releasing affect,' unaware that affect is not something you strive for in itself but a by-product of the way you give yourself to a life situation."

Hedda Nussbaum entered therapy while she was working at Appleton Century Crofts, after she had crossed the sobering divide of her thirtieth birthday. At twenty-one the thirties *are* the future. But what if one arrives there and finds them empty? She went faithfully to two private sessions a week and one group session with Dr. James Bradley Norton, a Freudian therapist. She loved her new editorial job—she could really lose herself at times in the absorbing, exacting work—but she had not found a husband. Perhaps Dr. Norton could help her understand why she had recently been so tremendously attracted to a man with sadistic tendencies. It had taken a lot of will power to extricate herself from this person, particularly since her rejected lover kept calling up, trying to lure her back.

She felt the need to tell her next boyfriend, Bill Mutter, about him, but didn't go into the specifics of the "really unhealthy stuff" that had frightened her away. In any case, she had escaped and she was proud. Dr. Norton was helping her to take control of her life.

Bill Mutter did not scare or intimidate Hedda. They had a comradely, joking relationship in the office before they discovered they were drawn to each other and started going out. The pretty new editor had what Bill immediately appreciated as a "playful mind." Bill Mutter was an artist and looked much more like a hippie, with his mustache, flowing beard, and shoulder-length hair, than a man who had a nine-to-five job as an art director. He was three years younger than Hedda, intense, kindly, rebellious and garrulous, with charismatic, piercing eyes. (A similar look in the eyes later attracted Hedda to Joel Steinberg.) Bill Mutter had passionate feelings about many issues; he was opposed to Richard Nixon and the Vietnam War. He also had some esoteric ideas. "She knew I was a nut," he told Susan Brownmiller cheerfully, when she interviewed him for an article about Nussbaum in *Ms.* Some of Mutter's thinking had been influenced by Charles Henry Fort, an ideologue of the 1930s, who "had this wonderful, cynical view of the established scientists of our culture. If a doctor says something, you tend to believe it. They're like holy, holier than everyone else. Charles Fort would tear these people apart." He urged Hedda to read Fort's books.

She introduced Bill Mutter to things as well. In fact, she was always coming up with inspired ideas for their dates. On one of their first evenings together, they went to Lincoln Center to hear Nikos Theodorakis, who thrilled Bill by his singing of Greek labor-movement songs. Hedda had obviously wanted to create a left-wing night out for them, although she herself was no leftist.

She knew Bill liked beer even though she didn't care for it much herself. Whenever he came to her apartment, he would find that Hedda had bought him three or four bottles of different foreign beers. They would be in the refrigerator waiting for him, perfectly chilled.

Hedda had recently moved into her own apartment—a one-room studio that Bill remembers as "a beautiful little place in a big old brownstone." A ridiculous quarrel over the ownership of a Mixmaster had made Hedda and Risa decide it was time to live separately. But Hedda had only moved right across the street. She could look out of her windows and see the lights in Risa's place. As usual, the two women had patched things up. Hedda didn't have a lot of friends, but neither did Bill, for that matter. He found Hedda distinctly cautious about getting to know new people— "not an outgoing, running-around, making-friends-all-over-the-place kind of person."

For nearly a year, he spent every weekend with Hedda in her Seventy-fifth Street studio apartment. Bill was too embarrassed by his own funky living quarters in a low-rent district on the Lower East Side to take his fastidious girlfriend there. They shared many a pitcher of sangria in Victor's Cuban restaurant in Hedda's neighborhood, talking about everything under the sun— the latest headlines, the novels Hedda was always reading, Bill's desire to quit his job and stay home and paint. Often Hedda's conversation focused on her sister Judy and her kids. Bill remembers her liking those kids "a whole lot." Still, Hedda never said she wanted to have kids of her own. Nor did she lead Bill into discussions about the possibility of the two of them getting married. Although Bill knew Hedda wanted to write novels, she didn't say much about that either. It seemed she was content to let him be the artist.

It was the heyday of the women's movement. Personally, Bill Mutter admired feminists. As he saw it, feminists let guys like him off the hook. They weren't obsessed with getting married and having husbands to support them. Hedda didn't seem to be a feminist, though she wasn't exactly antifeminist. In fact, the woman he was spending his weekends with seems to have been quietly intent on shaping herself to please him, to hold him. It was done very subtly, really—so skillfully that later on Mutter would remember Hedda as a woman who had not hesitated to assert herself. But in truth, she only asserted herself on minor points— suggesting they go to see a terrific off-Broadway play called *When You Comin' Back, Red Ryder?* or that Bill wear suits, shirts, and ties when he took her out. And even then, she never ordered him, Do this for me, do that.

Bill Mutter enjoyed dressing up for her. It made him feel adult. And Hedda was very lovely, he thought, with her long, curly, black hair and smooth olive skin and the pretty skirts, slacks, and sweaters she wore. He didn't even mind that she was taller than he was, but was grateful that she had enough consideration not to put on high heels. Hedda was Bill's first mature girlfriend. She never criticized him, as other women had, for not being aggressive enough in life. All in all, he thought of her as quite sophisticated. His previous girlfriend had been just out of college.

They had a good enough time in bed, Mutter told Brownmiller. Hedda was by no means passive about lovemaking or interested in anything kinky. But as time went on, Bill began to feel their lovemaking lacked something. It wasn't the most passionate affair he'd had in his life. Perhaps he sensed a lack of authenticity in Hedda's sexual responses. A man like Bill who didn't try to subjugate her, who carefully maintained boundaries—*space* was the popular word for it—left her alone with the emptiness in herself, imprisoned in her freedom.

"Cautious with her feelings is the way I would describe her," Mutter told Brownmiller. "I don't remember her pouring her heart out to me. But *willing* to feel and *willing* to give."

*

Hedda and Bill were both deeply interested in therapy. Another bond between them was their mutual acknowledgment of buried rage. Both had come from families where the expression of anger was not accepted. But of course it was very much the fashion then to be brutally critical of the older generation. Hedda didn't seem more angry with her parents than anyone else Bill knew. She even took him to meet the Nussbaums at a family seder, warning him beforehand that her mother was the worst cook in the world. And she was right—the meat was roasted to death. Bill thought Hedda and her parents got along pretty well, though not with a great deal of warmth.

Why was there so much anger in Hedda? Once she told Bill Mutter she was afraid that if she ever released any of this anger, she could never keep the rest from pouring out of her. There would be no end to the rage Hedda Nussbaum felt. Was this merely fear or the expression of a desire to feel something—anything—deeply? It was like the idea she'd had about sex when she was twenty-one: Once you start, you can't stop. In Hedda's mind there was some connection between sex and rage—torrential forces that could carry you away. In the danger of going to extremes, there was also the promise of great excitement.

Bill, too, confessed to a fear that if he ever lost control of his anger, he might literally go crazy. In the conversations he had with Hedda, this problem of what to do with anger became a recurrent theme. Hedda never really discussed the problem concretely. If some of her secret anger was now focusing on Bill, if she began to want much more from him, wondered what kept him from asking her to live with him, why he was content to see her only on weekends, she never communicated such feelings. But perhaps she herself was ambivalent about what she really wanted from Bill Mutter.

During the period he was involved with Hedda, Bill Mutter was also going to a Freudian therapist. About a year later, he turned to one of the new alternative therapies the 1970s had spawned. The Kasriel Institute focused on suppressed anger. Its patients unburdened themselves by learning how to scream. Bill screamed and screamed and didn't go crazy. There were big pillows all over the floor of the studio. "You pounded the shit out of them." Hedda, too, would eventually learn to pound pillows—during her 1988 recovery time at Four Winds Hospital. She would think of Joel Steinberg during her psychodrama workshops and pound and pound.

Bill did get to experience Hedda Nussbaum's anger—just once, in 1973, at the very end of their relationship. He had guiltily recognized that what he felt for her would never be more than mere attraction. He assumed Hedda was the one who cared much more. Bill's reinvolvement with a former girlfriend was another factor that made him decide to break off with her. For a while he handled the situation by being evasive, although he still spent every weekend with Hedda. If he was showing "funny signs," she gave no indication that she noticed them. Finally, he went to see her at her apartment to tell her the truth. Hedda seemed totally unprepared for it. Bill hadn't expected them to have a friendly discussion, but he was shaken by the fury of Hedda's response, although he told himself it was "healthy as hell." Hedda was crying and screaming, "Get out! Get out!" literally trying to throw him out the door. So he let her do it, and that was that. Fortunately they no longer worked in the same office, since Appleton Century Crofts had been sold a few months before, and they had both been laid off. Unlike the man who had both tempted Hedda and scared her so badly, Bill Mutter never tried to get in touch with her again. But she, too, made no efforts to revive their relationship. Despite her sense of injury, the ending was evidently not so unbearable. The loss of Bill Mutter did not threaten Hedda Nussbaum's survival.

Looking back at Hedda Nussbaum at thirty, Bill Mutter reflected: "I always felt she was no more confused than anybody else I knew at that time. We were all dealing with the pain of trying to find someone to love, or trying to deal with living alone. And if you meet somebody and you go out and you like them and they don't like you, there's pain in that. We were all through that a number of times."

Even after the Steinberg trial, Bill Mutter still thought of Hedda Nussbaum as "someone who was just trying to live and be happy."

THE THIRTY-ONE-YEAR-OLD woman who boarded a subway one afternoon in 1974 and rode up to Washington Heights for a doctor's appointment was a Hedda whose façade was nearly perfected. Dr. Richard Grossbart was an old friend who had known Hedda and her family since she was in her teens. He was an intellectual man, with a literary bent. Hedda had always looked up to him. That day she was going to tell him about her triumph—her new editorial job at Random House. Perhaps the glow of confidence she had when she walked into his office was almost the real thing.

The doctor would always remember how "unusually personable and self-assertive" Hedda Nussbaum seemed to him during her visit for her annual checkup. He was quite bowled over by the success she had made of herself, although even as a girl she had been bright and outspoken, in contrast to her shy, reticent parents. Hedda's self-assertiveness, he told me, when I talked to him in 1989, seemed so much a natural part of her that "she didn't have to raise her voice." Grossbart listened appreciatively to Hedda's enthusiastic description of Random House and the work she was doing there on children's books. He was the kind of thoughtful, liberal-minded doctor women patients often confided in, but Hedda Nussbaum had not come to him to seek advice. Apparently, she herself had no complaints—even in the male/female department. "Well, listen, if there's a problem, I'll handle it," Grossbart remembers her saying at one point in their conversation.

The doctor often formed his judgments of people on the basis of body language. Perhaps he did so too readily. That day Hedda Nussbaum's seemed flawless. He still has a picture in his mind in which Hedda is in his office standing up very straight, "regal—like Wendy Hiller walking down the stairs in *Pygmalion.*"

Fourteen years passed after Hedda Nussbaum walked out of Richard Grossbart's office. The next time he saw her, she loomed up before him on his television screen, giving testimony. He thought to himself with a feeling of terrible sadness, "My God! Even now she's sitting up straight, shoulders back," still the proud Hedda Nussbaum he had known.

There was something he had to tell me about this Hedda—a thought that had been preoccupying him a great deal. He couldn't imagine this woman putting up with competition very graciously—especially competition between herself and a child. And of course, Lisa wasn't a little girl of her own. Not every mother loves her adopted child, he reminded me. If it had been another woman who came between herself and Steinberg, Hedda would have been furious, Dr. Grossbart thought, but might have been able to say, I can handle it.

"How do you follow a child star?" he asked me. "You can't handle that. It happens all the time."

As a physician, he had seen many inexplicable and terrible permutations of human behavior. "Again and again," he reflected, "things may not be what they appear. If you don't recognize that as a given, you're a bad observer."

Things may not be what they appear. Like a leitmotif, this warning runs through the story of Hedda, Joel, and Lisa. Even by the age of six, Lisa had learned to be a little actress, how to look people in the eye and lie to them—she could even simulate "happiness." To this day, Joel can still charm and manipulate certain people, although his self-aggrandizing stories have always been rather transparent. But who was Hedda Nussbaum? Which of the Heddas was the real one? Or was what lay underneath as unreal as her façade?

Hedda Nussbaum worked at Random House for nearly eight years. "I would have said she had it all," one fellow editor remarked to me ruefully, "intelligence, talent, looks." The Random House people, too, went by what their eyes told them. Hedda Nussbaum made heads turn when she showed up in the office for the first time in the fall of 1974. Louise Price was somewhat older than the other women in the department, the tough-minded mother hen. She recalls thinking to herself, " 'Oh boy, what a good-looking person this is.' Hedda carried herself like a dancer. I thought she looked just like Faye Dunaway, only with dark hair." She had beautiful eyes, remembers Walter Retan, who was editor-in-chief at the time. "They had a warmth about them when she smiled—which wasn't a lot."

Hedda's style in her Random House days was "a little bit Villagey." At Appleton Century Crofts, she had dressed rather formally, cultivating the look of a young businesswoman. By the mid-seventies, however, jeans had become a uniform for serious and independent working women, even in the genteel world of publishing. In this latest version of herself, Hedda wore no makeup and had a fondness for bright scarves, which she tied around her waist or her shoulder-length hair. There was a definite flair to the way she put herself together.

Betty Kraus, who became Hedda's closest Random House friend, remembers that fairly often Hedda would have lunch with Judy and her children. Judy would come to the office to meet her. Betty couldn't get over the physical difference between the two sisters. "I was always surprised," she told me, "that Hedda didn't think she was as pretty as I thought she was. I always wanted to probe her psyche. I thought there was some tragedy in her life." But Hedda never indicated what it could have been. Perhaps her tragedy was that she lacked the capacity to have one.

Betty was the only one of Hedda's Random House friends who ever visited her in her studio apartment. Betty was impressed by how immaculate and orderly it was, cozy as well with its plant-filled windows, its neat shelves of books. Hedda even had a piano. "There was a place for everything and everything was in its place. You couldn't even see a cat hair," Betty remembers, despite the fact that Hedda's cat had just had kittens, one of which Betty was going to adopt. Hedda brought the kitten into the office, as she would later bring Lisa, and was "very sweet with it," Walter Retan remembers.

Hedda's office was right next to Retan's. Compulsive order was maintained there, just as it was in her apartment, and it, too, was filled with plants—quite exotic ones. By now the passion for them had become one of Hedda's memorable attributes. She took superb care of her "green things," never failing to water them before she left for the weekend. The work she did on manuscripts was just as reliable—impressive for a relatively inexperienced editor. Hedda worked hard in her pristine office and late. Quite often Walter Retan would hear her on the phone, her voice rising and falling in the after-hours silence, passionate and full of anger, though he couldn't make out the words. Who was she talking to? he wondered. Who on earth had angered her so much?

The books assigned to Hedda Nussbaum were unglamorous, semieducational, and highly lucrative: the Easy-to-Read series, the *Charlie Brown Books of Questions and Answers.* Over the *Charlie Browns* Hedda was given total control, according to Nadine Simon, a free-lance art director who worked on them with her. She did a good deal of the actual research and writing, as well as editing the final manuscript. After a few years, Hedda began proposing to write books of her own, compilations of interesting facts about plants and animals that would carry the credit line "by Hedda Nussbaum" right on the jacket.

If Joel Steinberg's most cherished credential was "criminal lawyer," "Random House editor" was Hedda's. Years after Nussbaum had been fired from there, Lisa Steinberg would inform strangers that her mommy wrote books for Random House.

The juvenile books department was almost entirely staffed with hard-working young women. It had a cozy, gossipy atmosphere, a little like a dorm in a women's college. When the graduates left and went on to better jobs, they tended to keep in touch with each other. Over sandwiches and salads in various Greek coffee shops in the East Fifties, the women chatted about their plans for the weekend, the men they were dating, the male/female conflicts that weren't evaporating overnight despite all the devastating insights Simone de Beauvoir and Betty Friedan had brought to bear upon them—between theory and practice, there was still a huge gulf. Was Hedda going out with anyone? No one knew. Did she have a *life?*

For over a year Hedda Nussbaum probably didn't think she had one. Without a man, her life was like a hat on a shelf, waiting to be claimed and worn. Hedda Nussbaum was inert. Only the façade kept moving in its everyday rounds—showing up punctually at the office, going to therapy and to art classes, having dinner with Risa or Judy. To walk out of the busy, fluorescent-lit office at night was to step into a void.

"Hedda was b-o-o-o-ring," in the opinion of Diane Margolies, a young editor fresh from some adventurous years in radical student circles in Berkeley, California. Hedda made it clear she didn't want to be "girls together." Cool, rebellious Diane was the kind of woman Hedda preferred to keep away from. She felt on more secure ground with Betty Kraus. With Betty, who had a steady boyfriend and longed to get married and start having kids, Hedda would have earnest discussions about how motherhood might be successfully combined with a career.

"Everybody was so out there and she was so in there," says Diane, remembering the lighthearted spirit in the office. "We were pretty, smart, and Jewish. And we all were 'Mary Hartman' freaks." But Hedda stayed noticeably aloof from the sessions in Walter Retan's office where everyone gathered for hilarious analyses of Mary Hartman's latest crisis. It was not only that Hedda lacked what Diane calls "middle-class socialness," it was as if she had never learned to play. Where was the Hedda with the "playful mind" who had flirted with Bill Mutter at Appleton Century Crofts? At Random House there were no eligible males to appreciate her wisecracks—only other young women who felt at ease enough in the world Hedda had entered so recently to let down their guard with each other.

"Do people wear masks in everyday life?" In 1978, after three years with Joel Steinberg, Hedda Nussbaum would pose this playful rhetorical question in *Charlie Brown's Fourth Super Book of Questions and Answers.* Skiers, divers, and even bank robbers did, she informed her juvenile readers. One wonders now what else went through her mind. By that time, the reserved and proper mask she wore at Random House was often marred by a black eye.

They met through an ad in *The Village Voice* that sought prospective shareholders for a summer house in East Hampton. Each spring Herbert Alpert, a lawyer who once shared office space with Steinberg, would rent a house with another bachelor friend and run a similar ad. Interested prospects who called up for further information would be invited to small gatherings where Alpert and his friend could screen them. Risa and Hedda showed up at one such party and made a favorable impression as very pretty girls. Risa naturally did most of the talking. Hedda stood back rather shyly. "The moon children," Alpert amusedly called the two dark-haired young women.

Joel Steinberg had no interest in buying a share. Nonetheless, Alpert had invited him that evening. "We brought Joel along as the shill," Alpert later recollected to a Greenwich Village writer named Linda Gordon. "He was good looking. We thought he would attract good-looking young women to our group."

Joel Steinberg's eyes immediately captured Hedda Nussbaum's attention. "Bright, shining, alive eyes," as she recalled nostalgically on the witness stand. She was also quite taken by his boundless self-confidence and his air of success—he made some references to his powerful Mafia clients and looked quite dashing and substantial in his tightly vested navy-blue suit, with his aviator glasses and his longish, rumpled curly black hair. A scent of risk about Steinberg may also have appealed to her. Pathological liars often seem a little larger than life.

Hedda and Risa signed up to spend every other weekend in the Hamptons. They were both thirty-two—and rather despairing in their incessant search for marriageable men. The sexual revolution had created the group house, just as it had created the singles' bar. With long-term commitments fallen out of fashion, intimacy could be achieved very quickly; mere proximity and availability were enough to bring about sexual encounters. By 1975, the crowd of young men and women looking for pickups was so thick on one stretch of beach in Amagansett that people stood up in their bathing suits as if at a gigantic cocktail party; the place became known as Asparagus Beach. Some group houses had a reputation for wildness—there were rumors of drugs and group sex. Others were quite sedate. In fact, the shareholders would enter into explicit agreements *not* to sleep with members of the household, dinners would be elaborate and protracted, with men and women rigorously splitting the chores, thrilled by the novelty of eating a home-cooked meal with others. For people who lived by themselves in small New York apartments, the group house could provide a substitute family.

Hedda felt no sense of community with her housemates. She kept to herself, took long bicycle rides to get away from everyone. But one Monday morning when she walked into Random House, she was able to announce to her colleagues that there was a man in her life, at last having news they might envy. She was uncharacteristically eager to broadcast the details. This man was perfect in every way—a brilliant, successful Jewish lawyer, who was begging her to move into his wonderful apartment in the house where Mark Twain had once lived on the best block in Greenwich Village. In other words, Hedda Nussbaum had finally *arrived*—now that she had found her lawyer, she would shake off the last traces of Washington Heights.

"*Well*, little mousy Hedda!" Diane Margolies thought.

Joel Steinberg had nothing against houses in the Hamptons, but he never spent a penny unless he had to. He'd been able to mooch a free weekend from Alpert and ended up in bed with the pretty brunette he'd met a couple of months before. It is doubtful that he felt he'd met his destiny.

It was ESP, Hedda told Naomi Weiss.

From a purely pragmatic perspective, one of the most miraculous features of Joel Steinberg must have been his availability. In Manhattan, an unattached, affluent heterosexual thirty-three-year-old male was a rare prize. Joel Steinberg had become available because a schoolteacher who had lived with him on Tenth Street for a number of years had recently broken off their relationship.

The schoolteacher was another pretty brunette, though rather emaciated-looking, according to Karen Snyder, who socialized with Joel and his girlfriend in the apartment across the hall, which was kept quite nicely in those days. Others who remember the schoolteacher say she acted helpless and never asserted herself much. One ex-friend of Steinberg's described her as passive-aggressive, "the type of person who just drives you crazy." Another ex-friend remembers witnessing a screaming fight between Joel and Hedda's predecessor on a sailboat off Fire Island. The schoolteacher later let it be known to investigators that Joel had severe sexual problems, difficulty in maintaining an erection under normal circumstances. He would knock her to the ground and jump on top of her, which was what he did the day she finally asserted herself enough to tell him she was moving out. Years later, when Steinberg was in the grip of paranoid fantasies, he would imagine that his former girlfriend had been "psychoed out of the school system" and that she had been a member of a satanic cult.

After her departure, Joel was alone on Tenth Street. His only faithful companion was a black Great Dane named Sascha, whom he would often take for walks in the Village and buy hamburgers for at Orange Julius' on Eighth Street. Joel was very proud of Sascha and had devoted considerable effort to his conditioning and training. When Joel roughhoused with his dog, so much noise issued from apartment 3W that the neighbors frequently complained.

IF YOU seek out Joel Steinberg's oldest, closest friends, you mostly come up with people who *used* to know him, and even the relationships they had with Steinberg ten or fifteen years ago can hardly be described as intimate. Mel Sirkin, for example, saw a lot of Joel from 1975 to 1977, when they were sharing office space with a group of other attorneys. Then Sirkin lost touch with him until 1987, when Joel called him out of the blue from Rikers Island and asked him to handle his financial affairs, which he continued to do throughout Steinberg's trial. When I asked Sirkin whether Joel had ever talked to him much about his early history, he laughed: "A lot of things I thought I knew, I didn't know—his schooling, his military career. The stories he told ten years ago were just untrue. Even Hedda was certainly misled about a lot of things Joel told her. Nobody knows him."

One of the experiences Joel used to point out he and Mel had in common was that they'd both gone to Catholic colleges—Mel to Georgetown and Joel to Fordham. Not that Joel himself was really Jewish. My mother is Italian, he informed Mel, as well as another friend, an entertainer named Marilyn Walton. When Marilyn visited Charlotte Steinberg before Joel's trial, she asked the eighty-one-year-old woman whether it was true she was Italian. Charlotte Steinberg was amused: "Oh, that's Joel and his stories." She seemed neither shocked nor hurt that her son had made up a different mother for himself than the one he'd really had. Charlotte, like Joel's father, Maurice Steinberg, came from a German Jewish family.

Then there were the tales Joel told people about his outstanding achievements at Charles E. Gorton High School in Yonkers, from which he'd graduated in 1958 at the age of seventeen. Joel conferred upon himself a glorious all-American adolescence; he'd been a football hero and a golf pro, as well as a top student. Mel doubts that Joel was any of those things, although he does seem to have been a rather frantic joiner. The Charles E. Gorton year-book records Steinberg's participation in an inordinate number of extracurricular activities, not only the varsity football team, but the school newspaper, the biology club, the yearbook, the color-guard band. Mel thinks Joel was a loner, never accepted as one of the boys. Perhaps he'd hopefully keep joining things, then find himself still on the outside. Nonetheless, Steinberg's fellow stu-dents came to think of him as something of an operator. The yearbook predicted that he would be an oil millionaire by 1973. Another notation was less flattering. In a list under "Last Will and Testament," the graduating seniors bequeathed to their succes-sors "Joel Steinberg's alibis."

What seems clear is that from the time he was very young, Joel Steinberg didn't know who he really was and compensated by making up stories in which he starred as the person he'd like to be. When Lisa was three, he even felt impelled to improve on the story of her "adoption," telling a friend that the child's natural father had been a basketball pro, who gave Lisa to him in lieu of legal fees. That lie made the papers the week Lisa died.

Charlotte Steinberg wanted her son to be strong and tough in accordance with her image of masculinity. She let it be known that neither Joel nor his father lived up to that ideal. Maurice Steinberg was a small-time Manhattan lawyer, who never earned enough to support his family with any real style. Charlotte still tells people about her late husband's lack of ambition and drive. While Joel was growing up, she had to work as a secretary in the Child Welfare Department. She dedicated herself to pinching pennies.

Joel was eleven when he and his family moved from a Jewish neighborhood in the Bronx to a garden apartment on Cascade Avenue in Yonkers, an Irish and Italian neighborhood, where Jews were quite unpopular. Frequently Joel would get beaten up on his way home from school. Charlotte was unmoved when he came to her in tears. What she would always say to him, she later told Marilyn Walton, was, "Why don't you fight back?" On the one hand, Charlotte's son wasn't manly enough for her taste. Yet she also let him know she hadn't wanted a boy at all; what she'd really wanted, she used to tell Joel, was a little girl.

Charlotte's elderly mother lived with the Steinbergs, and the two women banded together to run an immaculate household. The women made the rules Joel lived by and were strict disciplinarians. Joel was not allowed to sit down at the dinner table unless he wore a shirt and tie. In 1987, Charlotte couldn't understand why there was so much fuss about Mitchell's being tied to his playpen; after all, she had used a halter on Joel when he was little. She was also of the opinion that Joel had erred in letting Lisa run wild. According to Mel Sirkin, Joel vehemently denies that he was ever physically punished or that his upbringing was unusually strict. There's too much denial there, Sirkin says.

Elderly Yonkers neighbors of Charlotte's remember Joel Steinberg as a boy with nice manners who worked as a caddy at the Fairview Country Club. He also did a great deal of baby-sitting for people, although most boys did not earn their spending money that way. Joel seemed to seek out the company of little children. Perhaps it was because they believed whatever he told them, looked up to him as a hero, followed his orders. He may also have been drawn to them sexually in ways he didn't understand.

The profession Joel Steinberg picked out for himself when he was still in high school was the one in which his father had failed to distinguish himself. One wonders whether that choice was a gesture of loyalty to Maurice or a final bid for the attention of an ineffectual father who had meekly bowed out of having a say in the upbringing of his son. At Fordham University, where he is said to have had a scholarship, Joel was one of the few Jewish students; he majored in political science there and was accepted into New York University Law School in 1962. He showed little aptitude for the law; his grades were poor, and in 1964, after he flunked two courses, he was suspended. He took a job for eleven months, then enlisted in the Air Force. At Fordham, Joel had been in the ROTC and enjoyed strutting around the campus in the blue Air Force uniform. The Air Force held out an opportunity for adventure, a brand-new chance to become "a man's man." It also provided an escape from the Steinberg household and from Charlotte's sharp tongue; she would not have had much sympathy for her son's humiliating failure in law school.

While Joel was in the service, Maurice Steinberg developed a brain tumor and had to retire from his practice. Soon he was completely dependent upon Charlotte. Steinberg has told Marilyn Walton as well as the court-appointed psychiatrist who examined him in 1989 that he felt Charlotte Steinberg did not treat his father very kindly during this period, and that while he was in the service, he was very upset by a letter about the situation that he received from an aunt. Of course this may have been only another of Steinberg's fabrications. Maurice Steinberg survived until 1972. After his death, Joel was estranged from Charlotte for two or three years.

Even by the late 1980s, Joel was still talking nostalgically about Southeast Asia and his James Bond–like exploits there as a pilot for the Defense Intelligence Agency. One of his more macho duties had been conducting tough interrogations of Vietcong prisoners. Joel intimated to various acquaintances that he had been involved with the counterinsurgency Phoenix Program and had learned to use torture to extract the information the military was after. He had just returned to civilian life, however, when the notorious Phoenix Program went into action in 1968. The Manhattan district attorney's office did unearth a photo of Joel Steinberg in a pilot's uniform when it was conducting its investigation in 1987. In reality, however, Joel Steinberg spent four years of the Vietnam War in the United States. He was merely a supply officer and never got to fly a plane. He did have one opportunity for heroics when he rescued an airman from a fire that had broken out in a hobby shop on the base.

When Lieutenant Steinberg received his honorable discharge, a number of his superior officers thought well enough of his performance and character to call him "highly motivated," but one officer described him as a person whose word was of "little or no value in the determination of the truth." Another had previously made a notation on Lieutenant Steinberg's record to the effect that he was unfit to be a leader: "For these men, namely subordinates, to be exposed to an officer of Lieutenant Steinberg's caliber at this time will more than likely have a disastrous effect on what attitudes they do form."

Among Joel Steinberg's bad attitudes in and out of the service was the assumption that rules other people had to follow did not apply to him—an attitude that later thrilled the conventional Hedda Nussbaum. During the Vietnam War period, for example, a New York State ruling exempted law students who had been drafted from taking the bar exam if they had completed two-thirds of their studies at the time they were interrupted by military service. Joel had re-enrolled himself at NYU Law School. He graduated in 1970, used the ruling to duck the bar exam, even though he himself had not been drafted, and became certified as a lawyer. According to Adrian DiLuzio, one of Steinberg's defense attorneys, "Joel's attitude was, 'I wasn't drafted, but I served. That isn't fair. People who volunteer should be rewarded.'" "In a way," said DiLuzio, "Steinberg had a point there." In time, Joel Steinberg evidently came to believe that he had dropped out of law school voluntarily in order to serve his country. Perhaps he nearly convinced himself he had served in Vietnam; certainly his "experiences" there had become a key element in the creation of a new persona.

In 1970, Joel Steinberg found the one-bedroom apartment in the Mark Twain brownstone and moved in. It was the perfect address for an up-and-coming bachelor lawyer, and the rent was so low that seventeen years later it had only gone up to seven hundred dollars a month. The apartment 3W had what the realtors who advertise in the *Village Voice* call "Village charm": parquet floors, high ceilings with ornate plaster moldings, French windows, two marble fireplaces. It was a place where a young attorney would not be embarrassed to entertain an important client.

Joel Steinberg never actually joined a law firm, although he was always proposing to other young lawyers he met that they go into partnership with him. It was almost as if he didn't want to be alone, that he was seeking companionship rather than a working relationship. In the early 1970s, he became acquainted with Ivan Fisher, now a prominent criminal lawyer, when Fisher took over a federal case from him. As Fisher remembers it, somehow Joel "inveigled" him into becoming involved with him professionally in the sharing of an office. Joel volunteered to act as the administrative and business person. He negotiated to rent a floor in a building, renovate it, and sublet it to other lawyers. When it suited him, Joel would casually refer to his co-tenants as "my partners." Joel was the one who collected the rent checks.

One of the tenants was Albert Krieger, who was making a solid reputation for himself defending radicals and activists. He had previously shared office space with Steinberg, but in their new quarters he soon found that he had little patience with him. "I could never figure out how anyone could practice who knew so little law," he told me, "or how Joel could possibly get clients." "How the hell did Steinberg pass the bar?" was a standing joke in the office.

Fisher, who was working for Krieger at the time, had a more positive view of Joel's abilities. As he put it when I talked to him, Joel had a way of becoming involved in cases beyond his level of expertise: "He was a damn good internist. When it got to the point you had a tumor, he'd send you on to the next guy." Joel kept referring clients to Fisher when it came time to go to trial. Even after he gave up a case, Joel would remain emotionally involved with it. Fisher considered him "extremely thoughtful and caring about his clients' interests."

Although the shared-office arrangement lasted for nearly four years, Krieger became increasingly allergic to Joel Steinberg. He couldn't stand anything about him—the way Joel expressed himself, the way he postured, what appeared to be his interests. Unsuccessfully, Krieger tried to avoid contact: "He was boring, pretentious, full of shit—so who would want to carry on a lengthy conversation? Words would creep in that would stop you and make you think, *What* is he talking about? You had to be foolish to get involved with Steinberg," Krieger told me. "You didn't know what you were going to be held responsible for." When Steinberg asked Krieger to try one of his cases, Krieger angrily declined the referral.

The tension between them was defused for a while, when Krieger opened a second office in Florida. He made Ivan Fisher his junior partner in New York, and commuted back and forth, keeping an apartment on Tenth Street and Fifth Avenue, right around the corner from Joel. Somehow Krieger ended up going out to dinner with Joel one evening and went so far as to let Joel pick the restaurant—some Italian place, where Joel swore the food was "extraordinary." Krieger thought it plain and not very good, but Joel went into raptures over a plate of mushrooms. He kept urging Krieger to taste them "because they had such a *sincere* flavor." He put some on his fork and tried to get Krieger to eat them. Krieger told Joel that if there was one thing he hated, it was people passing food around in restaurants, but Joel wouldn't take no for an answer.

In 1973, Krieger spent six months in South Dakota, defending Indian activists in the landmark Wounded Knee case. During this period his partnership with Fisher dissolved. When Krieger returned to the New York office, he discovered that Joel had been pocketing rent checks from the other co-tenants and took him to court to collect the money. "He was a thief," Krieger said indignantly, "and I was partially victimized." After the litigation, Krieger moved out. "You run by instinct, by intuition—if you find you can't rely on the people around you, you get away."

Oddly enough, as if Joel Steinberg had no memory or understanding of what had happened—or as if he couldn't bring himself to let go—Steinberg kept seeking Krieger out over the years, finding excuses to call him up. He felt no compunction about occasionally dropping Krieger's name, referring to him as "my former partner" or even "my current partner." His last phone call to Krieger was shortly before Lisa's death. As Krieger remembers it, Joel had evidently "shot off his mouth to his client" about his partnership with Krieger and put himself in a position where he had to make the call. "I told him to get stuffed."

Both Albert Krieger and Ivan Fisher went on to have the kind of professional success Joel Steinberg could only fantasize about. Krieger's office is in Miami now; he no longer defends activists but big-time Mafiosi like Joe Bonanno. Around 1975, Joel Steinberg tried to impress a young woman he had taken to dinner in Little Italy by telling her that some of his clients were leading mob figures. The young woman had grown up in Chicago, and her negative image of Joel was reinforced when they strolled around the area and Joel was greeted familiarly with "Hi, counselor!" by various heavies. When I asked Krieger about Joel Steinberg's work with the Mafia, he said sarcastically, "Those must have been shopkeepers who said hello to him that night. You think Joe Bonanno would be represented by someone like him?"

Ivan Fisher's offices occupy an entire townhouse in the East Sixties in Manhattan. His private quarters are an enormous, strangely empty floor-through room on the second floor, where no papers are visible. You sit on leather couches and gaze at Fisher's collection of modern art—his taste seems to run to surrealism. In 1974, however, he was still struggling to build up his practice. When Krieger moved out, Fisher found another large suite—four thousand square feet of space on Park Avenue—and sublet it to nine other lawyers, including Mel Sirkin and Joel Steinberg. Despite the contretemps over the rent checks, Fisher had evidently not lost trust in Joel. In fact, he continued to find him helpful in many, many ways. "Joel was always wanting to help people. One could question what his motives were." As he looked back thirteen years later, Fisher didn't want to commit himself to saying he'd ever *liked* Joel Steinberg: "I didn't like him, I didn't hate him," was the way he put it. Although in the past he had been truly appreciative of some of the "help" Steinberg had offered, he did not take on the task of defending Steinberg when Joel approached him in 1987. He did, however, become one of Dr. Sarosi's attorneys.

It was quite true, of course, that Joel was "bizarre," that even in the early 1970s, as Fisher said, you sensed "some black hole in him you didn't know about and didn't want to," that it was difficult to accept him or to be comfortable with him because he seemed to have such an excess of personality. For a time, however, perhaps that very excess made Fisher see Joel as "guruish" and "verbally spiritual sounding," even after an argument between Joel and Fisher's male secretary exploded into a fistfight. Ivan Fisher had listened thoughtfully when Joel expounded on the value and responsibility of relationships—one of his favorite topics. A relationship, Joel Steinberg often said, was "the most important achievement of a life," although his own relationship with the schoolteacher was unraveling at the time. Fisher could still remember some of the exact language Joel had used: "A relationship was a trophy, like money in the bank. It was how you got ahead." I wondered if Fisher considered *trophy* a peculiar choice of words. It was hardly tender, more a hunter's term.

Fisher is a short, slightly built man with dead-white skin and black hair that's beginning to thin quite noticeably in his middle age. He had admired Joel's muscular physique, had never really questioned his "tough guy" image. Joel had never dared to tell Krieger about his intelligence exploits in Southeast Asia, but with Fisher he felt able to make those claims. When Fisher admired the khaki Air Force dress shirts Joel often wore to the office, Joel presented him with one. Fisher still wears it occasionally. "It's a great shirt," he told me.

In those days, Fisher was a bachelor and Mel Sirkin was recovering from a divorce. Mel had a three-year-old boy whom he saw on weekends. Joel would often tell Mel how much he envied him his fatherhood. In fact, it seemed to Mel that Joel wanted children more than he wanted a wife. He bragged about all the babysitting he'd done in his teens, how great he'd always been with kids. Sometimes Mel would have to remind Joel that finding a wife had to come first.

Joel had "raised" a little girl named Dawn, the child of a Canadian nurse whom Joel had lived with before he met the schoolteacher. Joel had thought of her as his own daughter; it sounded to Mel as if little Dawn had enchanted Joel far more than her mother had. As mementos of his relationship with the child, Joel had even kept some articles of her clothing, although he did not tell Mel about that.

Steinberg was living with Hedda in 1976, when Dawn was killed at the age of ten in a Christmas tree fire in a house on Long Island. She would remain one of Joel Steinberg's obsessions. Even Lisa knew all about little Dawn and how she had died.

Around the time Joel started seeing Hedda, he made Mel an offer: he and Hedda would take care of Mel's three-year-old for an entire Saturday—this trial run seemed to be very important to Joel. Mel brought the child to the apartment on Tenth Street. Joel hit it off with the little boy right away; but Hedda seemed "downright uncomfortable" with him. Mel had the feeling she resented the arrangement. This kid is going to ruin my Saturday, seemed to be her attitude. "You remember what Risa said about Hedda not caring about other people?" he asked me. "That was the quality she had with my son."

Whenever Joel dated a new woman, she was on approval. He'd solicit opinions about her qualifications to be his girlfriend. What do you think about Hedda? he'd ask Mel. Mel never thought much of Hedda Nussbaum. The way she retired into the woodwork got on his nerves. She acted like someone much younger than she really was. Neither Doctor Grossbart nor Bill Mutter would have recognized the childlike Hedda Joel Steinberg introduced to Mel Sirkin, who seemed so unsure of herself socially and intellectually.

"Joel had such a dominant personality," says Mel. "I thought she didn't fit."

As time went on, what Mel saw as the poor fit between the two became painfully pronounced. By 1978, Mel stopped seeing Steinberg outside the office because neither he nor Tina, his fiancée, could stand the spectacle of Hedda numbly submitting to Joel's humiliating attacks: "Hedda, you're wrong. Hedda, you're stupid." Mel was unaware that Joel's verbal battering of women was nothing new. A few times Mel tried to talk to him about his behavior. "Joel would say he was trying to improve Hedda, make her more independent. Of course he didn't want to make her independent at all."

Ivan Fisher interpreted Hedda's submissiveness to Joel quite differently. He found Hedda "lovely, an attractive person, not just physically." Admittedly, Joel was not a "regular kind of person. I thought he was fortunate to find someone who cared so deeply and could absorb the irregularities of his personality." Fisher did, however, say that their relationship did not strike him as "bilateral—more unilateral, with Joel being the *uni* in the phrase. He was the one who seemed to be in charge." As far as Fisher could tell, Joel seemed "pleased as punch" to be involved with her.

Fisher even felt a little jealous of Joel's good fortune in attracting Hedda. He was feeling lonely at the time, still unattached, still struggling to establish himself professionally; 1977 was Fisher's hardest year. "My level of emotion was extreme," he told me. "I would frequently lose my temper." Oddly enough, only Joel Steinberg could cool him down. Joel would put "strong hands" on Fisher's shoulders, tell him to take deep breaths—to fill up the top part of his chest with air. Joel's relaxation technique worked like a charm. "Guru that he was, he was putting out peace, tranquility."

Guru and healer. That was beginning to be Joel Steinberg's new concept of himself, supplanting Military Intelligence Officer or even Criminal Lawyer. If Fisher became an appreciative patient, healed to some extent by his willingness to believe in the man with the strong hands, Hedda Nussbaum became a fanatical follower.

"I THOUGHT," recalled Hedda Nussbaum on December 2, 1988, "he was probably the most wonderful man I'd ever met."

"What qualities was it that attracted you to him, Miss Nussbaum?" Assistant District Attorney Peter Casolaro asked her.

"Well, he seemed to be extremely intelligent and bright, and I loved to listen to him talk for hours."

And talk for hours he did. Probably no one Joel Steinberg had ever met had favored him with such rapt attention, drinking in his every word, especially since his favorite and most fascinating topic was Hedda Nussbaum herself. Right from the start, they would have long nightly sessions in which Joel tried to help Hedda "to come out more. I was very shy and I guess tense, and he was trying to make me more spontaneous, more natural, freer."

Spontaneous, natural, free. These benign but essentially amoral words, so much the credo of the 1970s, had different meanings for different people. You owed it to yourself to be yourself, but many were quite uninterested in what obligations they had beyond that. Hedda Nussbaum was thrilled when Joel talked of freeing her because she had always imagined she was a superior being. Only now was her true self being discovered. Finally, she had met a man who instinctively seemed to recognize that the earnest, schoolteacherish young woman who had sought the approval of so many people was really only a cowardly fake. It was Joel's genius to undertake the liberation of the proud, unfulfilled, outlaw self, the one who had always been rigidly kept from breaking through to the surface and causing trouble. This Hedda burned to break the rules, to violate taboos, to plumb every experience life had to offer—to become like Steinberg, as a matter of fact, bold enough to seize his kind of freedom. The Hedda Joel attacked so viciously on occasion was only the false Hedda, who had to be shucked off now like a useless, withered skin. Steinberg made Hedda Nussbaum so interesting to herself that for thirteen years she could never quite tear her gaze away from her own image.

Joel would tolerate no barriers between them, no pretense. He demanded an involvement so total that the rest of the world ceased to exist. She had never dreamed that any man would need *all* of her, that anyone so perfect would want to fuse with her in this amazing way, as if the two of them in their profound love were pieces completing a jigsaw puzzle. No one could have convinced her that only a man with many missing parts would crave such a dangerous fusion.

One of Joel Steinberg's primary concerns was truth. Perhaps his own tremendous difficulties in that area made him particularly sensitive to Hedda's inability to communicate her feelings with real honesty or reveal what thoughts underlay her silences. How could a consummate liar trust a cunning dissimulator who would say anything to please him? "Stay in truth," was his commandment to her.

What this meant, Nussbaum earnestly explained to Peter Casolaro, was "to have your mind in a truthful place, even if your words aren't truthful. It means to be honest with yourself, really."

In other words, in Joel Steinberg's mind, the only truth he and Hedda could hope for was the inner knowledge that they were lying. He was not really trying to cure their mutual affliction, but seeking a way to validate it.

The kind of truth Joel Steinberg was concerned with was exactly the kind that preoccupies lawyers when they are attempting to interpret a witness's alibis or evasions such as "I don't know" or "I can't recall." In a sense, no one could have prepared Hedda better for her brief future career as a witness against Joel Steinberg.

"Stay in harmony" was another thematic phrase in Joel's teachings. If Hedda and Joel were in harmony together, he and Hedda would be in truth. There's a biblical ring to the phrasing of both commandments. No doubt they had their genesis somewhere in all the psychobabble Joel Steinberg had absorbed in his own quest for mental stability.

For years Hedda Nussbaum's nervous tension had caused her to have a spastic colon. Joel Steinberg cured it, she swore to the court. Perhaps Bill Mutter was surprised to learn that for years

Hedda had also suffered from pains in her feet and "had to wear what I considered old ladies' shoes. Because of it, I couldn't wear high heels, and that disappeared, which I credited to [Joel]." Indeed Steinberg could not have helped noticing that she had walked into the courtroom that very morning wearing sling-back pumps with three-inch heels. His cure was evidently still effective.

During Hedda's childhood, her parents had never encouraged her to take up sports, as parents who lived in Westchester might have. But Joel wanted his Galatea to achieve physical as well as mental fitness. Like a father with a small daughter, he worked with her "throwing a ball, catching a ball, making a basket," just as he would later teach Lisa how to skate, swim, and ride a bike. Hedda faithfully did her exercises, started running, took up ballet for a while. All these were wonderful things she had never imagined she'd be able to do.

At Random House, people noticed changes in Hedda Nussbaum. For one thing, she no longer went to Washington Heights to have William Nussbaum cut her hair. Her new downtown haircut was much more stylish. So were the clothes she wore that Steinberg selected for her—expensive, more sophisticated outfits replaced the blue jeans and artfully tied scarves. Hedda proudly came to work in her new high heels just as feminists were making a point of abandoning them for more comfortable and less sexy shoes. Betty remembers that Hedda suddenly lost a lot of weight because Steinberg liked his women very thin. Hedda had made herself too thin, was Betty's private opinion.

Many unself-confident people in those days were concerned with learning how to be more assertive, how to put their own needs first. *Don't Say Yes when You Want to Say No* was the title of a best-seller on the subject. The new very slender and stylish Hedda Nussbaum was getting a crash course in assertiveness training from Joel Steinberg. While he may not have wanted to teach her how to assert herself with *him* (that was not quite what he meant by achieving a state of truth), he did set out to show her how to ask for promotions and raises at Random House.

In 1975, Hedda wasn't sure she merited a promotion and a raise; after all, she hadn't worked at Random House much more than a year, and she was still thrilled she had landed there at all. Nonetheless, she did begin to speak up more at meetings, and to consciously try to be more "outgoing" and "sociable." Soon she found she was able to go to a sales conference, present the books she had edited to the sales force, and "give a fantastic talk, spontaneously. And everybody would tell me how great it was, and I credited him for my improvement, my growth in personality." One day she was able to walk into Walter Retan's office and ask to be promoted from associate editor to editor. That's a bit premature, thought Walter Retan, both piqued and amused. Still, Hedda was promoted.

"Her job was to do books that kids would enjoy and get something out of," said Gerald Harrison, a Random House executive in 1987. "She had a joy for the job."

One night after work, Betty and her fiancé went out for drinks with Hedda and her new boyfriend. At this first meeting, Betty was dismayed by Steinberg. She found him "obnoxious, loud, and full of himself. He wasn't unkind to Hedda, but he wasn't particularly nice to her. She was a pretty girl for him and that was about it." A second evening out only strengthened Betty's initial negative feelings. They were all supposed to have a drink together after seeing an Off-Broadway show, but Betty and her fiancé made up an excuse to go home.

Walter Retan also met Steinberg at a departmental party for writers and illustrators. When Joel overheard Retan tell someone that he was thinking of drawing up a will, he horned in on their conversation: "Oh, I can do that for you," he said. "Oh no, you can't," Retan thought to himself. The office gossip generated by Hedda herself was that Hedda Nussbaum was running around with a Mafia lawyer. It bothered Retan that Hedda was so proud of having such a disreputable boyfriend, that she was positively showing him off at this party.

Hedda had always come to work very early and been one of the last to leave. Soon she seemed to be on a different schedule, oversleeping in the mornings, dashing out of the office at five. Hedda was clearly leading a nocturnal life. She had to go to a lot of very late dinners with Joel and his clients, she explained to Retan. She and Steinberg even seemed to be socializing with underworld types—"people involved in drug deals," one woman remembered. "All kind of in the fast lane." Far from being troubled by these encounters, Hedda seemed to relish them. In a conversation with Betty, she made allusions to experimenting with cocaine. Betty thought Hedda was talking about cocaine just to see if she could shock her.

Hedda Nussbaum not only believed that Steinberg was "extremely talented" but that he was "probably one of the best lawyers in the whole country." Since she knew little about legal work, she was quite enthralled when Joel came home from court and performed the proceedings of the day for his audience of one. It didn't occur to her to wonder whether he was "reenacting" imaginary events. Unlike Joel's mother, Hedda was incapable of doubting him, of brushing him off derisively with, "Oh, that's Joel and his stories." Given Hedda's capacity for boundless acceptance, it may have become harder and harder for Joel to remember that he was lying.

Although Steinberg's preferred designation was "criminal lawyer," he had also branched out into family law. He had something of a reputation for winning cases in which divorced fathers sought custody of their children. Private adoption was becoming another specialty. Since it did not involve complicated litigation, it was not a particularly taxing way of amassing a sizable income.

Through frequenting a Village nightclub called the Eighth Wonder, Steinberg found a couple of show-business clients. A young comedian named David Heenan, who lived in the neighborhood, came to depend on Joel for personal as well as professional advice and thought of him as a father figure. Folk singer Chad Mitchell, however, remembers him as being "bizarre sometimes, in the sense that he was an aggressive person who could be somewhat obsessive."

Much of Steinberg's criminal work was fairly routine. It was a matter of making brief appearances with clients before calendar judges. One such judge was Harold Rothwax, who would later preside over *The People* v. *Joel Steinberg.* When a case was more complex, Steinberg would still step aside and turn it over to Ivan Fisher or one of the other attorneys he knew.

Hedda had never met anyone who knew so many people. Visitors were always coming in and out of that apartment on Tenth Street. Since she was so shy herself, Joel's gregariousness was very appealing. He was not a man who discriminated when it came to making friends. As he often said to Mel Sirkin, he drew no lines between his personal and professional relationships. Steinberg was proud of this accepting attitude, but Sirkin was very troubled by it. While it was reasonable for a corporate lawyer to socialize with clients, a criminal lawyer who did so flirted with disaster. Joel wore his underworld associations like a badge of courage, Sirkin told me.

He did have a few respectable friends. One was Detective

Jimmy Levison at the Sixth Precinct. And then, of course, there was Dr. Michael Bergman. When they had roomed together at NYU, Bergman had been studying medicine. Now he was a gynecologist with a flourishing practice on University Place. Bergman, like Joel, had a taste for the fast lane. (He reportedly had a cocaine habit and died in 1986 after suffering a sudden massive heart attack.) Perhaps from identifying with Michael Bergman, Steinberg came to believe that he, too, was a healer.

Once, in 1980, as a kind of joke, Bergman took Joel behind the scenes to satisfy his curiosity about how abortions were performed. When Joel walked into the examination room in a white coat and surgical mask, Bergman introduced him to the unsuspecting woman on the table as "my assistant."

Steinberg continued to seek out the companionship of doctors. Dr. Michael Green, a Long Island pulmonary specialist, became his next medical friend, and finally, of course, there was Dr. Peter Sarosi.

Now that Joel had become her therapist, Hedda saw no need to continue her three sessions a week with Dr. James Bradley Norton, who had encouraged her to keep making lists of her problems, but who had been unable to cure her spastic colon or help her get a promotion at Random House. With Joel she'd had tangible results. Joel Steinberg had the power to bring about quick fixes. So what did it matter that he'd get carried away by anger and disappointment because she wasn't changing fast enough or that he kept mercilessly tearing her down? Everything he did was for Hedda's own good. And it could never be said that he neglected her. The feelings he aroused through his unappeasability were very powerful ones.

He had wanted her to move in with him almost from the start. But she kept telling him she wasn't ready. She did love her studio, the first place that had ever been all hers. And Joel's place was rather small for two people, particularly when one of them was a writer. A writer needed a study of her own. He was already talking, though, about the two of them having kids, moving to a big house in Westchester.

Whenever Joel Steinberg pressed her to give up her apartment, perhaps Hedda was reminded that she did have a great hold on him. Joel Steinberg needed her as his soulmate, as the only person on earth who had ever understood him. Finally, of course, she had to say yes. In January 1976, she moved down to Tenth Street, but kept the lease on the studio for a while just in case things didn't work out. Joel arranged for Mel Sirkin to move in as a subtenant. She had to leave a lot of things behind, among them, her piano. She offered it to a friend of Nadine Simon's on extended loan. But then Joel said that was the wrong way to go about it, and that he was going to draw up a legal agreement for the transaction. Nadine Simon's friend was quite hurt. "In that case, let's forget it," she told Hedda.

Soon after Hedda moved in with him, Joel Steinberg evidently realized that their relationship was not on the road to perfection. Hedda continued to have great difficulty with truth and spontaneity. The Steinberg treatment was not getting fast enough results. Now that the novelty of the new relationship was wearing off, perhaps Joel was plagued by the same sexual inadequacy he'd experienced with the schoolteacher, and he may also have begun to worry about his inability to control his anger. He was living with a woman who regarded him as a god. But a man who hates himself cannot overcome his contempt for a woman who is fool enough to worship him; he may even believe she is deluding him by faking her feelings, particularly in the area of sex.

He looked around for a guru of his own and found one a few blocks farther west. Edward Eichel had a degree in human sexuality from New York University and had been meeting for a couple of years with groups of troubled couples. According to Nussbaum, Eichel called himself a Reichian behaviorist, although he did not subscribe, as Wilhelm Reich did, to the use of an orgone box to treat his patients. The complete Eichel treatment took two years. Steinberg went through the entire process, although Nussbaum dropped out after the first twelve months.

Reichian behaviorism, Nussbaum testified, concentrated on modifying one's present behavior rather than dealing with one's history. Eichel worked "on the physical ways to deal with emotional difficulties, basically trying to get you centered in focus, making eye contact with people, speaking clearly."

Joel Steinberg was also something of a behaviorist. He believed in the efficacy of negative reinforcement in retraining the psyche. Steinberg's obsession with punishment was certainly reflected in the stories he concocted about the methods he'd been taught to use when interrogating enemy prisoners.

For a time Steinberg was so enthusiastic about Eichel's treatment that he wanted everyone he knew to benefit by it. He did succeed in persuading a very skeptical Mel Sirkin to go to one of the sessions at Eichel's apartment. But Mel did not care to be centered by Eichel, and he never came back.

In 1977, possibly through Eichel, a second guru came into Joel's life—a long-haired Christly young man who was a carpenter and had a consciousness-raising group of his own. The carpenter's goals were spiritual—tranquillity and inner peace. Joel and Hedda started attending those sessions as well. Steinberg was very anxious to share his "spiritually deepening experiences" with Ivan Fisher. Finally, he brought "Carpenter Tom" to the office and lined up some work for him building bookshelves.

Ivan Fisher found Steinberg's guru a "mellow man. You could feel the leaderliness in him." And the bookshelves he built were so well crafted that Fisher has them to this day in his townhouse. But for all the carpenter's charisma, Joel and and Hedda failed to achieve inner peace.

Hedda tried Biofeedback next; then it was back to psychiatry for a few sessions with Dr. Albert Ellis, a best-selling authority on sexual responsiveness. In 1980, she had herself Rolfed for a few months. None of these therapies succeeded in liberating the real Hedda. In 1981, the year she and Joel tried parenthood, she stopped shopping around for new ones.

Manhattan can be like a small town. When you're in a public place, you're apt to run into a friend, even a former lover. Around 1977, Bill Mutter and a business partner saw Hedda Nussbaum on a subway train. The partner had also known Hedda three years before. The two men stared. "My God! She's turned gray!" they said to each other.

IN THE spring of 1977, a second woman came into Joel Steinberg's life. Marilyn Walton is a black, Texas-born jazz singer, who testified as a defense witness at Steinberg's trial. In her conversations with me, she has frequently pointed out that Joel Steinberg has mostly treated her with great respect and generosity—quite differently, in other words, from the way he treated Hedda Nussbaum. Today Marilyn Walton remains Joel's confidante, even though she will never forgive him for not having the strength to abandon the life-style that eventually led to Lisa's death. She blames him for the life-style but does not believe he could have killed his daughter, although she is the first to admit there is a great deal Steinberg has never told her. In fact, he always seemed to "clean up his act" when she was around. Now she has taken on the task of his spiritual redemption. While Steinberg was awaiting trial, she visited him on Rikers Island and presented him with "the Bible, the Koran, and the Torah." "Pick one," she told him sternly; together they sang "Amazing Grace." Marilyn is hopeful that Joel, having an "addictive personality," will become "addicted to religion." Not Judaism, "but one of them stormtrooper religions—Catholicism or the Baptist church."

Her own addiction is food. In her late thirties, Marilyn is a massive woman with an appealing heart-shaped face, surprisingly light on her small feet. The sequined satins she selects for her gigs are as flamboyant as they used to be when she was younger and eighty pounds lighter and singing at an East Side club called Jimmy Westin's.

When Joel Steinberg walked in one night with Mel Sirkin and a lawyer who was interested in managing Marilyn, his first sight of her was on a platform in a clinging red gown that bared one shoulder. It was one of her first singing engagements. Joel Steinberg, Marilyn says, couldn't take his eyes off her. When the set was over, he walked up to her and said he wanted her to dance with him. "We danced and we talked," Marilyn remembers. By the last dance Joel was holding her so tightly that she became aware he was having an orgasm. Understandably, she "freaked out." Nonetheless, when the club closed at three, Marilyn asked him if he wanted a lift home. To her surprise, Joel preferred to ride home in a cab by himself, so she shared a cab with Mel. To Marilyn, men like Joel and Mel were in the category of "what the *Cosmo* Girl was looking for."

Marilyn Walton tends to look at white people rather too categorically, missing some important nuances, although in other ways she is a shrewd judge of character. She wrongly persists in seeing Hedda Nussbaum as a "Jewish princess," for example, viewing that as a key to her personality. Marilyn is very proud of her churchgoing Dallas family and the struggles of her parents to educate themselves. Her memories of her high-school-principal father are her solace in life and her touchstone for what is right and what is wrong. She's tolerant of Steinberg, and of white people in general, in the way of one who does not expect the best behavior from them; none of them will ever measure up to Marilyn's family, that's for sure. With white friends, she's a little imperious, expecting deference, just as she probably always expected it from Steinberg.

He kept inviting her out to dinner after that first meeting at Jimmy Westin's, often suggesting that she pick him up at his office. It appeared he was going out with her very openly. The relationship, according to Marilyn, was both romantic and platonic, and she was absolutely determined to keep it that way. Although she had fallen in love with Joel despite what had happened on the dance floor, "he never could get me in bed. I had this thing about white guys using black chicks. Those were the house rules." In any case, Marilyn had a black musician boyfriend that she didn't tell Joel about. "Joel didn't know if I was a virgin or not and he was scared to death to find out."

Marilyn Walton's house rules may have been a great relief to a man beset with fears of inadequacy, a man with what Steinberg's attorney, Adrian DiLuzio, calls a "dirty idea about sex." Undoubtedly Steinberg hoped a relationship with a black woman would prove sexually therapeutic; just like Hedda Nussbaum, he was seeking to become spontaneous, natural, and free. Marilyn bossed him around and set limits, yet obviously cared for him. The fact that Marilyn had a graduate degree in criminal justice and had briefly worked for the U.S. district attorney's office in Chicago and as a Pinkerton detective in Dallas certainly must have reinforced Steinberg's image of Marilyn's toughness. She may have seemed like the kind of woman he wished he'd had for a mother.

For months, Joel neglected to mention that he was living with someone. Hedda's name, in fact, never came up—not until November when Marilyn had to return to Dallas for Thanksgiving and the annual Deb Ball, the high point of the black social season. Joel and Mel took Marilyn and a girlfriend of hers to the airport. As they waited for Marilyn's 7 P.M. flight, Joel decided on the spur of the moment to go to Dallas with her to meet her family. He bought himself a ticket and said to Mel, "Call Hedda and tell her to look at my calendar to see if I have any court dates." Marilyn thought Hedda must be Joel's secretary. They all made jokes in the airport about how funny it would be if Marilyn were paged as Marilyn Steinberg. Wouldn't people be surprised when a black "Marilyn Steinberg" showed up?

The Dallas trip was a disaster and nearly ended Marilyn's friendship with Joel for good. As Marilyn explained it, Joel started clowning (the word she always used for Joel's bad behavior), being unbearable to live with. "When you come down South, everything has to slow down. Joel couldn't slow down. He was very short and very tense."

Soon after they arrived, Marilyn and Joel had a fight because Joel started wrestling with her while she was trying to cook breakfast. Joel had "clowned" this way with Marilyn before; he was always trying to roughhouse—grabbing her, tickling and pinching, shadow-boxing, getting her in holds around the waist and refusing to let go. Oddly enough, Marilyn still doesn't consider any of this behavior "sexually aggressive," although it did lead to arguments between them. "A dog will be aggressive with you," Marilyn reflected to me, "if you're an aggressive person. Hedda was into a lot of shit. I wasn't." On this particular occasion, Joel wouldn't stop clowning when she asked him to, so she slammed down the skillet and walked out of the kitchen. Her father, who had traditional ideas about a woman's duties, as well as southern hospitality, ordered her back to the stove to cook for her guest. When she cooled down enough to return to the kitchen, she was amused to find Joel contritely making eggs for himself and her father.

The Waltons, who were used to their daughter bringing both black and white musician friends home with her, had given Joel a cordial welcome, although Mrs. Walton, privately, was not very taken with him. Joel admired Mr. Walton, the most important man in Marilyn's life. Marilyn's handsome father had been an athlete in his youth and had fought in the Second World War. Marilyn describes him "as proud, stubborn, principled, and quiet"—everything Joel Steinberg was not.

Perhaps Joel had fantasies about being regarded as a son by Marilyn's father—as if the answer he sought to what was lacking in him could be found there. But he was not about to marry Marilyn, although Marilyn brought up the subject every time he tried to get into bed with her. "If I sleep with you, I will be married to you," she'd warn him. Joel would back off and start talking about birth control, as if anxiety about that was the only obstacle to their sexual relationship. He swore the last thing he wanted was to make Marilyn pregnant. When she got back to New York, he wanted her to consult his gynecologist friend, Mike Bergman, right away.

Soon enough Joel made himself offensive to Marilyn's parents by refusing to escort her to the Black Debutante Ball. Since the Waltons considered this an important social obligation, they felt deeply insulted. But Joel Steinberg wasn't in the mood for apologies. He decided to leave Dallas and go to Miami, offering Marilyn the choice of accompanying him or not. Marilyn confronted her father and told him she was going.

Reluctantly, Mr. Walton drove his daughter and Joel to the Dallas airport. Again Joel started "clowning," telling Marilyn's daddy he wasn't driving fast enough. The two men got out of the car and had a fistfight. "Daddy won, hands down," and Joel was docile for the rest of the ride. On the airplane, though, he started being obnoxious again, flirting with a blonde whom he found attractive. Cruelly, he told Marilyn she was fat. The two of them berated each other until a flight attendant made them move to separate seats.

In Miami, Marilyn called Mel Sirkin and asked him to meet her at Kennedy Airport because she was flying back to New York. After that, she refused to speak to Joel for three or four months. Mel gave Marilyn "intellectual" companionship during this period.

Out of loyalty to Joel (the two men were so inseparable in those days that Marilyn used to call them "Pete and Repeat"), Mel Sirkin told Marilyn nothing about Hedda, although once he hinted that Joel was a "sadistic son of a bitch." Joel soon grew jealous that Marilyn was seeing so much of Mel. Again he started courting her with dinners at expensive restaurants, and even presented her with a large antique emerald ring. Marilyn was afraid it would be stolen from her dressing room at the club where she was performing, so she gave the ring and some of Joel's other gifts back to him and told him to keep them for her in his safe deposit box. She has never seen this jewelry again.

As time went on, Joel apparently decided that "three was company," as Marilyn put it. Perhaps wanting to needle Hedda, he took her and some friends to hear Marilyn sing. But Marilyn was still in the dark about the place Hedda occupied in Joel's life. He was careful to invite Marilyn to the apartment only in the daytime when Hedda was not around. Finally, Marilyn called him there one night and got Hedda on the phone. That was when she realized that Hedda Nussbaum was not his secretary. When she confronted Joel, he told her that he had no intention of ever marrying Hedda, although he had felt guilty when he went to Dallas with Marilyn.

Marilyn Walton believes that even then Joel knew his relationship with Hedda had the potential to destroy them both. As long as he wasn't married to Hedda, Joel knew he had the option of pushing her out the door and turning over a new leaf with a much better woman.

On December 7, 1977, shortly after Steinberg's impulsive trip to Dallas, Hedda Nussbaum spent some time setting down what she later told Ira London were her "unconscious thoughts," although London pointed out that once they were on paper, they were not so unconscious. Perhaps she was alone after hours in her office at Random House, for the paper she used was Random House stationery. If Hedda did not yet know whom Steinberg had visited, his abrupt departure must have raised her suspicions. In any case, she was feeling very troubled, and so she made a list for herself of fourteen "unconscious thoughts" in all.

Number 1 was the cornerstone of the others:

I must have Joel's approval and love in order to survive.

Number 2 stated Hedda's worst feelings about herself:

I am worthless and helpless, and a piece of shit.

In other words, there was the awful possibility that she was unworthy of Joel's love. Nussbaum continued:

> I can never do anything right. And I will always be rejected for it.
> I can't change. I need someone's magic formula or magic wand to
> do it for me.

In Number 4, the tone changed to one of defiance:

> I don't want to take care of anyone else. I want to be taken care of.
> I want to be loved the way I am. I don't want to change to be loved.
> I deserve to be loved because I exist.

Developing this line of argument, she petulantly declared her right to be selfish:

> I don't have to do anything to earn it. I don't have to give. I'm not
> going to do anything I'm told to do. I will do what I want. So there.

Following the naughty "so there," Nussbaum's mood deflated:

> I am hopeless. I've got to control myself. And everything around
> me. I can't go out of control.

Hedda may have had faith that she could control Joel by the act of surrendering herself to him completely. Yet this strategy of control through submission was obviously not working if Joel could be attracted to someone else.

But now there was another striking change of mood. In the midst of all this misery, Hedda seemed to discover ecstasy in herself. Was this merely one of her false notes? Or was she ecstatic *because* she was suffering?

> Being me feels so good it scares me to death. I'm afraid I might be
> happy. I don't deserve it. I don't want the responsibility for keeping
> it up.

Surely she was emoting a bit in "I don't deserve it." A childish, whining voice immediately took over:

> I need everyone's love and approval, even people I don't like.
> I must please everyone. No one has a right to criticize me. I'm a
> good girl.
> I try *so* hard. *So* hard to please.

In the next to last item, "I don't want to take responsibility for really living. I want someone to do it for me," Nussbaum truthfully confessed her need to be put back by Steinberg into an infant state. The infant does nothing for itself, is the supreme taker, but is loved because it exists.

She concluded the exercise:

> I don't want to take the responsibility of dying, but maybe if I'm lucky I'll get hit by a truck.

*

Marilyn Walton makes no bones about it. "Hedda considered me a rival. Well, I was. And I didn't like it, which made things even worse." Joel Steinberg was the one who enjoyed the situation— enjoyed it so much that once the two women became aware of each other, he would often take them out jointly, making it plain to Hedda that although Marilyn did not share his bed, she was getting better treatment. Marilyn claims that when Steinberg invited her to the apartment, he'd make Hedda wait on her "hand and foot."

"*Nothing* Hedda did pleased Joel," says Marilyn, voicing the classic misconception one rival is apt to have about another. Seeing no positive qualities in Hedda Nussbaum, Marilyn Walton still finds it difficult to believe that what she perceives as the most negative aspects of Hedda's personality were precisely what did please Joel—what, in fact, bonded Steinberg and Nussbaum together for so many years.

THE SEXUAL behavior of Joel Steinberg and Hedda Nussbaum never became an issue in the Steinberg case. If it suited the purposes of the defense to suggest from time to time that Nussbaum was a masochist, it was detrimental to Steinberg's image to paint him as a sadist. The prosecution, too, had a great deal to lose by presenting its star witness as a participant in a sadomasochistic relationship, thereby calling into question Nussbaum's will. So both sides worked to exclude sexual material—after all, Steinberg was on trial for murder, not deviation. The prosecution was content to portray him as a monstrous but essentially standard batterer.

It was clear from the public reaction to the case—even the assumptions immediately made about the two suspects by the press—that people were most reluctant to believe that Lisa Steinberg's death had come about as a result of anything more alien and perverse than a man's brutal and ungovernable rage and a woman's fear and weakness. Steinberg and Nussbaum were interpreted as having only played out the roles traditionally defined by gender—though taken to extremes.

The acknowledgment that the possibility of inversion is always present in heterosexual love is immensely threatening. It is perceived as being against nature, even though men are often cruel to women and women experience suffering in relationship after relationship, frequently when they believe themselves most deeply in love. For twenty years, the women's movement has crusaded to stamp out male cruelty and domination and to argue women out of passivity and submission. Various therapeutic and quasi-religious groups have sought to create less politicized versions of an ideal world, where sexual tension is abolished either by making sex so available that it becomes meaningless or by imposing abstinence. Middle-class marriage has meanwhile been tamed and deromanticized, with lovers turned into "partners" with equal shares in the family enterprise, both dedicated to the erotic acquisition of status and worldly goods. Yet the polarities of male dominance and female submission continue to exist, and so do the Steinbergs and the Nussbaums.

Psychoanalyst Jessica Benjamin is one of the few feminist intellectuals who has taken on the unpopular study of the dynamics of the sadomasochistic relationship. In her introduction to *The Bonds of Love,* she warns her readers: "To reduce domination to a simple relation of doer and done-to is to substitute moral outrage for analysis." Whereas "domination begins with the attempt to deny dependency," voluntary submission "is a paradox in which the individual tries to achieve freedom through slavery, release through submission to control."

Hedda Nussbaum has testified that she is quite unable to recall the circumstances surrounding the first blow she ever received from Joel Steinberg. Marilyn Walton believes it happened in January of 1978, when Hedda found out Joel had visited Marilyn in Dallas. But Marilyn Walton tends to see herself in a pivotal role throughout the story she tells.

Nussbaum did remember being struck in the eye and also had no difficulty recalling how surprised Joel was by what he had done to her, and how affectionate he was afterward, promising it would never happen again. Joel's contrite apologies no doubt thrilled Hedda to the core. Yet Steinberg's behavior with Hedda's predecessor, and even his attempts to roughhouse with Marilyn, suggest that the sadomasochistic element in his relationship with Hedda probably manifested itself physically as well as verbally from the start. In Hedda, Steinberg had found the willing partner he had been searching for—the perfect mate that Marilyn Walton could never be, the woman who would let him do anything. Whether or not there were previous blows, Steinberg directed this one at a place where it would be visible and unmistakable, as if he wanted Hedda to wear the sign of his ownership, a bruise rather than a gold ring. The relationship had entered a new phase—he was upping the ante.

Many a woman has walked out on a man the first time he raises a hand to her, instinctively recognizing that the acceptance of one blow will only lead to another and another. Some women are paralyzed, of course, for fear of violent reprisals following their departure. Housewives with small children often feel so bound to their husbands socially and economically that they cannot bring themselves to sever the relationship. But Hedda Nussbaum was more than adequately equipped for independence from Steinberg—in fact, in 1978, she was at the peak of her Random House career. She would merely have had to move into a new apartment, as Joel's previous girlfriend had done. Instead she stayed. Rather than fearing Joel Steinberg, she only worshiped him more devoutly. But perhaps Hedda was also worshiping herself. Was she not God's handmaiden, the martyr/heroine of the Hedda Nussbaum drama? Without Joel there would be no drama, none of the pain she mistook for wild passion, no feeling that only she could satisfy this extraordinary being who had selected her to be with him out of all other women. If Hedda Nussbaum were alone again in some pathetic little studio apartment, nothingness would swallow her up.

She did start worrying about her eye, however, when she began seeing "slashes of light in front of it," so she went to have it examined at Manhattan Eye and Ear Hospital. When she was asked how the accident occurred, at first she told the hospital the truth. She was probably not even ashamed that she had been beaten if she was still feeling the glow of the aftermath. "But then when I thought about it, I decided—I didn't think it would be a good idea to put that on the record because the doctor had written it down and I asked her to change it, and she crossed it out and wrote something else." In the future, Nussbaum would continue to protect Steinberg from legal repercussions.

Joel went to the office that Monday with an irresistible desire to talk about the incident. He sought out Mel as his confidant and told him he had struck Hedda accidentally while they were "playing." Then he quickly altered his explanation: Actually, he had reacted in a moment's anger and was very shocked by what he had done. He claimed he had never hit a woman before. Of course this confession was "all bull," Mel says, in view of what he now knows about Joel's relationship with the schoolteacher. In all probability, the act of telling a portion of the truth titillated Steinberg. He wanted very much to know whether anything similar had ever happened to Mel.

Hedda, too, showed up at work that day, with an elaborate story to explain her black eye. Over the weekend, she'd been mugged by a purse snatcher as she came out of Bloomingdale's. The women in the office were very upset and asked her if she had reported the incident to the police. A few weeks later—another Monday—Hedda appeared wearing dark glasses. This time she'd walked into a door when she was refinishing kitchen cabinets. Then there was the branch that struck Hedda across the face when she was on horseback. . . . Then she was "mugged" a second time. With a kind of tacit understanding, the women in the juvenile department came to the conclusion that there was something going on at home. A couple of them walked into Walter Retan's office and closed the door. "These aren't accidents," they told him. After a while, Hedda no longer bothered to give excuses, and people started looking the other way.

Among themselves, the women had long discussions about what they could do to help Hedda Nussbaum. But Hedda never asked for their help. In fact, nothing infuriated her more than solicitude. She made it plain that no one was to interfere in her affairs. Everyone wanted to believe that this was because Hedda was so terrified of Steinberg.

Michelle LaMarca, who worked in the production department, invited Hedda and Joel for a weekend at her house in the Hamptons. She watched Joel Steinberg closely and found him "extremely intense and intelligent," but for the life of her she didn't see anything strange about him; nor did she have the feeling that Hedda was unhappy or fearful. Michelle's main impression of Joel was that he was a perfectionist who wanted to excel in everything he did—that seemed the root of his intensity. She remembers him telling her he skied well enough to be on ski patrol.

Louise Price had a more mature perspective on the irrational aspects of human relationships than did the younger women in the department. "I never had the sense Hedda wanted the beatings to stop," she told me. "She wasn't denying what was happening, but she wasn't apologizing for it either. It was almost as if she was proud of her bruises."

One day Hedda was in Louise Price's office. Looking at the black-and-blue marks on her face, Louise said quietly, "Hedda, take care of yourself."

"What are you saying?" Hedda demanded. "Oh, I know what all of you are thinking," she said proudly, even arrogantly, "But you just don't *understand.*"

"Uh oh," Louise thought to herself, "they're engaging in some kind of game, but she's a willing participant. I thought, Wow, she's not afraid of him. Or if she's afraid of him, there's something else in it for her. It's a game that occasionally goes too far."

Louise did not feel that Hedda's attitude was inconsistent with her previous demeanor. Unlike Betty, she had never considered Hedda shy or retiring.

Although Hedda was aware of the gossip about her in the office, this did not prevent her from continuing to press Walter Retan for more increases in salary and a second promotion—Retan found her positively "militant" on the subject. In 1989, Hedda Nussbaum could not resist bragging in court about how far she had risen at Random House with Joel's coaching: "Eventually, each time I would ask for the promotion or the raise . . . I always got them . . . Well, I went from associate editor to editor to senior editor, and I ended up at Random House earning more than—I believe, more than any other editor in that department had ever earned." Meanwhile, at home, the most talented lawyer in America told Hedda Nussbaum that she was a "much better editor than any of the other editors at Random House." Sometimes Steinberg would even tell Hedda she was smarter than he was. At work, Hedda was known for taking a firm hand with her authors, yet making her recommendations on their manuscripts in a tactful, considerate way. In fact, the only fault Walter Retan could find with her performance was her late arrival in the mornings. He spoke to her about being more punctual, and she did mend her ways for a time.

During 1978, Hedda Nussbaum made the same discovery that thousands of other white, middle-class professionals were making—that nothing was a better substitute for really feeling alive than cocaine. For Hedda, coke must have seemed a panacea—not only a physical and psychic anesthetic, but an avenue to instant spontaneity and a feeling of superiority. A line or two of coke could turn Hedda Nussbaum into a free spirit, the delightful life of the party that Joel wanted her to be. Once Joel had fed her LSD to see if that would make her "come out more": she had obediently taken it and he had served as her "guide." But LSD, unlike cocaine, could not be incorporated into one's everyday life.

Steinberg didn't even take aspirin, according to Hedda Nussbaum, and would have nothing to do with coke. Undoubtedly he knew something about its effects since so many of his clients were dealers or substance abusers. Among the Me Generation, cocaine was the fashionable way of getting high—one reason for its enormous popularity was the mistaken belief that it couldn't make you crazy. Since so much of Joel's tension came from the effort to remain in control—of himself and everybody else—he may have been wary of any substance that would make him too loose. But of course it was different with Hedda. Hedda didn't have to be in control of herself because Joel was in charge of her. Hedda's problem was not being able to let go.

During those glamorous late nights out with Joel's clients, Hedda snorted coke whenever it was offered. In court she could recall only one occasion when Joel actually stopped her. They were in a movie theater with a group of other people, and everyone except Joel was making liberal use of "snorting keys." "They took keys, door keys out of their pockets and there is like a little indentation, a line in the key, and they were putting cocaine on that." Joel took their keys away, she said. "He didn't want them to do that, especially in a public place."

Steinberg's new doctor friend, thirty-two-year-old Michael Green, a graduate of Georgetown University Medical School, was a pulmonary specialist who had recently gone into practice on Long Island. He indulged in cocaine, according to Nussbaum's testimony. Green and his wife, Shayna, were the most exciting of their recent acquaintances.

Joel had met him in late 1977, just before he and Mel set up a new office with a third attorney named Marty Rappoport. (Ivan Fisher had prospered defending Tony Provenzano in the Jimmy Hoffa murder case and had moved out of the Park Avenue suite into private quarters.) That year Joel had believed he was suffering from heart palpitations and went to Green as a patient. When he heard Green had tax problems, he referred him to Mel, who found him a difficult client. Mel was even more irritated by Shayna Green, who phoned him incessantly. But Joel was very taken with these people—with their big house in Fort Salonga and their money and the kind of entertaining they did. On the weekends the Greens liked to party; between 1978 and 1983, Hedda and Joel spent approximately fifty weekends with them on Long Island.

The hospitality was reciprocated in their own much smaller quarters. Michael Green would spend the night at Tenth Street when he came into the city. He would just call up and say he was coming. For quite a while, according to Hedda, he did that on a fairly regular basis. With all this visiting back and forth, if we are to believe Nussbaum as to the extent of it, it is almost as if some merging of the two couples was going on. It is quite common for people like Steinberg and Nussbaum to seek to draw others in,

one psychotherapist told me. In any case, the idiosyncrasies of Joel
and Hedda did not seem to trouble the Greens.

Thirty-one-year-old Shayna Green was wild about small children. Two and a half years before their friends aquired Lisa, she
and her husband became the parents of a son. No doubt the
Greens, like Joel and Hedda, believed in the right of children—if
not everybody—to be spontaneous and free. It wasn't enough for
Shayna to have just one child in her life, so she worked as a
volunteer helper at a local daycare center to which Michael
Green made financial contributions.

Despite Michael Green's stimulating visits with Steinberg and
Nussbaum and the fulfillment Shayna found through her work
with kids, the Greens were evidently a deeply bored couple—as
bored with themselves, perhaps, and as empty as their two Greenwich Village friends. Possibly they had come to view themselves
as daring explorers on the frontiers of suburban sexuality.

Suburbia did provide more privacy for certain kinds of experi-
mentation than did Manhattan apartments. Stories of Long Island
wife-swapping parties often hit the newspapers in the 1970s.
Some swingers on the Island even engaged in the making of
pornographic videos, abetted by the new technology.

By 1980, one of the things Joel and Hedda allegedly did with
Michael Green during his visits to Tenth Street was to smoke
freebase, passing a glass water pipe from person to person. Hedda
cooked up the mixture herself in the small kitchen, taking an
almost aesthetic pride in the process of purifying the white crystals of cocaine. After two years of refusing to snort, Joel took to
freebasing like a duck takes to water. Joel and Hedda had first
experienced this intensified high during a visit to one of Joel's
clients. They knew exactly what this man was going to offer them
and how they would respond even before they went to see him.
The client had taken them into a discreet little office he maintained across the street from his regular place of business and
brought out a freebase pipe. When Joel and Hedda reached for
it that night, they were sealing not only their own fates, but Lisa's.

For both of them, freebasing was a deliberate choice. Joel has
been silent on the reasons for his sudden decision to freebase after
his avoidance of cocaine in its milder form. Hedda, of course, has
come to blame her entire addiction on Joel in keeping with her
consistent unwillingness to take responsibility for her own life.
Shortly after the Steinberg trial, Hedda told Naomi Weiss:
"Freebasing made me feel like I wanted more and more, and I

hated that feeling. But Joel loved it and demanded that I smoke with him. Although Joel said the cocaine helped us communicate better, he used the drug to force his will on me." Yet sitting on the witness stand just a few months earlier, she had recalled her freebase cookery with the rapture of a connoisseur or a religious devotee. It had also been revealed in the courtroom that Hedda collected freebase recipes on index cards, and planned to write a book on cocaine. Her research files had been discovered in the apartment.

Despite the amount of freebasing she was doing with Steinberg, Hedda Nussbaum continued to be a productive employee at Random House. For a year or so, she seemed to do better than ever, even writing and publishing three children's books of her own, *Animals Build the Most Amazing Homes, Ranger Rick's Nature Magazine*, and *Plants Do the Most Amazing Things*. The plant book was dedicated "to Joel, my everyday inspiration."

In addition, Hedda continued to work with other writers of juvenile nonfiction. One of them, Larry Weinberg, became a friend of hers and a client of Joel's. For a few years, Weinberg would consult Joel whenever he needed advice on a book contract. Joel fascinated Larry Weinberg, who had once written a play about Adolf Hitler. Here was a man with a Hitler-like personality, he thought. But Weinberg was horrified by Joel's relationship with Hedda. As time went on, it seemed to him that Joel was "using his fists on Hedda to create a Dorian Gray image of himself."

One of Hedda's responsibilities continued to be the *Charlie Brown* series. According to Nadine Simon, who worked with her on all these books, the *Charlie Brown*s constituted a large part of Hedda's workload. Although her byline did not appear on the title page, she composed most of the questions and answers herself, as well as doing the necessary research and matching the art to the text. In the fourth Charlie Brown book, about customs and holidays around the world, one can find the question, "Is there a Children's Day?" Yes, indeed there is a Children's Day, celebrated by the Methodist Church. The second half of the answer, however, is hardly appropriate for very young readers:

> One unusual custom is practiced in Yugoslavia. Parents tie up their children on that country's Children's Day. They set their children free when they promise to be good for the rest of the year.

How did such a bizarre passage creep into the text? Did Hedda write these sentences herself or were they the work of one of her free lancers? Nussbaum claims that a free lance must have written them. As a conscientious editor, however, she should certainly have decided to omit such disturbing information. It could hardly be called information, though, since in point of fact the Yugoslavians have no such colorful custom.

Inserting the passage into the text may well have been a convoluted private joke, a reference to Hedda's and Joel's sexual practices. It may also have been a gesture of contempt for the well-meaning colleagues who still kept offering her unwanted help and foolishly trying to separate her from Steinberg.

"Let's hear it for the Yugoslavians!!!" says the beloved hound Snoopy in a balloon issuing from his mouth.

At Random House, Hedda was socializing much less with the other women by now, although she still went out to lunch with them from time to time. Everyone was alarmed by a new theme that had cropped up in her conversation: her overwhelming desire for a baby. Hedda was desperately trying to get pregnant and couldn't figure out why she and Joel were unable to conceive, so she'd started going to fertility specialists. She'd tell her strongly disapproving listeners what a wonderful father Joel was going to make, how he'd once raised a little girl named Dawn as his own. It's a good thing Hedda can't get pregnant, the women would think to themselves. It's a good thing she and Joel can never have a kid.

One day Hedda strode into Betty Kraus's office and had a confrontation with her. This was not the soft-spoken Hedda with the private tragedy, but a woman in a state of fury, who warned Betty to stop spreading malicious lies. Steinberg had learned that Betty had told a mutual acquaintance, "I think Joel's going to kill Hedda," and had brought the remark to Hedda's attention.

"I stepped back," Betty told me. "I became obsessed with the whole question of how someone could stay with a man who abused her. But my husband said, 'Lay off.'"

GREEN THINGS

WHY DID they want kids? people kept asking each other in the fall of 1987 in puzzled, horrified tones. In a sense, the question was rhetorical, yet people also asked it as if there had to be some rational answer, forgetting that there are people who want children for irrational yet compelling reasons. Almost involuntarily, we believe in human goodness. It is difficult for us to acknowledge the existence of "illogical" behavior that seems to go against nature. Why would a woman seek out pain? Why would an educated middle-class couple beat a defenseless child? We want to believe that the desire for children comes out of a profound human need to nurture. Yet the nurturing instinct is not universal; there are women as well as men who lack it. "I don't want to take care of anyone," Hedda Nussbaum had truthfully written during the very period when she was trying to get pregnant.

When Hedda proclaimed, "I want a baby," the baby she must have been thinking of was an undemanding doll. She counted on this doll, the product of Joel and herself, for one more necessary transformation. Without it she could not turn into Hedda the mother—or more to the point, Mrs. Joel Steinberg.

In the summer of 1979, when the three of them were spending a weekend in the Hamptons, Hedda even complained to Marilyn Walton that she wished Joel would have his fertility checked out. To while away one long, hot evening, Marilyn read Tarot cards. She could not resist telling Hedda that she would never have a child of her own, even though the cards contained no such prediction. She remembers that Hedda got very upset.

The following year Hedda continued to make the rounds of doctors, in addition to having herself Rolfed—the painful, deep massage was supposed to liberate you from the emotional tension stored in the body's muscular system. Perhaps Hedda felt enormous inner tension was preventing conception. In any case, like Joel, she had come to believe in the curative powers of physical pain. A book called *Body/Mind* that Hedda read at the time, may have served to reinforce this idea. According to Hedda, "it talked about the relationship between the body and the mind . . . and about different kinds of therapy that would work on one and affect the other." It stimulated her to do some further list-making; "I made up this list of different parts of my body," Nussbaum testified, "and wrote down all the associations, whatever came to my mind with regard to it." Of course she showed the list to Joel.

Joel called Marilyn long distance one night in 1980 to give her some heart-rending news: "I'm not perfect anymore." A doctor had just told him he had a low sperm count.

Marilyn thinks Joel decided to adopt a child in August of that year, when he was feeling renwed anxiety about his arhythmic heartbeat (Green had made him give up caffeine and cigarettes, though not cocaine.) That same month, Marilyn's father died very suddenly. Joel, Marilyn theorizes, suddenly started feeling his own mortality.

The fear that one will die and leave nothing of oneself behind is an acceptable reason to want a child. Indeed, it may have acted as a stimulus for Steinberg, just as it has for many normal fathers. But Steinberg was in no sense normal, and less rational by far than he had been before he began to freebase, although he was still trying to locate his feelings in his grandiosity and hyperactive behavior. Undoubtedly he hoped parenthood would be one of the ultimate therapeutic experiences. Through having a child constantly available for him to love, who knew what greatness and caringness, what depth of emotion, might be liberated. He couldn't have recognized that he hated children, too, just as he hated the small, weakling Joel who had once cowered in fear before Charlotte Steinberg.

In the early 1970s it had been fashionable for people not to have children, the better to explore total freedom, By 1980, it was becoming fashionable to have them. If the singles life hadn't brought people happiness, maybe the revival of the despised and rejected family would be the answer. In an acquisitive decade, The Child—the white, middle-class child—became the prime acquisition, the essential accessory for the good life. This message was taken up by the mass media and given a special twist. In movies, television, and books, Daddy or a surrogate Daddy was often shown to be better at nurturing a small child than a mother. These daddy/child romances were so completely satisfying to the male protagonists that adult female love objects, with their strident, uppity demands, were rendered superfluous. There was also the popular belief among the affluent and the ambitious that children could be managed so as to disrupt grown-up life as little as possible. Babies could be turned into superachievers, given an early push down the road to becoming tiny adults, stimulating companions for their parents.

Some of this superbaby philosophy was in line with Joel Steinberg's "behaviorist" ideas. Any child of his, of course, would have to be perfect. What an adopted child lacked genetically could be compensated for by his advanced training methods. After Steinberg had achieved fatherhood, he would often brag to his mother, "The children are making progress"—as if Lisa and Mitchell were overcoming their innate genetic defects.

When Steinberg strolled in Washington Square, he saw middle-aged daddies carrying infants in Snugglis or pushing toddlers on swings. At last a man could be a child-lover without shame—he could even go public with it. It was quite consistent with the redefined image of masculinity.

Birth can be an inevitable event that overtakes both suitable parents and men and women who are drug users and have violent sexual relationships. Antiabortionists would hold that to give birth to a child, whatever the circumstances, is to do the right thing. But adopting a baby involves conscious choice and decision.

Steinberg seems to have had some inkling that there was something morally questionable about adopting Lisa. Naturally, he concocted a story to justify it, which he told to Marilyn Walton and others. At the end of it—no surprise—Joel Steinberg turned into a do-gooder, and Lisa into a foundling thrust upon him by fate.

According to this version of events, Joel never intended to adopt Michelle Launders's baby. In fact, he went to some trouble to find an appropriate home for it with another couple, after Anita Launders, whom he characterized as tough and street smart, pressed five hundred dollars on him. Neither she nor her daughter wanted any part of that baby. Michelle, he claimed, was in no way a good Catholic girl. She had let that pregnancy go in order to force her lover to marry her—she gambled and lost. When Michelle unfortunately developed toxemia and diabetes, Joel's deal with the prospective parents fell apart. The prognosis for the baby was poor—Michael Bergman said it would be riddled with birth defects. But Joel Steinberg found it in his heart to take the possibly defective baby home with him. He kept her because he didn't know what else to do, figuring that if she didn't turn out to be perfect he'd put her into an institution. That was why he didn't take immediate steps to adopt Lisa. It took six months to see that she was okay, although she did have problems with physical coordination. In a second, more heroic version of the story (at least by Joel's standards) Joel goes to see the couple who reneged on the deal and vents his moral indignation by beating up the husband.

While it seems entirely consistent with his character, that Joel Steinberg would have put an imperfect infant in an institution or that he would have a fistfight with a client who angered him, he did in fact begin planning the "adoption" soon after he met Michelle in the winter of 1981. Initially, Hedda, bitterly disappointed at not being able to give birth to Joel's child herself, was very opposed to the whole idea. Since she didn't want to be in the business of taking care of anyone, she may have been particularly unwilling to take care of a baby who wasn't her own. And what if Joel should prefer this child to her, as her parents had preferred her sister?

Perhaps it was conflict over Hedda's resistance to Joel's pet project that provoked a particularly savage beating on February 19, 1981. Most women would remember quite clearly why and how such a terrible thing had happened, but Nussbaum's courtroom account of Steinberg's attack was devoid of any cause for it. It was as if she had been knocked down by a storm or an earthquake. Hedda could only remember what she *hadn't* felt—anger. There had been no anger—she made a point of that, then launched into a detailed description of her trip to the hospital.

Nussbaum had stoically sat up all through the night because the pain was so bad. In the morning, she decided to go by herself to St. Vincent's. She left the house quietly, so as not to wake Joel; she didn't want him to stop her from going. Nussbaum didn't tell the hospital that Steinberg had hit her "Because I again—I was protecting him. I didn't want him to get in any kind of trouble." The emergency-room doctors warned her that the injury she had suffered was potentially fatal and that they would have to remove her spleen. There wasn't even time for a second opinion, Nussbaum testified. Yet the operation wasn't performed until midnight.

Joel showed up at her bedside the following day. He did not apologize; nor did she ask him to. "Why not?" Ira London asked her, interested in Hedda's peculiar acceptance of Joel's brutality. "I was feeling like—" Hedda answered slowly. "I was feeling very connected to him, not like he was someone who had hurt me." It was a classic answer, though not the answer of a typical battered woman. In the kind of relationship Steinberg and Nussbaum had by this time, flirting with death constituted a peak experience for both the master and the slave.

Ira London's next question was, "Are you familiar with the term masochist, Miss Nussbaum?"

"That means someone who likes pain, I think," she answered.

When Hedda came home from St. Vincent's, Steinberg, the medical expert, was outraged by a bad scar the residents had given her and felt Hedda should be, too. Fortunately, he had been able to pull strings and get her a good surgeon through a doctor friend of his at the hospital.

When Hedda testified, she recalled herself as being wholeheartedly in favor of adopting a child, despite feeling a little reluctant at first. When asked why she had not questioned Steinberg's ability to be a good father in view of the fact that he had nearly killed her, she could only reiterate her belief that Steinberg would excel in fatherhood as he did in everything.

Probably the truth of the matter was that the fate of any child was quite unimportant to Hedda, compared to what Joel wanted, and to the benefit to her in finally acquiescing and selflessly letting him have his dearest wish. That benefit was immediately apparent. The months before and after Lisa's arrival were, Hedda told Casolaro, "the best number of months in our relationship and in my whole life."

According to Hedda, she and Joel were kept fully apprised by Michael Bergman of Michelle Launders's health and progress throughout her pregnancy. As Joel started looking at houses in Westchester because the addition of a baby was obviously going to make their apartment too crowded, Hedda may indeed have come to believe that this "adoption" was going to solve a couple of her problems. A nice house in Westchester was something she truly wanted. Perhaps Joel's next step would be matrimony, which would be required if they were going to legalize the adoption.

Hedda did not keep the reason for her newfound happiness a secret. Betty Kraus was the first of her publishing friends to hear about it. Perhaps telling Betty was particularly satisfying for Hedda after the awful remarks Betty had made about Joel. Betty had left Random House for a new job, but she and Hedda had lunch now and then, although their relationship had cooled considerably. Hedda announced the upcoming adoption over one of their lunches, just as she had once dropped the news to Betty that she had tried cocaine. This time as well she may have been amused by the look of absolute shock on Betty's face.

Yes, wasn't it wonderful that she and Joel were finally going to experience parenthood? Hedda had only one tiny area of concern. Both the baby's parents were Catholic. There was no reason, however, why she couldn't disregard this and raise the baby as a Jewish child.

Betty was truly appalled. It had never occurred to her that a couple like Joel and Hedda could get a child through adoption. Obviously, this adoption was going to be private if not illegal, and would proceed without an investigation.

Betty went back to her office and got on the phone to her old friends at Random House. "They're looking for someone else to involve in this dreadful role-playing," was Louise Price's immediate reaction.

Louise and the other women, Elma Westley, Jenny Fanelli, and Ann Christensen, mobilized themselves to see if there was any way to stop the adoption, unaware that this baby would simply be fraudulently acquired. Louise called the Spence-Chapin adoption agency and asked them for help. They told her nothing could be done to rescue the baby unless someone had actually witnessed Joel beating Hedda and would be willing to press charges. "Frankly," Louise told me, "we weren't about to tangle with Joel. He was big, he had connections. How could we prove anything?"

Baby Girl Launders came into the world on May 14, 1981, perfectly equipped to have a wonderful life—by all accounts, an unusual infant, rosy and beautiful, exceptionally alert. Karen Snyder was the first of the neighbors to see Joel and Hedda carrying her into the house. She went right into her apartment and made a fruitless phone call to the Bureau of Child Welfare.

Joel hadn't succeeded in finding a house in Westchester yet, or even a penthouse in the Village—nothing was quite good enough—so he and Hedda prepared for Lisa's arrival by borrowing an antique cradle, which they put in a corner of their bedroom. Hedda bought a layette and read some books on baby care.

In those days the apartment still looked like the dwelling of well-to-do middle-class people. The living room was rather attractive with its shelves of books and Hedda's plants. There was a round oak table with a Tiffany lamp hanging above it and a beige couch over by one of the French windows, where Lisa would later sleep when she outgrew the Porta-crib that succeeded the cradle.

The place seemed bigger without Sascha, the black Great Dane who had died of heart failure the year before, but it was beginning to get quite cluttered. Joel no longer had an outside office and was conducting business from a desk in the bedroom. His arrangement with Mel Sirkin and Marty Rappoport had lasted only eighteen months. Increasingly, Mel had been feeling the need to separate himself from Steinberg; Mel's fiancée was certainly in favor of a complete break. Joel seemed to get the message, because when Mel and Marty Rappoport moved to a new suite, he decided not to come with them. "Joel retreated to the cave," Mel Sirkin says now, although he didn't see it that way at the time. When Mel got married in 1980 and moved to New Jersey, he had dutifully invited Joel and Hedda to the wedding. He saw Joel only once or twice after that and then lost touch with him until 1987. During that period Joel did not try to revive their friendship.

Mel and Tina Sirkin were not present at the baby shower organized by Hedda's sister. Invitations were sent out to Betty as well as to the other Random House women, but almost everyone found a reason why she would be unable to attend. Only Jenny Fanelli accepted the invitation. Afterward, she told the others she had not felt comfortable at the party.

When Joel phoned Marilyn Walton to announce he'd become the father of a beautiful little girl, he told her that Lisa was all his. He was just keeping Hedda around to take care of her. This attitude did not seem unreasonable to Marilyn, given her animosity toward Nussbaum, though she did think it might lead to trouble.

Nonetheless, the period of great harmony between Joel and Hedda lasted a while longer. At Random House, everyone believed that the baby was responsible for Hedda's glow of happiness.

"I'm so lucky to have her," Hedda had told Naomi Weiss at the baby shower. It was a perfectly conventional expression of enthusiasm. One wonders, though, just how Hedda Nussbaum defined her luck. Perhaps she was enthralled for a while with her tiny daughter, but she must also have enjoyed the attention she was receiving from everyone, especially from Joel, when she played the role of the thrilled new mother. Even the interfering busybodies at the office gathered around to admire Lisa when Hedda brought her there to show her off.

Among themselves, the women theorized that Hedda must have wanted the baby as some kind of protection from Joel. Of course it made perfect sense to think so, if one also believed she was afraid of him. They thought it was terrible for Hedda that Joel was spending all his time now at home.

The cave to which Joel Steinberg had retreated was the only small piece of the world where he was totally in control. As a man's man, he had failed to win the respect of his peers—the Kriegers and Fishers. As a lawyer, he was certainly not going to have a brilliant career, even though already he had made over a million—more money than his father had earned in a lifetime. (Some of Steinberg's wealth came from shrewd investments; the bulk of it may have resulted from extralegal activities—drug deals, baby selling, pornography.) The Tony Provenzanos wanted Ivan Fisher to represent them; they felt no confidence in a Joel Steinberg. The people he serviced were only small-timers, perpetrators of penny-ante crimes. And always Joel must have feared getting too much out of his depth, having that little matter of the bar exam catch up with him. When he freebased, of course, he felt on top of the world—there was nothing Joel Steinberg couldn't do. Joel even began to snort cocaine during his diminishing appearances in court. It increased his brilliance and confidence, relieved the tedium of waiting around for hours. He'd devised an ingenious way of carrying it, concealing it in little Sweet'n Low packets, which he'd take out in the men's room. Sweet'n Low was Sweet'n High. Sometimes he suggested to certain clients that he be paid in cocaine rather than cash.

One irate client was John Novak, whom Steinberg represented in 1981 at a federal trial in Rutland, Vermont. Novak and his wife, Donna (represented by her own attorney), had been charged with smuggling a shipment of Colombian marijuana into the United States via the tiny airport in Bennington, Vermont. Joel hit it off with them, or so he thought, and spent some sociable time with them on their farm. Hedda joined him there with Lisa. The Novaks made a big fuss over the baby, especially Donna, who was pregnant.

Although Novak alleges Steinberg extracted over one hundred

fifty thousand dollars from him plus his Mercedes, his trial didn't go well at all; neither did Donna's. Novak was sentenced to five years and Donna to slightly less than a year. Novak was very concerned about Donna because she was expecting. He arranged to borrow twenty thousand dollars from Donna's sister to post bail for his wife. The couple later accused Steinberg of convincing the sister to hand over the money to him for his fees and blamed his poor performance during the trial on his frequent trips to the bathroom. Donna Novak claims he even partook of cocaine in court, dipping his finger into it as he hid behind a book and putting the finger in his mouth. She went to jail for twenty-one days and had a miscarriage. In 1983, John Novak unsuccessfully tried to sue Steinberg for inadequate legal representation and the missing bail money.

After Lisa's death, the Novaks were happy to give the authorities the lowdown on Joel. "I held that beautiful baby in my arms," said a tearful Donna Novak.

The Novaks weren't the only clients outraged by Steinberg's professional misconduct. He ran afoul of another couple when he defended the husband on a minor charge of possession. Actually, Joel felt he got along beautifully with his client; it was the man's bitch of a wife who started talking against him, telling even mutual friends, people Hedda knew at Random House, that Joel Steinberg was totally inept. "Why doesn't your wife like me?" Joel asked him when the client told him his wife wanted Joel fired from the case. In the end, the client didn't have the guts to do it himself; he had his wife tell Joel they were getting another lawyer.

With humiliations like that, it was a good safe feeling to be at home. Now that he had, so to speak, dropped out of the rat race, he was learning to take pleasure in the simpler things. He started picking up broken furniture and electronic equipment from the street and bringing it home to tinker with—it was perfectly good stuff; all he had to do was get it functioning again. He also sought ways to improve the apartment. When he became fed up with the bathroom sink, he ripped it out of the wall and demanded a new one. The landlord was very upset by the holes in the plaster and started eviction proceedings. Joel retaliated by counterthreats and by withholding the rent. He could put five hundred dollars a month to better use by investing it. By 1987, he owed the landlord twenty thousand dollars.

A man's home is his castle. Joel kept looking at penthouses and places in Westchester to humor Hedda, but really he liked it just where he was, in his two and a half rooms in the heart of the Village, where he had now found a way of living free of charge. He could sit in his bedroom-cum-office and know what the two females in his kingdom were up to, listen in on Hedda's phone conversations and reassure himself she wasn't talking against him, wasn't making dates with other men, that she was still as devoted as ever. And now that the baby had come, the gorgeous, wonderful baby, he could oversee every step of her development into a highly sensitive, intelligent, and loving daughter, leaving nothing to chance or to Hedda, who was already beginning to fuck up.

SINCE JOEL, like Hedda, liked to use a camera, perhaps it was he who took the photo of Hedda, holding a six-month-old Lisa. "A beaming Nussbaum," said the caption in *People* when the photo ran with Naomi Weiss's article. The photo also appeared in many newspapers to show how pretty Hedda was before Joel's beatings ruined her face. At the time, Hedda was still an attractive woman, but her wide grin, baring her white teeth, seems a little forced—Hedda striking a pose in her prim blouse. It looks as if the woman in the photo has been handed someone else's baby to hold. Rather stiffly, Hedda props Lisa up in her lap, holding the baby's tiny wrists; a wedding band can be observed on her left hand. The proud mother is not gazing down at the baby. Her eyes are flirtatiously focused on the photographer.

There is a father-and-daughter picture as well, probably taken by Hedda. The main feature is Joel's bare, manly chest, with its dense growth of curly black hairs. The infant is stretched out before him on his bed like an offering, as Joel bends over her, communicating with her already, only two weeks after her birth, through the long fingers that cover her torso, the intense downward gaze of his eyes. It is Joel as he would like us to think of him—the sexy daddy, the natural, spontaneous man, the naked prophet enveloping the tiny female in his overpowering love—the way Hedda always longed to be enveloped, too.

As the baby became less like a doll and more like a miniature person, who favored those who pleased her with smiles and cried when something frightened her or when she wanted attention, Hedda felt insecure with her. It was desperately important to be a hit with this baby, but they seemed to have difficulty in communicating. When she saw how Lisa behaved when Joel paid her attention, how she would be "overwhelmed with joy" whenever she played with daddy, Hedda would have to compare it with how relatively unresponsive the baby was with her. Maybe if she'd had her own child, she wouldn't be making these comparisons; everything would have been so much easier, much more natural. It was Lisa who was the ungiving one; Hedda was making a great effort, wearing herself out what with going to the office and having to take care of an infant and trying to keep up with Joel by staying up with him till all hours as they smoked freebase and discussed Hedda's psychological problems. Joel had a cute little new plaything, but it was Hedda who had all the shitwork, literally. He wouldn't lift a finger to change a diaper. If the baby cried in the small hours of the morning and woke him up, it was Hedda's fault. And when he went out now on his nocturnal prowls, Hedda had to stay home. Instead of providing a peak experience for the two of them, which was the whole point of getting this baby in the first place, Lisa seemed to be driving them apart, creating new areas of tension and disharmony. Ironically, after Hedda had struggled so hard not to become a dreary housewife, that was exactly what the baby threatened to turn her into.

When Hedda Nussbaum was on the witness stand, she seemed to remember her experience of motherhood mainly as a list of the tasks she'd had to perform. She enumerated them as if giving a job description: "Well, from the beginning, I prepared the formula, sterilized the bottles, bought the food when she was eating food, cooked it, fed her, changed her diapers, bathed her, dressed her. . . . Originally I bathed her in the kitchen sink because it was large, and then when she got older, in the bathtub." She had also taken Lisa to the pediatrician once a month when she was an infant. When Ira London asked her what other responsibilities she'd had, Hedda obliged with another list—in this one, her language had a little more affect: "Well, I used to rock her to sleep at night in a rocking chair. I would sit with her on my lap, and sing her a lullaby, play with her. As she grew up, I would read to her, do schoolwork with her."

Joel, on the other hand, would "play with her, talk with her, supervise—if I had a problem in anything . . . there was a period I remember when she was crying a lot, when I put her in the crib, and I would discuss with Joel what was the best way to deal with that." "Discuss" was one of Hedda's favorite words—there's something unemotional and businesslike about it. She and Joel were forever "discussing" things. But most parents don't have discussions when their baby is crying; instead they react, pick the infant up and try to soothe it, see if it's wet or hungry. Hedda seemed to lack those instincts, just as she lacked empathy with others in general, unless it was in her own interests. She could be servile with Joel, solicitous with an author, keep the foreign beers Bill Mutter liked in the refrigerator. But the demands of an infant are unceasing, and the payoff is years down the road.

Sometime in 1982, perhaps at Joel's therapeutic insistence, Hedda wrote a note to herself: "How to accurately feel Lisa and overcome resistance to her. Know that I love her. Look at her, see." Babies have ways of learning things about people—not from the content of what's said to them, but from the tone of voice, the way they're picked up and held. Lisa already knew a lot about Hedda and could not help responding accordingly. When Lisa was two, Hedda jotted down another memo to herself: "Lisa. Look at her. Do nothing. She reached out after rejecting me. Talking sensitively to Lisa." It seems odd that a mother would have to remind herself to look into her child's face. As she dealt with Ira London's questions, Hedda was able to remember what had prompted this note. Lisa had not been "terribly responsive" until "Joel told me to look at her and do nothing. Then she responded to me in my simple honesty." Was it the honesty of nothingness, of feeling no genuine emotional connection?

If there was one area in life where Hedda retained some autonomy, where she was still effective, it was in her career as editor. When she went uptown to her neat office at Random House, for a few hours she was beyond Joel's reach. There she continued to work with authors who accepted her suggestions; continued to make deals, go to meetings, even supervise others—the free lancers who worked on the *Charlie Brown*s. Random House was still Hedda's success symbol for her climb out of Washington Heights. But now that Joel had retreated to the cave, he wanted to make sure he had company there. After Lisa's arrival, he did not make it easy for Hedda to continue to be Hedda-the-editor. Although he was home a great deal of the time, he made Hedda fully responsible for arranging Lisa's care.

For a while Emma Nussbaum came to the house to look after her granddaughter. Then Hedda hired a baby-sitter for the job. Next she took Lisa to daycare at the home of another Greenwich Village mother. When that arrangement ended, she started bringing Lisa to the office with her.

Walter Retan had left Random House and Janet Shulman had

risen from the ranks to replace him as editor-in-chief of juvenile books. Shulman was very sympathetic toward the plight of a working mother—particularly one in Hedda's difficult situation. According to Betty Kraus, Shulman made a courageous phone call to Joel and told him she suspected he was beating Hedda; Steinberg's response was a burst of laughter. For quite a while, Janet Shulman made no objection to Lisa's presence and even let Hedda work at home for a few days at a time. Among themselves, the Random House women whispered that Hedda was afraid to leave the baby at home with Joel—afraid of what he might do to her. The baby began looking "washed out," not as rosy and bouncy as it had at first, and there was no trace of Hedda's glow. She was coming in again with black eyes and bruises on her arms and neck.

As Lisa grew older and more active, her presence in the office became disruptive, and Shulman had to ask Hedda not to bring her in so often. Lisa was just learning to walk on one of the last times Hedda came in with her. That day Hedda looked as if she'd been beaten within an inch of her life. "She walked like a scarecrow," as one person put it. "She was appalling." What was even more appalling was the spectacle of Lisa toddling along beside her mother—the child had a cut lip! One woman who saw them fled back into her cubicle, where she burst into tears. No one took any action, of course. No one knew what to do.

That August, Janet Shulman went away for four weeks' vacation. Simultaneously Hedda Nussbaum vanished, without so much as an explanatory phone call to the office. (Nussbaum claims she was embarrassed by having another black eye. According to Steinberg, she and Lisa spent the month in Vermont, accompanying him on a business trip.) The day Janet Shulman returned, Hedda Nussbaum also reappeared, but Shulman reluctantly fired her. Hedda had gone too far, taken advantage of her leniency. She did, however, promise to supply Hedda with free-lance assignments, and gave her a manuscript to take home.

At first Joel encouraged Hedda to keep up her editorial work. But soon his attitude changed. One day he ripped up one of her manuscripts and threw the pages out the back window. Hedda had to retrieve them, with Joel's help, from a neighbor's backyard; they told the woman their baby had misbehaved. Another time, when Hedda was supposed to turn in a fully edited book the following day, Joel hid it and refused to tell her where it was. He explained to her that this was just one more thing he was doing for her own good. His tactics proved successful. Shortly after that Random House stopped sending Hedda Nussbaum work. Hedda was totally dependent on Joel—financially as well as emotionally. She could make no purchases without his approval. He doled out small amounts of money like a father giving an allowance to a little girl. He also began to restrict Hedda's movements, according to her testimony. He didn't want her walking around the neighborhood with bruises on her face.

Ira London asked Hedda whether she had ever tried to talk to Joel about his hitting her. She assured him she had—many times—but simply could not recall even one specific conversation, only the gist of what she claimed to have usually said—that she hated being hit, that she didn't want him to keep doing it. "It's not me," Joel had protested once. It wasn't really him, he'd explained, because it wasn't his natural way. Joel Steinberg didn't do things like that. He said he hated the *him* who hit Hedda.

There was often something suspiciously generic about Nussbaum's insights into her extreme passivity with Joel. She seemed to be reflecting some coaching when she told Ira London that every time Joel hit her, she thought it would never happen again. This explained why she never threatened Steinberg that she would leave if he didn't change his behavior.

A paper published by Nussbaum's psychiatrist, Samuel Klagsbrun in June 1989, made exactly the same point in more elaborate language. Battering became tolerable, Klagsbrun theorized, because a woman in love with a batterer had a "peculiar mechanism" that made "history discontinuous. It chops up a long series of experiences into unrelated small incidents, each one treated as if it had no past and no future."

The true and unmediated voice of Hedda Nussbaum can probably be heard in an extraordinary statement she made to one of her psychiatrists in 1988: "Joel was a little boy and I was his teddy bear with a broken leg and a torn eye." The martyred teddy bear secretly believed herself much stronger than her master, because she could endure and forgive him for his infantile behavior.

From the summer of 1982, Joel's intensive supervision of Hedda, his unceasing efforts to improve her, went on full time. In fact, it was Nussbaum who became Steinberg's primary work and obsession, as he attempted to wrestle her into a state of truth. Why should Joel have had any reason to doubt this woman whose flesh was stamped with the marks of his dominance, who faithfully cared for the infant he had acquired for his pleasure, and who, when he told her he was having affairs, now cheerfully responded that she was pleased he was being honest and not having them behind her back? Perhaps it was impossible for Steinberg to believe that any woman, any human being, could become that submissive. He may have resisted believing it, in fact, because then their relationship would become worthless to him—exhausted and discardable, despite all that he had invested in it so far. It was much more energizing to think that Hedda Nussbaum was really holding out on him, merely playing along, cleverly telling him what he wanted to hear. How could he ever be sure he was uppermost in her thoughts at all times, that he was aware of all her activities?

On New Year's Eve, 1983, Joel took Hedda to the Greens' annual bash. Steinberg invited a new client, Bobby Merlino, to join them there. Merlino didn't find the party at all festive. He later told investigators that the Greens' twenty-five or thirty guests just sat around staring like zombies.

That night Steinberg was introduced to a woman named Paula and her husband who owned a couple of video shops in the area. They were apparently quite well acquainted with Hedda. A few days later, Steinberg phoned Bobby Merlino and told him he needed his assistance. He wanted Merlino to help him break into one of the couple's shops to retrieve what he claimed were pornographic videotapes that featured Hedda Nussbaum.

Steinberg claims that Hedda frequently went out to Long Island on her own to visit the Greens, taking Lisa with her. When Ira London questioned her about this, Nussbaum claimed that there had only been one such overnight visit.

SINCE 1978, Marilyn Walton had spent little time in New York. She had become disillusioned with Joel Steinberg. In 1980, when her father died, Marilyn had called Joel and told him she needed him in Dallas. Despite his stated admiration for her father, Joel didn't, as Marilyn put it, "have the backbone to deal with death."

Although they kept in touch intermittently over the phone, Marilyn didn't see Steinberg again until February 1983. When she called up and told him she was back in town, Joel said, "Come right over. Just be sure to call before you come." Marilyn was running around, doing errands, so she forgot to call. Nonetheless, when she arrived at Tenth Street, Joel pressed the downstairs buzzer and admitted her to the building. It was two-year-old Lisa, "buck-naked," who opened the door of the apartment and gave her a big welcome. Lisa was already, Marilyn remembers, "a coherent, walking person" and even knew exactly who Marilyn was. "She hollered, 'Daddy! Daddy! It's Marilyn and she's *pretty!'*" An observation Hedda Nussbaum certainly must have overheard.

Hedda herself was walking around the apartment, "without much on." Joel was embarrassed by this, Marilyn thought. The thing that really shocked her, though, was that Hedda wasn't pretty anymore. She walked with a limp and her face looked so bad that Marilyn asked her whether she had been in a car wreck. Hedda shook her head and made shushing gestures, pointing to Lisa. A little later, while Joel was putting Lisa to bed for a nap, Hedda explained to Marilyn why her appearance had changed so drastically. Hedda said she had gotten herself involved in what she referred to as a "cult." The people in this cult had made her believe she had been incestuous with her father and had to be punished. Fortunately, Joel, her savior, had rescued her. Now he was keeping an eye on Hedda, and she was slowly getting better. It was hard for Marilyn to believe what she was hearing.

When Joel came back into the room, he gave the story a somewhat different twist. Hedda had been doing things to herself— "jumping off shit, burning herself with cigarettes." Like Hedda, he claimed that a dangerous cult was to blame for her condition, and he mentioned some people called the Greens. The cult was making Joel look like an abusing husband and father. "Marilyn, you should see the doctor bills!" he said grimly.

Marilyn remembers just staring at him. She couldn't help having a different idea of how Hedda had come by her injuries.

The story grew even more elaborate. Joel had gone to the police and the D.A.'s office, but everyone thought he was crazy. Now he needed the names of deprogrammers. He asked Marilyn if she knew anyone who could help them, since she'd had experience in law-enforcement work.

Then Lisa woke up, and they all changed the subject. Joel decided to take Marilyn and Lisa out to get ice cream, leaving Hedda alone in the apartment. He walked them to an ice-cream parlor in the neighborhood, then said he had to go to the supermarket (these days he'd had to take over all the shopping). He wanted Marilyn to meet him there with Lisa when they'd finished their ice cream. Marilyn was confused about which supermarket Joel had gone to, so she decided to take Lisa back to the apartment. It was very cold and had started to snow. The child was wearing a thin pink nylon jacket with a hood.

When she buzzed the apartment from downstairs, Hedda spoke over the intercom and said she couldn't let anyone in. "Goddamn it, Hedda. Open the door," Marilyn yelled back. "It's cold out here!" Hedda repeated, "No! No one can come in." "Are you nuts?" Marilyn yelled. "I'm standing outside with Lisa." Finally someone who was leaving the building opened the door for them.

When they went up to the third floor, Marilyn furiously kicked at the door. There was no response, so she kicked harder. Finally Hedda opened, and Marilyn quickly pushed Lisa inside. Hedda meanwhile positioned herself in the doorway, blocking Marilyn's path. According to Marilyn, she had a grimace on her face and her teeth were clenched. "Why wouldn't you open?" Marilyn asked. Hedda never answered that question. Instead she turned on Lisa, grabbing her by the neck of her jacket and flinging the two-year-old girl seven or eight feet across the living-room floor. Lisa barely maintained her balance. Marilyn said, "Hedda, what are you doing?" But Hedda ignored her and started to unzip Lisa's jacket.

As soon as Hedda reached for her, the child started squirming. At that point, as Marilyn remembers it, Hedda raised her arm and said, "Stop! Be still!" She raised her arm to slap Lisa's face, but the child ducked away from the blow, so the side of Hedda's hand struck her on the neck. "I asked Hedda what she was doing. I went over to Lisa, tried to shield her. I was pretty much up in Hedda's face—Lisa was half hidden in the corner. I told Hedda if she ever struck that child again in my presence, I'd put my foot up her ass." And in fact, Hedda never did strike the child again in front of Marilyn Walton.

Nussbaum seemed on the verge of making an angry reply to Marilyn when Joel walked in with the groceries. Lisa was still looking dazed and frightened, but Hedda's demeanor underwent an abrupt change. She relaxed and became very docile. It was as if nothing had happened. Everything was back to "normal," except for the look on Lisa's face.

Marilyn didn't tell Joel about what she had just witnessed—not until 1988, and then she told Mel and he told Joel. She has very firm ideas about propriety and it may have seemed improper to carry tales about Hedda to Joel. She may also have thought that Hedda's old jealousy of Marilyn's special relationship with Joel had triggered the attack on Lisa.

Since the atmosphere had now changed for the better, she visited with them a while longer. Despite the way she looked, Hedda was stepping out with Joel that night. They had been asked to a party given by one of Joel's clients, a manufacturer of sexual aids. Mischievously, Hedda kept urging Marilyn to come with them. They could arrive as a threesome, just like the old days. Joel said he didn't think Marilyn would enjoy this party because she'd have to take off her clothes. "I ain't going," Marilyn said firmly, but Hedda persisted in daring her to join them. In the past, Marilyn had often heard Hedda complain that Joel wasn't very hip. She, Hedda, was the party person. It was just like Hedda, Marilyn told me, to be "gung ho. She'd always go a few steps further than Joel and then he would join in."

It was ostensibly because of Hedda that Joel Steinberg sent Lisa to the Greens six months later. If we believe Marilyn Walton's account of her February visit, Joel's action doesn't make much sense—in fact, Joel's choice of what he apparently had come to believe was a "cult" household as a refuge for his daughter seems perverse. But then, it seems just as puzzling that Joel and Hedda were still socializing in August with the very couple they had allegedly feared in February.

Hedda Nussbaum, who testified a few weeks *before* Marilyn Walton did, evaded this very issue of continued contact with the Greens. Her story was that she and Joel did not become fearful and suspicious of the Greens until *after* October 1983, although she did let slip that earlier that year she and Joel had begun to talk about the Greens's ability to hypnotize people.

In 1989 Marilyn Walton flew in from Dallas to be a surprise witness for the defense; the decision to put her on the stand was made only a few days before she appeared on January 5. If Nussbaum had known Walton was going to testify, she might have brought up that February 1983 visit and given a very different interpretation of it as well as of the relationship she and Joel had with the Greens by the summer of 1983.

According to Nussbaum's testimony, Joel thought the Greens would "take good care" of Lisa because of a little trick he was playing on them—letting them assume he would allow them to adopt her. Joel wasn't *giving* her to them, Hedda Nussbaum insisted. No, she had never believed Joel really intended to give Lisa up.

She herself was having some mental trouble that summer, though she wouldn't go so far as to say she was having a breakdown: "Well, particularly, after I left Random House, I started having certain difficulties in—well, in remembering where things were. Things would get lost. And as an example—" Evidently, she decided not to go into that example. "That's not accurate. That didn't happen." Then she took control of her story again, summoning up an example of the most harmless kind of difficulty. "Like I would look for a pair of socks and find them in the refrigerator. I had been putting things in strange places. I was a person who always remembered," Hedda said emphatically, and one couldn't help wondering whether that was still the case, despite all the relevant material she had been unable to recall as a witness. "Joel always relied on me to remember things, appointments and things like that. I kept forgetting things, losing things." Nussbaum's voice trailed off childishly.

As it turned out, the Greens only kept Lisa for three weeks. Hedda was unable to characterize her state of mind during the period she was separated from her little daughter. "Depressed? Despondent?" Ira London prompted her sarcastically.

Joel Steinberg's decision to send Lisa to Michael and Shayna Green suggests that he was as deeply involved with them as he claimed Hedda Nussbaum was. If he had any real or even imaginary reasons to fear them by this time, the child may have been a propitiatory offering. There were vague allusions to blackmail in Hedda's testimony. In 1989, Steinberg would protest to writer Maury Terry that he had never dreamed the Greens would harm Lisa; it was an article of faith that you didn't do certain things with "one of your own." Even Nussbaum, in her evasive statements on the witness stand, would never commit herself to saying that everything she and Steinberg had once believed about the Greens was only fantasy.

In September, Michael Green returned Lisa to the Steinberg household. The child seemed changed. "She was behaving," Nussbaum recalled, "in a more withdrawn manner than usual. At some point—I can't remember specifically—I can only assume I changed her diaper, she was still in diapers"—Hedda "observed" something else. The little girl's vaginal area was bruised black and blue. She reported what she had seen to Joel: "I believe I showed him Lisa. And he saw the injury or discoloration."

Certainly the two reacted in an extraordinarily apathetic way. Nussbaum's recollections indicated no shock or outrage over what they believed had been done to the two-and-a-half-year-old girl. Hedda naturally had one of her classic discussions with Joel, but they did not think of reporting Lisa's injury to the police or of taking her immediately to be examined by a pediatrician. A pediatrician, of course, would have asked a great many questions and might even have suspected them of abusing the child. Hedda asked Joel to help Lisa, "and he did. . . . I guess I believed he healed her because she came out of it after he—I think—just held her for a few minutes and she was—just back to her normal behavior, so it seemed to me." It must have seemed another of Joel's homegrown miracles, like the time he cured Hedda's spastic colon, and of course it is widely believed that little children have amazing recuperative powers. Hedda did not describe how she herself tried to comfort Lisa; the laying on of Joel's hands seemed to do the trick. She admitted she never tried to talk to her little daughter about what had happened to her, even though Lisa, at that age, was precociously verbal.

Notwithstanding the bruise they allegedly noticed on Lisa's vagina, Hedda and Joel went on seeing the Greens.

*

In October, Michael Green came into Manhattan and stayed with them for ten days. It was a very eventful visit, a kind of marathon day-and-night encounter group, fueled, according to Nussbaum's testimony, by the daily smoking of freebase. Shayna had been left behind in Fort Salonga. Michael Green was planning to divorce her. That was one of the reasons he had come to see Joel—he needed his expert legal advice.

The apartment must have felt quite crowded. In addition to Green, their good friend Gregory Malmoulka was also present. And of course Lisa was there, too. Perhaps she was included in some of the adults' activities.

The grownups were playing a truth-telling game, and the truths were down and dirty ones, nasty and sexual. Joel was acting as leader of the group; after all, it was his house, and truth was still one of his major preoccupations, if not his and Hedda's lifelong quest. Hedda may have found it thrilling to be the only adult female present.

For a while everyone's attention focused on the absent Shayna Green. As therapist, Joel was trying to induce Michael Green to act out his feelings about his wife. Dr. Green's feelings were apparently hostile, according to what Nussbaum recollected in her testimony. She claimed that Green accused his wife of having various sexual activities with other partners. On her last day on the witness stand, Hedda described with a stifled giggle how Green had seized a large pepper mill and demonstrated what he would like to do to his wife.

Dr. Green not only wished to talk about Shayna's sexual trans-gressions but about Hedda's. Green actually accused her, Hedda said, grinning broadly, "of having sex with just about the whole world." Of course, earlier that year, Joel himself had indicated that "his broadness of mind and caring for me had made him very understanding" about Hedda's need to be with other men. "He was very understanding to me because this was something that I was involved in, I wanted, and he wasn't jealous. He even allowed me to go out on dates."

Following this disclosure, Ira London naturally inquired, "Did you go out on dates?" "No," Hedda replied, poker-faced. She apparently knew that even she was a potential victim of the double standard. It certainly would have improved her image had she ever walked out on Joel and not turned right around and gone back. Paradoxically, unfaithfulness to him would have cost her some of the sympathy of the public. As an example of how pecu-

liarly accepting Joel Steinberg could be, Hedda recollected another of Green's visits when Joel had come home and found that
she and his friend had spent the entire day together; both were
fully dressed, of course. It took Joel three years to tell Hedda he
thought adultery had occurred that day. Had he been right?

Neither Nussbaum nor Steinberg has given a full account of Michael Green's ten-day visit in 1983. Each has disclosed only pieces
of what happened, according to their separate agendas. And undoubtedly some of these pieces may be fabrications. But there
seems no question that *something happened*—something that
drastically loosened Joel Steinberg's grip on reality.

Could Green have been intent on proving to Joel Steinberg that
he had exacted submission from Hedda Nussbaum? It would not
have been difficult for him to arrive at the idea that whoever
controlled Hedda also controlled Joel. Hedda was a woman whom
Joel had almost reduced to zero. But if a man cannot even control
his abject slave, his power means little. Anyone can get to him,
penetrate his façade.

The encounter group on his home turf may have been Steinberg's last-ditch effort to assert the gurulike power he so badly
needed to believe he possessed, to show Michael Green that no
one could control Joel Steinberg. Hedda Nussbaum testified that
the subject of hypnosis came up. Green had allegedly taught
himself to hypnotize people. He asked Joel to be his subject, and
Joel refused.

Nussbaum testified that Dr. Green described an episode to
Steinberg in which he made sexual overtures to Hedda and had
struck her when she rebuffed him. But had she really rebuffed the
doctor? Nussbaum told the court that for many years she believed
that Green had raped her. If this was so, why did she then recall
her reaction to Green's story as "one of great surprise. There were
so many strange things going on at that time in the house that I
don't think I reacted more than that." Perhaps if she and Green
had indeed been having an affair, Hedda never imagined Green
would dare to tell Joel about it. But, according to her recollection,
Green evidently felt enough contempt for Steinberg as well as
Nussbaum to do just that. Green also told Joel, Nussbaum claimed,
that a number of times over the years, he had "stolen money out
of the drawer where Joel kept money. And that I told him where
the money was kept . . . and then he had taken it."

Her most sensational claim was that on the ninth day Green

finally talked about Lisa, alleging that he had seen—or perhaps more accurately watched—Shayna sexually abuse the little girl. Presumably this was the most unpardonable violation of Steinberg's property and trust. Did Hedda react with rage and horror? Did she take any action? "No, I left it to Joel's wisdom to take care of that," she recalled. "Yes, that's how I felt at the time." Joel, normally a man of many words, responded to Green's revelation with silence.

The following day, however, "Michael Green left our house with two black eyes, and had to have surgery to repair the orbits." At first, Hedda could not remember how Green had come by his injuries. As far as she knew, there had been no fight. A few days later, on the witness stand, she did recall something that had happened to the doctor after Joel had sent her out of the room. Green had been lying facedown on the floor with his hands over his eyes and Gregory Malmoulka "had stepped on his neck," as she delicately put it.

The fact that Hedda was so well versed in the details of Green's ensuing plastic surgery suggests that the involvement with the Greens continued even after the doctor had been beaten.

Nussbaum could not help opening up the subject of the Greens when she testified, even though she had probably been strongly advised not to. It was as if she felt a compulsion to talk about them, as well as a desire to protect Joel. Steinberg's delusionary ideas about the Greens, as Nussbaum described them, virtually gave his attorneys the basis of an insanity plea, if Steinberg would agree to go for one. As London led Nussbaum deeper into testimony about the Long Island couple, Hedda's lawyer, Barry Scheck, gnawed on his fist in his front-row seat, visibly anxious.

One thing Steinberg told Maury Terry about Michael Green never came out explicitly in court. During Green's October 1983 visit, Steinberg allegedly found Green and Hedda in compromising circumstances. He claimed to Terry that one day when he let himself into the apartment after having gone out, he discovered the two of them together in the bathroom only half-dressed. If this was so, then Steinberg had been confronted with the evidence of a sexual union between the two most powerful figures in his life. But of course it could also be just one of Steinberg's stories.

After Lisa's death, Dr. Green was questioned by the police. He told them he had been held captive in Steinberg's apartment for twenty-four hours and had been beaten up by both Joel and Hedda when he raised questions about the legality of Lisa's adoption. Hedda had swung at him forty or fifty times and was said to have enjoyed it. Green had only been released by Steinberg when he had signed a document attesting to Shayna's abuse of Lisa. (Steinberg may have filed it away in case he ever wished to blackmail the Greens.) As for the so-called bruise, Green claimed it was merely diaper rash.

During Steinberg's trial, the prosecution would claim that the document had been fabricated solely for the purpose of slandering Shayna and thus furthering Green's suit against her (although no divorce ensued). The implication was that perhaps Lisa had not been sexually abused. Yet although Hedda denied a great many other things on the grounds that they were merely beliefs she no longer had, she was still very sure she had seen a bruise on the child's vagina in the summer of 1983.

After Green left, Joel demanded from Hedda the names of all the people she had been having sex with. As far as their two-and-a-half-year old daughter was concerned, neither Hedda nor Joel took any immediate action on her behalf, even now that their "suspicions" had been confirmed, as they both claim.

At the end of December, however, Hedda did contact a deprogrammer named Paul Engel. On December 31, Engel phoned his associate, Priscilla Coates, who took some notes on their conversation—notes about a sex ring called the "We Love" group on Long Island, buzzwords, the use of kids for porno films, and "Daughter—catatonic—labia bruised black and blue."

On January 3, 1984, Hedda placed a call to the Cult Awareness Network. She had been in a cult, she told them, and was having difficulty readjusting.

By 1988, the idea that the Greens had been the leaders of a cult was as nonsensical an idea to Hedda Nussbaum as her previous notion that she had ever "had sex with practically the whole world." Both were in the category of what she *used to believe* when she was under Joel Steinberg's influence rather than Barry Scheck's or Samuel Klagsbrun's. Still, she did claim credit for originating the cult idea. That way of characterizing the Greens had first dawned on her when she read a book called *Snapping* in 1984—which again puts the birth of the cult idea one year *after* Marilyn Walton's visit, as well as several months *after* the encounter group with Michael Green and Hedda's December 1983, call to Paul Engel, the deprogrammer.

Whenever it was that Hedda and Joel actually did read *Snapping,* it became a kind of Bible for them, giving them a rationale that justified what they had been doing with and to each other, and perhaps to Lisa as well. Subtitled *America's Epidemic of Sudden Personality Change, Snapping* had been written in response to some of the most alarming manifestations of the widespread anomie that Rollo May had identified just before the 1970s. Flo Conway and Jim Siegelman had first published their book in 1978 in the wake of the Patty Hearst kidnapping, the Charles Manson and Son of Sam mass murder cases, and the rapid growth of cults such as Scientology, est, TM, and Krishna Consciousness. "To us," Conway and Siegelman wrote, "it depicts the way intense experience may affect fundamental information-processing capacities of the brain." The following year, right after Jim Jones and 912 members of his People's Temple had drunk poisoned Kool-Aid in Guyana, an ominous postscript was quickly added to the paperback edition.

Hedda's heavily annotated copy was found in the Steinberg apartment, as well as a carbon of an urgent letter Hedda sent the authors on March 29, 1984, after showing it to Joel for approval. She informed them that she happened to be a particularly interesting example of a person afflicted with what they had called "information disease," and offered herself to them for further study.

Throughout the text, she had no doubt come upon passages like the following that made her feel the book had been written about herself and Steinberg: "Without warnings or guidelines, America's searchers, in their earnest longing to find something higher and their sincere desire for self-improvement, had no way of interpreting their experiences, of separating the truly spiritual from the sham, or of distinguishing personal growth from artificially induced sensation."

Like one woman who had great difficulty recovering from her experiences in est, hadn't Hedda herself been "personally encountered by the trainer and taken through a lot of trauma"? Hadn't she herself reached the point where "fantasies became real," as well as experiencing bliss and altered states of consciousness due to physical punishment and deprivations of food and sleep? Hedda, too, had been severed from family and friends. Oddly enough, she didn't blame Joel Steinberg for her loss of feeling and personality. Instead, some of her annotations indicate that she saw him as a victim of the Snapping phenomenon.

Did Hedda believed Joel had "snapped" during Green's visit? Certainly they had engaged in the kind of heavy psychodrama that, Conway and Siegelman warned, "took the imagination a step further than fantasy, engaging the individual in the physical dramatization of his psychological problems and past trauma. The power of this method lies in the conflicting patterns of information it gives rise to in the context of intense group interaction."

"Many admit," Conway and Siegelman also wrote, "that through lies and carefully contrived suggestions, a hypnotist could prompt his subject to commit any action, even a crime, in the firm belief he was performing the act to accomplish some greater good."

Apparently Joel Steinberg studied *Snapping* with equal interest. A sentence in the "information disease" chapter to the effect that the human mind could be programmed by an outside influence much the way a computer is programmed seems to have had a powerful impact upon him. He adopted the computer analogy and often verbalized it to Hedda as if he had invented it himself.

Like a primitive man, Joel Steinberg had come to believe himself to be possessed, though his evil spirits used modern techniques such as programming and brainwashing to direct his actions. For years he had sustained the illusion that he was a programmer, but secretly he must have known he was totally ineffectual, a perfect candidate to be a programee. In his entire life he had been able to subjugate only one other person—Hedda Nussbaum. And now she had been taken over by the Greens. Steinberg was the prize they were after, of course. But they knew they could use Hedda to get to him. She was the medium through which their will flowed into his. Their will was huge and forceful; his was an empty shell. Only Hedda Nussbaum was foolish enough to believe in Joel Steinberg's will. She was the weak spot in his defense system—so malleable that the Greens could even program her from afar by using the telephone. A buzzword coupled with her name (Hedda's personal buzzword was *teapot*) sufficed to put her into a hypnotic trance. Through Hedda, Joel could be buzzed by the Greens. No one else could be used to program him, because only with Hedda did Joel let down his guard.

Steinberg and Nussbaum had taken so much cocaine by 1983, that if there had been no Michael and Shayna Green, their demons would probably have operated under other names. But cocaine was the real demon that had seized them both. Steinberg had been absolutely right to avoid it for so many years—once he started freebasing, his mind deteriorated very rapidly. Perhaps his most fatal illusion became the conviction that nothing could destroy the sanity of Joel Steinberg. The mounting paranoia Nussbaum described in court is quite typical of massive cocaine abuse, so was Steinberg's increased propensity to behave violently. Just as Steinberg became paranoid about the Greens, Nussbaum may eventually have become paranoid about Lisa. Whereas Steinberg had always had a great fear of being controlled, Nussbaum's own worst scenario was that she could be displaced by a rival. Being infinitely suggestible, however, she also accepted and even consciously reinforced Steinberg's fears of the Greens. Of the two of them, Nussbaum always seems to have been both the "saner" and the more vacuous.

In a way, it was quite convenient for Steinberg and Nussbaum to believe other people had taken over their wills. It gave them the license to do virtually anything. The idea that the Greens were setting invisible control systems buzzing provided a logical explanation for the growing sense of disengagement they had from their acts, as their sexual relationship grew more extreme. Even in inversion there is a craving for logic, but the logic is inescapably insane.

Underlying Nussbaum's testimony about the Greens was the sense that she had found definite gratification in sharing Steinberg's madness. Joel's admission that he was only vulnerable through Hedda may have seemed to her as close as Joel would ever come to a declaration of love. Steinberg had lived with Nussbaum for nearly ten years in increasing isolation. What he may have been recognizing and fearing was how far they had gone in merging with each other. He was incorporating Hedda Nussbaum's "weakness," just as she was incorporating Joel Steinberg's "power." If he had made Hedda into a machine, he, too, could be robotized. Now it was Joel's turn to fear that he would have to do Hedda's bidding. According to Hedda Nussbaum, Joel actually came to believe that after she had been hypnotized herself, she "then learned how to hypnotize others and started a chain reaction and I was hypnotizing everybody . . . that we knew and using them sexually."

As she uttered these words, Ira London observed a smile cross her face. When the judge asked her, "Did you smile, Miss Nussbaum?" Hedda grinned widely. "Yes . . . The absurdity of the whole thing just hit me."

But in another exchange with London, Hedda indicated that the absurdity had hit her long before that day in court: "Joel kept encouraging me to come up with buzzwords of various people, especially himself, so that I could protect him from getting buzzed. But I was never able to come up with any of the buzzwords, even though I tried by every means I could."

As for the word *cult*—"I never believed there was any actual cult," she told London. For her, it was merely a "convenience word," inspired by their joint reading of *Snapping*. Joel's actions, however, indicated that for him the cult continued to be very real. Between 1984 and 1986, he kept attempting to put a halt to its activities, especially in the area of child pornography. Of course Steinberg never had his own activities investigated.

Hedda clearly knew her man—knew exactly how to play along to keep his obsession with her alive. Once when Marilyn Walton suggested to her in a phone conversation that she think about getting plastic surgery, Hedda answered that if she ever did that, Joel would leave her.

It was not until her very last day of testimony that Hedda Nussbaum suddenly remembered why it was that Joel Steinberg used to beat her. It never did have anything to do with hypnosis, or a cult. It was that old preoccupation of his with bringing her into a state of truth. He'd say, "he was trying to help me, that it would snap me out of the state I was in. That I'd been lying to him."

Whatever the reason, the beatings occurred with greater frequency after Michael Green's visit. Certainly during 1984, Joel intensified his efforts to control Hedda's thoughts and limited her movements more stringently. In the past Steinberg had encouraged Hedda to focus a great deal on herself and her needs; now he came up with different sets of "beneficial ideas" about his own needs that he made her copy by hand over and over as if she were a schoolgirl kept in detention. He even called these her "assignments." On one page Hedda wrote the sentence, "I want to care about Joel's hair, I will care about Joel's hair," twenty-six times. Other "beneficial ideas" constituted a veritable laundry list of assorted domestic and psychic duties: "I want to care about Joel's clothes, I will care about Joel's clothes and his work and his problems and his shaves and his feelings and his shirts and dinner and what he eats and what he wears and what he does for exercise and his health, his insurance, his happiness, his teeth, his thoughts." This, too, Hedda had to copy out quite a number of times. Joel Steinberg had a naïve faith in the efficacy of repetition. Perhaps he hoped that if nothing else, he could program Hedda into becoming a perfect housewife. In his mother's house, at least you could have eaten off the floor.

Late at night, quite often, as they smoked freebase together, Joel and Hedda pursued truth by a brand-new method. Conway and Siegelman had warned of the dangers of a therapeutic technique called "guided fantasy," but Joel evidently saw no reason not to use his own version of it on Hedda. "For approximately a year," according to Hedda, "Joel was encouraging me to come up with stories, fantasies, what I call images of supposed events." His idea was that as Hedda unleashed her fantasies, it would cause her to "unblock the block"—information she either found too painful to remember or that hypnosis had made her suppress. "If I talked about what happened, it would relieve my soul." Joel, of course, was not only her therapist but her priest.

Most of the "supposed events" that Hedda dredged up for Steinberg on those long sleepless nights were events of a sexual nature. That was what Joel was after—graphic descriptions of what he had come to imagine Hedda had been doing with the Greens as well as with other members of their circle. When Ira London asked Hedda whether in fact other couples had been involved, her syntax became rather elaborate: "There were supposedly other people involved, yes." *Supposed* and *supposedly* were words she was leaning on a lot in this part of her testimony. These things Hedda had "supposedly" done "were ideas that were in my head—basically I would say that were put in my head by Joel Steinberg."

"I believe," Nussbaum finally allowed, after Ira London had worn her down a bit with questions about what had constituted reality in 1985 and 1986, "that I had been involved with a lot of—Well, I believe [oddly enough, again she slipped into using the present tense] that these things had occurred and Joel would not allow the ideas to lay at rest and say, O.K. these are in your past, let's go on from here."

Now, it turned out that, for at least four years, Hedda had shared Steinberg's paranoid delusions about using hypnosis, blackmail, and programming to get her to "remember acts in particular ways." What Nussbaum had apparently once believed in most while under Steinberg's influence was the reality of her own "supposed" acts in the past.

Until her months of therapy convinced her otherwise, Hedda Nussbaum claims to have had a rather persistent fantasy that she had been involved in the sexual abuse of children: "Well, I believed that another woman who was a friend of Shayna's, named Paula, was also hypnotizing people, and abusing children, taking videotapes of sexual encounters with them; that she was forcing the people she hypnotized into having sex with these children, and she was videotaping it and selling them at a video store that she supposedly owned." Lisa "supposedly" had been one of Paula's little victims. Until 1988, Hedda imagined that she had been hypnotized into making Lisa perform on some of these tapes, and had participated herself. Joel, of course, wanted to hear all about these pornographic acts. And Hedda naturally obliged, unlocking further memories of "supposed" events of the same nature. As she put it at one point, almost proudly, her imagination got "very creative," but then she had always had a playful mind. On those nights when Hedda spun her "fantasies," with Joel giving her all his rapt attention, she must have felt as powerful as Scheherazade.

By 1984, Hedda Nussbaum's thoughts about the little girl Joel had brought into their household were downright perverse. Mothers who love their children may have deep fears that their children could be abducted, molested, or raped, but it would be much too painful and frightening for them to imagine scenes in which such things occurred.

Nussbaum evidently had no difficulty in visualizing Lisa's violation and supplying Joel with the brutal details. Did Joel find her memories of these "supposed" events merely painful and upsetting? One can't help suspecting they may have been very sexually stimulating to both parties. The fantasizing of a sexual act is often the prelude to its actualization; at the very least, it reflects a desire. In this case, the desire was one that broke the ultimate taboo.

The kinds of fantasies they shared could certainly have been inspired by child pornography. Such material is often amassed by people who use children sexually and can become important evidence when perpetrators are put on trial, as Steinberg was no doubt aware. Judy Cochran, one law-enforcement expert I talked to, suspects that on the morning of November 2, 1987, he and Nussbaum spent some hours before they called the ambulance disposing of an incriminating collection of pornography. Nussbaum may have continued to carry on the operation while Steinberg was at the hospital and she was alone in the apartment, unsupervised by the police. The only pornographic photograph later found in the house was one nude, spreadeagled shot of Hedda.

By the time Lisa Steinberg was four, Joel and Hedda had a new friend who sometimes stayed with them at the apartment, just as Michael Green had done. This young woman was a part-time prostitute who had been implicated in the murder of one of her customers in a New Jersey motel. She later claimed to investigators that she had sex with both Steinberg and Nussbaum and had been invited by them to put her mouth on Lisa's vagina, which Joel said was "the most beautiful part of her." Was this merely fabrication on her part or a recollection of something that really happened? Was this the kind of thing that happened to Lisa Steinberg throughout her life?

IV

THE SHORT LIFE OF LISA STEINBERG

A PERSON WHO dies at the age of six does not leave behind much of a biography—no deeds, few memorable quotes. Testimonials quickly level the personality of a child victim: an adorable little girl. She was always very sweet, etc. In Lisa's case, what one almost cannot bear to contemplate is the question of her awareness, the education she received in the Steinberg household.

Whenever Joel Steinberg talks to the media, he boasts that Lisa Steinberg was his creation, a credit to his love and care. Adjectives erupt from his mouth: bright, joyous, and affectionate; highly articulate, athletic. In one TV interview he even claimed that "Lisa never had an unhappy day in her life." Hedda, in contrast, has so far seemed incapable of describing her daughter; she can scarcely find even the tritest words to say what kind of child Lisa Steinberg was. The most notable thing Hedda could remember about Lisa when she testified was that she had always been a very sound sleeper. Perhaps she had been made to recognize how much violence had been done to the child's consciousness, and now wanted to convince people that Lisa had somehow managed to sleep through most of the nightmares of the Steinberg household.

Sometimes, when I meet other bright, spirited children, I try to imagine Lisa. The five-year-old daughter of friends ran into my garden in Vermont and stood amazed at the edge of a lush overgrown meadow where ferns towered above her. "This is the world!" she said in an awed voice, and I remember thinking, Lisa Steinberg could have said something like that, my mind connecting it with a surprising thing Marilyn Walton once said about Lisa: "Lisa was a celebration of life."

But could a child with Lisa's history have had the capacity to celebrate life? And how soon would the celebration have stopped altogether?

Marilyn remembers a child who seemed "a very old soul. Even at two, Lisa had the ability to penetrate your skull and get right to your heart. She instinctively knew what was inside a person." Yes, I think that's probably how Lisa Steinberg managed to survive. Growing up in extreme circumstances sharpened her perceptions from the start. But would she have become an extraordinary person or an utterly destroyed one? What would she have done with so much terrible knowledge? What would it have made of her?

The Swiss psychoanalyst Alice Miller, who has made a lifelong study of children, writes in *The Drama of the Gifted Child* that it is not uncommon to encounter narcissistically disturbed patients whom adults had once considered remarkable children. In analysis, "the well-behaved, reliable, empathetic, understanding and convenient child, who in fact, was never a child at all," wakes up and discovers "the small and lonely child hidden behind the achievements," the child's lost and unacceptable true self. "What became of my childhood? is the essence of the question such patients often seem to ask. "Have I not been cheated out of it? I can never return to it. I can never make up for it. From the beginning I have been a little adult. My abilities—were they simply misused?"

It is precisely children like Lisa Steinberg—children described by Dr. Miller as "intelligent, alert, attentive, extremely sensitive"—who learn exceeding well how to become "completely attuned" to the well-being of a powerful parent, entirely at the parent's "disposal" and "ready for [the parent's] use." As resilient as she may have been, Lisa Steinberg in all likelihood would have grown up to become more narcissistically disturbed than Hedda, even if she struggled not to be at all like her. Ironically, on the face of it, Lisa appears in no way attuned to Hedda; the parent whose wishes she constantly adapted herself to was Joel.

"Daddy's girl" is how Marilyn Walton sees Lisa. In one of our conversations, Marilyn equated Lisa's love for Joel with Marilyn's adoration of her own father. "In Lisa," Marilyn declared, "Joel Steinberg found the only human being who ever loved him without reservation." Uncritical love, however, is an ideal only when it is a love between equals. What reservations was Lisa capable of having? By what known standards of behavior could she compare her daddy to the daddies of other little girls? What was the knowledge of an exceptionally bright six-year-old compared to Joel's or Hedda's?

Tragically, until the last months of her life, Lisa Steinberg seemed to have a false sense of her own power—on this basis, she faced life with poise and confidence, perhaps even at times with joy. She could always be sure she was the favorite of the most powerful person in the world. If Joel fondled her sexually, it probably only contributed to her sense of her importance. If other adults did so as well, the psychological damage would have surfaced only in the future Lisa would never grow into. As for Joel beating Hedda—in all probability, Lisa took that behavior for granted. Mommy did things that made him mad, so Daddy had to punish her all the time. Joel had reduced Hedda's status in the household to that of a dependent child. Except when Hedda played teacher with her, showing her how to read and even instructing her in writing the letters of the Hebrew alphabet, Lisa may have related to her as an older, bullying, dangerous sibling. The word *mother* would not have had the meaning for Lisa that it had for other children.

Many women would like to believe that Lisa identified with Hedda and even went so far as to try to protect her from Joel, but there is no indication that this was the case. The relationship between the middle-aged woman and the small girl was a "deep freeze" even when Lisa was two, according to Marilyn Walton. Although Lisa would defer to Joel, she'd talk back to Hedda. With Hedda, says Marilyn, Lisa would often assume a "confrontational posture." By the time she was six, she may have imitated Joel, responding to Hedda's slaps or scoldings by striking back.

Hedda claimed in her testimony that she never physically punished Lisa. Not even once? Hardly a parent can make that claim. Nor do most adults go through life, as Hedda swears she did, without ever feeling or showing anger. Certainly Bill Muller, Marilyn Walton, and Betty Kraus have vivid recollections of a wrathful Hedda. Hedda has never described the manner in which she did discipline Lisa. Discipline, according to her testimony, was something she left entirely to Joel. Until Lisa was four or five, the only form Steinberg's punishment ever took was verbal, Hedda said, although verbal abuse can also be tremendously destructive to a child.

Still one can't help wondering how Lisa got the cut lip at thirteen or fourteen months that horrified the women at Random House, or the bruise on her face that Diane Margolies noticed six

months later when she ran into Joel, Hedda, and Lisa in a drugstore in the Village. Nonetheless, Diane did think the little girl
seemed "extremely outgoing, friendly, and affectionate," that
day. Then there was the friend of Louise Price's who ran into
Hedda wheeling Lisa in a stroller: on that occasion Lisa had a
black eye—Hedda said the child had fallen in the playground. But
as any mother knows, small children generally bruise their fore-
heads or scrape their chins when they fall on their faces.

Joel Steinberg's statements about Hedda's care of Lisa have
always been wildly inconsistent. Before Marilyn Walton testified
in his defense, he sent her a message that he didn't want her to
say anything that would make Hedda out to be a bad mother. On
the other hand, he did once tell Maury Terry that when Lisa was
a baby, Hedda would sometimes leave her on the windowsill next
to an open window. (This was during Hedda's forgetful period
when she was putting socks in the refrigerator.) He has also
claimed that whenever he had to be out of town for a few days,
he had a detective friend from the Sixth Precinct sleep over at the
apartment as Lisa's "baby-sitter."

But Steinberg's actions in the summer of 1983, do seem to
indicate he had begun to realize that introducing Lisa into his
household had been a mistake. He called Marilyn Walton in Dallas and told her he'd like her to raise Lisa. Marilyn agreed to take
the child, and Joel promised he'd be sending the adoption papers
along very soon, not that there were any adoption papers to speak
of. Soon after that conversation, Joel changed his mind and sent
Lisa to the Greens.

Perhaps the worst thing about Joel is that he was capable of
having compunctions. He knew what he should have done for
Lisa, where she would be safe; instead he decided to do something that was clearly destructive. It is in such knowledge and
such choices that one finds true evil. His decision to obtain a baby
regardless of the way he lived involved the same kind of knowledge and choice. Hedda would like to believe she made no
choices. All she ever did was what she was told, following through
on whatever Joel wanted.

Escape attempts are quite important to Hedda Nussbaum's credentials as battered woman and victim. Between late 1983 and
1985, she did flee the house five times. Not long after each of her
departures, she would phone Steinberg and tell him where she
was, always mindful, as she told the court, that he might be worry-

ing about her. Perhaps her primary objective in leaving him was to be able to stage a dramatic return. Certainly before Lisa came into their lives and began to win more and more of Joel's attention, Hedda Nussbaum never tried "escape." On the two occasions she had slipped out of the house to go to the hospital, she had never burned her bridges by charging Joel with her injuries. Return was uppermost in Hedda's mind even after Joel had ruptured her spleen; after all, she was determined to live with him forever.

Many battered wives finally find the courage to run when they realize that their children are also in danger from the batterer. Hedda Nussbaum, it should be noted, never once considered taking Lisa along with her. "I thought she would be better off with Joel's care," Hedda explained to prosecutor Peter Casolaro in 1988. When he asked her why she had thought that, she was ready with a high-minded answer. Hedda had unselfishly believed Joel was a better parent: "Well, I thought that he had tremendous insight and ability to handle people, including children, and he was very sensitive, and that I had those problems and obviously caused problems in the house." Between the lines, though, you could imagine Hedda tearfully saying to Joel when she came back to him, "Well, I just thought you didn't need me anymore."

Of course the problems Hedda alluded to in court were only "supposed" problems, since they stemmed from her "supposed" involvement in the cult. By the time she testified, she no longer believed she'd had them.

As Assistant DA Casolaro took her through her futile flights, Hedda kept implying that she might have gotten away from Joel if only the outsiders from whom she sought help had given her a proper reception. No one wanted to do nearly enough for Hedda Nussbaum. In February 1984, when she allegedly sought refuge one morning at a women's shelter on Canal Street, she had merely been given bus fare by the callous administrators and told to go uptown to Bellevue Hospital. Then there was the time she took a train to Connecticut and phoned a friend from the train station. The motherly married woman who had once done freelance work for Random House had seemed "thrilled" at first, but her delight at having Hedda as an unexpected houseguest soon faded, and she took Hedda to see a social worker. That practical gesture had evidently been most insulting. Hedda had also once fled to the Greenwich Village office of the brother of an old friend whom she hadn't seen in years. She told this man that she was leaving Joel and asked if she could stay with him and his wife for a few days. "He was not comfortable with this idea and he also said, 'Look, you owe Joel more than just walking out on him without an explanation. Why don't you call him up?' And he encouraged me. He might even have dialed it, I don't recall . . . and so I spoke to Joel."

"Whenever I left," Hedda explained, "I always went to people who knew me and respected me and weren't really associated with Joel." But inevitably the people she chose to run to were never the ones who would have actually and effectively tried to help her. Why did she never get in touch with her sister or Naomi Weiss or even Risa? Or the Random House women who had been so concerned about her welfare—Betty or Janet Shulman or Ann Christensen? In 1987, when Ann Christensen sent flowers to Hedda at Elmhurst Hospital, Hedda wrote Joel that she was delighted the hospital wouldn't permit her to keep the unwelcome bouquet.

The February 1984 flight that landed Hedda in Bellevue Hospital sounded harrowing, but there is no doubt that its outcome—a bedside reunion with Joel—gave her tremendous emotional satisfaction. After arriving at the emergency room, Hedda told the personnel she had fallen down a flight of stairs. When they wanted to know about the older injuries on her body, she was ready with an explanation: "I had gotten them because I was a participant in a cult that was involved in S&M." When they told her they didn't believe the story about her fall, Hedda came up with another: "I said that I had been living in the street, and I was embarrassed that I had been living in the street, and in the street had been attacked by some men that had beaten me." Her mind was working very creatively that day, "so as to totally not associate Joel with the injuries."

When Casolaro asked her, "Why did you tell them the cult story?" Hedda answered, "Because I believed it." The Bellevue doctors hadn't, however. So, although Hedda had told them she had been living at the women's shelter on Canal Street, in the end she had to give them Joel's phone number. She said that if they called that number, someone there would verify her story. Joel, in fact, had a long conversation with the psychiatrist who had been examining her and helpfully suggested that the psychiatrist read *Snapping*.

Who should walk into Hedda's room soon afterward but Joel

himself. "I was lying in bed and he came over to me, lifted me up, turned me around; and made me feel very, very happy to see him. He treated me very specially and was very good to me. I remember even my roommate said to me, 'You seem to have such a caring man.' " Hedda was so happy to be reunited with Joel, that they left the hospital together forthwith. As she recalled this incident in court, her voice became almost rapturous.

Hedda Nussbaum had last seen her mother on May 14, 1983, when she came to the party for Lisa's second birthday. At that time, Joel had told Emma Nussbaum he never wanted her to visit them again. He didn't like the way she watched Lisa; she was upsetting the child. Hedda's mother was a liar and a bad person. Hedda made no effort to reason with him—as always, she accepted Joel's wisdom. But six or seven months later, in 1984, she did phone the Nussbaums and appeal to her father to come and get her. Although Joel was out with Lisa, she did not take the opportunity to flee to safety immediately. Steinberg returned with the little girl and found Hedda still at home, taking her clothes out of the hall closet. When she announced that her father would soon be coming to take her away, Joel responded by throwing her to the floor. After that, he told her to sit in a cold bath because the fall had hurt her leg. Joel relied on this cold water treatment "either to take down the swelling of injuries or sometimes he used it as a punishment, apparently." With Joel, she never could quite figure out what was punitive and what was therapeutic. Sometimes he would knock her down to teach her a lesson, but she couldn't figure out what the lesson was.

Hedda was soaking in the bath when William Nussbaum arrived. Joel directed the seventy-five-year-old man to take Lisa to the store and gave him a shopping list of things they needed. By the time William Nussbaum came back with the groceries, Hedda was out of the tub. "Everything's fine, Daddy," she told her father. Since there seemed to be nothing she wanted him to do for her, William Nussbaum left. Did he ever wonder why his daughter had not also begged him to rescue his grandchild from Joel?

Some months later, William Nussbaum turned up at the house unexpectedly. When he rang the downstairs bell, Joel had Hedda go to the intercom and tell her father to go to the phone booth on the corner and call them. Joel wouldn't permit her to let him in. According to Hedda, their phone wasn't working well. Sometimes they wouldn't hear it ring. "That's what happened that day and my father assumed that it was deliberate, that we weren't answering the phone. And I think in combination with my mother having been forbidden to come to our house, he decided not to return." It also could have been deliberate. The two of them could have sat there in the apartment, waiting for that ringing phone to stop. It could have been like that time Marilyn came home with Lisa, and Hedda didn't want to let them in.

By now Hedda's appearance was even more shocking than it had been on Marilyn's visit in 1983. Her nose had been permanently flattened and she had a cauliflower ear. Her face was indelibly stamped with the marks of Joel's dominance. She barely left the apartment. In addition to her household duties, which she performed with less and less efficiency, she acted as Joel's paralegal secretary. She kept his diary, answered the phone, and did research for him. In the process, Hedda herself became rather knowledgeable about the law. She still had her own projects as well—the research for the book about cocaine and two books on demonology for teenagers. If she wished to go out, she would have to ask Joel's permission. Sometimes she shopped very late at night at the twenty-four-hour Food Emporium on Avenue of the Americas. When her bruises were fresh, she wouldn't even go to the supermarket—the healing process generally took two weeks. The days when she accompanied Joel to parties and the late dinners with clients she had once found so enjoyable were over. Now Joel said Hedda looked too bad for him to be seen with her, and he didn't want to be embarrassed by her "inappropriate behavior." He felt that Hedda had regressed, gone back to her old ways. He had not succeeded after all in bringing out her real personality.

Of course certain people did visit them. The New Jersey prostitute, for example, and Greg Malmoulka and Joel's client Chubby D'Apice, the pornography producer, and Dr. Peter Sarosi, whom they had met in 1982, after Michael Bergman had his first heart attack and had to retire. Hedda thought of him as her good friend as well as Joel's, and of course he and Steinberg shared the *Aqua Viva*. Sometimes Sarosi would come over for dinner, sometimes just for advice from Joel on his investments. His last visit was shortly before Lisa's death, but he only stayed a few minutes.

Joel and Hedda may also have had some further contact with the Greens. (Michael and Shayna Green were still together; there hadn't been a divorce, after all.) At one point during 1984, Hedda had to write a note to remind herself once again how dangerous the Greens were "lest we forget"—how they "programmed, brainwashed and injured." Nonetheless, according to a police report, Joel and Hedda went to the Greens' New Year's Eve party that year.

In Steinberg's mind, the cult was expanding, sucking more people in all the time. Hedda's cautionary note about the Greens mentioned Bobby Merlino and her sister Judy. They as well as the Greens had the power to buzz Joel and Hedda and make them forget the danger they were in. The late-night talks Joel had with Hedda focused more and more on the growing peril. Joel kept begging Hedda to come up with his buzzword; he believed that once he knew it, it could no longer be used to program him. Once he hit her because she still couldn't tell him.

He grew increasingly fearful of Judy's power over Hedda, not that Hedda was seeing her anymore. Hedda last saw her sister when Judy and her son took Lisa out with them one day in 1984. When Judy brought Lisa home, she came upstairs with her, while her son waited in front of the house. Hedda had a black eye and didn't want Judy to see it. "So Joel told her that . . . I had been seeing a doctor and that the doctor said I should not look anybody in the eye because of all the staring I had been through." So Judy "sat at our dining-room table, which was in the living room, with her back to the entrance of the living room. I stood first in the entranceway . . . and talked with her and then I came over and stood behind her and she put her hands up like this. I held her hands and we talked and we never looked at each other."

Judy found Joel's explanation of Hedda's condition unconvincing. She followed up her visit with a letter, telling her younger sister that she still loved her. Joel intercepted the letter and told Hedda it was full of buzzwords. She couldn't read it or see Judy anymore because Judy could put her into a hypnotic trance.

A whole new set of nonsensical beliefs about Hedda's family and Hedda's history had erupted inside Joel's head—beliefs that reflected his growing fear of Hedda herself—the Hedda Nussbaum whom Joel had brought into being with his "therapies" and his fists. In the escalating brutality and perversion of their relationship he may have seen the potential for his own ruin. Someday he would go too far because Hedda permitted everything. What imperiled Joel most were the deadly suggestions implicit in her acquiescence. What had made Hedda the way she was? Certainly he had nothing to do with it—he had only tried to help her. He came to imagine she was susceptible to the Greens because of what she had learned from her mother. Emma Nussbaum was a witch, who practiced black magic rituals that came from the old country, in which she had also initiated her daughters. Hedda's father, Steinberg also fantasized, had irreparably damaged her by having sex with her when she was a little girl. In Joel's scheme of things, however, this wasn't really incest, since he also decided Hedda had been born in Europe and given away to the Nussbaums by her real family. He seemed to be creating a history for Hedda that to some extent paralleled Lisa's. Lisa, too, Joel convinced himself, had been violated by her grandfather. Between what Joel believed the Greens had done to Lisa and what Hedda's father had done, the child had certainly lost her innocence, through no fault of Joel Steinberg's.

Hedda seems to have accepted Steinberg's fanciful version of her history. Perhaps his stories seemed to make psychological sense—resonated with her old feelings of being a powerless and unwanted child. After 1984, she never tried to reestablish contact with her family; she obliged Joel in this even when she ran away. When they phoned her occasionally, she'd talk to them very briefly on the speaker phone with Joel listening in.

In contrast, from 1984 through October 1987, Joel's relationship with his own mother had never been better. Now that he was a family man, he paid Charlotte Steinberg fairly regular visits, almost like a conventional middle-class son, bringing Lisa along so that he could show her off. Charlotte Steinberg enjoyed her granddaughter, the girlchild she had always wanted. She fussed over her, taking off her clothes and giving her baths, dressing her up in the brand-new outfits she bought for her. Sometimes Joel would talk to his mother about his childrearing philosophy—he was teaching Lisa to be very independent, afraid of nothing. Charlotte Steinberg thought Joel was crazy to still be living in that two-and-a-half-room apartment now that he had become a father. Why didn't he and Hedda move into a house? Even though Hedda accompanied Joel on his visits more and more infrequently, Charlotte Steinberg was rather fond of Hedda. Despite everything, her son seemed to have turned out well. He had to be a pretty smart man despite all his cockamamie stories, because he was worth a couple of million dollars. Charlotte gave him some of her own money to invest for her in the stock market.

EVEN BY 1985, after the Greens had turned into deadly enemies and when it was clear that Hedda had never been further from making progress, Joel Steinberg no doubt still believed what he once told Ivan Fisher: "Relationships were trophies—like money in the bank. Relationships were how you got ahead." It had never been an altruistic philosophy; in fact, it was something that went along with the concept of networking, a process that Joel understood, Ivan Fisher told me, before most people caught on to it. When Joel spoke metaphorically about putting money into the relationship bank, what he meant of course was that you could look forward to collecting interest. For example, he was investing heavily in Lisa. He expected the rate of return on his investment to be very high.

Although Hedda took care of the little girl's physical needs, it was Joel who played with Lisa and sat with her watching the kiddie shows on TV Joel was the arbiter of her moral education and made all policy decisions concerning her upbringing. After Lisa's fourth birthday, Joel began to work harder at molding her into an ideal and delightful companion. With an adult woman like Hedda, the female personality was already formed, so an investment in the molding process would not necessarily bring dividends.

Joel wanted his four-year-old daughter to dance, swim, and become an all-around athlete. He wanted Lisa to be very thin, of course, in accordance with his ideal of feminine beauty. He also wanted her to be able to converse with him knowledgeably about art. Hedda was kept quite busy escorting Lisa to different classes in Greenwich Village. People who lived on Tenth Street frequently saw Steinberg out on the block with his little girl, steadying her two-wheeler or demonstrating to her how to rollerskate.

In fact, if you hadn't heard the alarming sounds coming from the Steinberg apartment, Joel would have looked to you like the model of the "involved father." The classes Lisa Steinberg attended were full of children of other ambitious parents, determined to make their preschoolers early achievers. Joel himself would often take Lisa to her ballet classes at Green House Music School. When he did so, he would stay the entire hour, peering through his thick glasses at the tiny ballerinas, the adorable little round bodies in the wrinkly leotards. No other parent showed such great interest, or even stayed to watch the class.

When Lisa was out with Joel, she did not act like a child terrified of her father. As far as Joel was concerned, says Marilyn Walton, "Lisa could do no wrong. Any woman would have to take a back seat to her." She sat in his lap, climbed all over him, told him her little jokes. Already she had an excellent sense of humor, and a good deal of common sense as well. "Oh, *Daddy!*" she would chide him, if Joel said something ridiculous, giving him a look that seemed to say, That's the stupidest thing I ever heard in my life. She had a thoughtful manner you'd expect to find in an older person. "If you told Lisa something," says Marilyn Walton, "she'd really think about it twice." Lisa was not at all bashful about giving adults advice. Joel, says Marilyn, would discuss adult decisions with his daughter rather than with Hedda. Marilyn used to kid Joel that he'd have his hands full when Lisa was eighteen.

It really did seem to Marilyn, despite the irregularities of Joel's household, like the kind of special relationship she'd had with her own father. Joel would take Lisa with him to softball games and roughhouse with her as if she were a boy. When she wore little dresses, he didn't seem to know what to do with her.

Marilyn kept in touch now, even when she was in Dallas or on the road. She'd talk to Joel and Lisa on the phone and would often send Lisa presents. Lisa would send back thank-you cards she'd made herself with crayon drawings. When she was older, Joel would supervise the writing of polite notes. Lisa had lovely manners, in contrast to Joel, who would often be deliberately boorish. His basic attitude in dealing with the outside world was: I'm rich and I'm powerful; I don't have to follow the rules everyone else does.

On the question of the rules of behavior for little girls, he would often defer to Marilyn, calling her long distance to consult her. "But she already has a mother," Marilyn once pointed out. "Lisa has two mothers," Joel told her. One of the things he taught Lisa was that if she were ever in trouble, Marilyn was the person to go to. Marilyn would take care of her.

Once when Lisa was five, Joel called Marilyn, sounding genuinely upset. His mother had given Lisa a little silk slip, and Lisa was running around the house in it, vamping, acting like a chorus girl. He said he wanted Marilyn to explain to Lisa how to be a little lady, so he put the child on the phone. Marilyn told her there were parts of the body you had to keep private. When Lisa grew up and fell in love, she could share those parts of her body. Until then, there was something called modesty. Joel listened in on the whole conversation on the speaker phone.

When Lisa had outgrown the Porta-crib provided by Hedda's parents, her sleeping place became the beige couch by one of the front windows in the living room. There she could play with her dolls, watch "Sesame Street" (her favorite character was Ernie), and draw pictures. Toys and drawings would collect beneath the couch; crayons would work their way into the dirt and crumbs and lint between the cushions. According to Hedda, once the lights were turned off, and Lisa was under her blankets, she soon became oblivious to the nocturnal activities in the apartment.

On certain nights, maybe a couple of times a week, Hedda would get busy in the kitchen, drawing some cocaine from the stash they always kept in the house and mixing it with ether, consulting her card file of recipes to vary the kind of high they'd get. She found all this very interesting "on an intellectual level." From her extensive reading, she'd learned to do a lot of different tests. When a new supply of coke came into the house, she was now able to test it to see what it was cut with; she found enjoyment in examining the crystals. She even carried on a correspondence with other experts on the drug. It was quite fascinating as well as very useful to learn how different mixtures affected different parts of the body. Although Hedda developed into a connoisseur of cocaine, by the time she testified she could no longer quite recall how freebasing had made her feel. Did it generally speed you up or slow you down? Maybe it slowed you down more, she thought.

Certainly the drug's anesthetic properties must have served her and Joel, allowing them to go further and further in their sadomasochistic adventures. After Lisa's death, investigators found certain telltale devices in the apartment. Handcuffs and a whip; an obdurator, used to stretch the anus. Karen Snyder had previously spotted a larger piece of equipment. One day when the door to apartment 3W was open, Karen was horrified to see a uterine aspirator lying on the floor in the hallway. Uterine aspirators are used to perform abortions; they are also sometimes used in the making of pornographic films. Joel, of course, later had an explanation for the presence of the aspirator in the apartment (actually it was one of two in his possession): he only used them as bilge pumps for his boat. As for the other sexual aids, they were free samples from the company he represented.

Perhaps on some of those endless white cocaine nights, a sudden burst of very loud music would awaken the child curled up on the couch. The music would blare and underneath it there would be other sounds, strange, awful wordless sounds that seemed to come from Hedda, all mixed together with the night noises from outside, the different universe on the other side of the windowpane, people talking to each other as they strolled down Tenth Street, people driving past the house, their car lights rippling across the ceiling. Perhaps Steinberg and Nussbaum had made a rule about the bedroom, where Lisa had slept in the Porta-crib when she was very little. Maybe now that Lisa was a big girl, she was not under any circumstances to get up at night when she heard music and walk in there, even if she felt frightened. Maybe Lisa could only sleep next to her daddy in the big soft bed that she loved if he told her she could. So what she'd learned to do was close her eyes and pretend to sleep. Maybe even when the music stopped and Joel or Hedda walked in to check on her, Lisa would turn her face toward the back of the couch and still pretend.

Joel Steinberg's obsession with the Greens was like his addiction to coke and sadomasochistic sex. It kept growing, developing new permutations, metastasizing in his mind. Now Hedda's eyes began to alarm him greatly; at times she had a certain fixed stare that seemed a sure sign she was entering a hypnotic trance, that the Greens or one of their numerous agents were buzzing her.

The Greens, in fact, would continue to buzz Steinberg until his separation from Nussbaum on November 2, 1987. For some time, however, they had been buzzing him from coal-mining country in Pennsylvania. In October 1983, coincidentally the same month as the encounter group described by Nussbaum that culminated in Green's beating, the doctor had run into professional difficulties. He was asked to withdraw from his partnership in a medical group of Long Island pulmonary specialists. Dr. Green "did not fulfill his coverage requirements" for the months "prior to his dismissal" was the rather ambiguous statement Dr. Jerome Weiner gave to the press in 1988. In June 1985, Green abruptly gave up his private practice and resigned from three Suffolk County hospitals. The the Greens left the area. Two years later, detectives involved in the Steinberg investigation learned there was a reason to suspect Green's departure could have been precipitated by a sexual-harassment complaint made at one hospital by a student radiology technician. Nothing had ever really been proven, however. Any follow-up on the part of the hospital had been cut short when Green relocated out of state.

After practicing briefly in the tiny rural communities of Williamsport and Lewiston, Green bought a handsome red-brick house near Sunbury in July 1987. He quickly established himself in the area with a blue-collar clientele and became director of the respiratory therapy department of Sunbury's 150-bed hospital. In September 1988, he bought a small medical center from a retiring doctor who had run it for thirty years. Many of the patients suffered from black lung disease. Green had set himself up in the kind of backwater place where doctors were desperately needed and were gods who could do no wrong. Shanya, too, was able to continue her work with children. She soon volunteered her services to a Sunbury daycare center.

An investigator from the Bureau of Child Welfare, who responded in 1985 to an anonymous complaint of suspected child abuse from Karen Snyder, found a happy, normal child without a bruise on her body. Did Lisa wonder what this stranger was looking for, why Joel and Hedda had taken all her clothes off? Was she fearful that she would be taken away from Joel? How old was she when Joel first instructed her that she must never tell anyone what went on in the apartment? He may even have explained, since Lisa was so mature for her age, that it would be very easy for people to come and take Lisa away from him, since she was only a chosen child and not his real daughter.

Now that she was getting old enough to enter kindergarten, Joel must have started worrying about what secrets Lisa might tell other children and, even worse, what she might confide to a teacher. Suddenly he may have realized that it would be very dangerous for him to believe that he controlled Lisa completely. She was too bright, she knew too much. How could he ensure that

Lisa was totally obedient to him even when he couldn't supervise her personally? Perhaps by constantly alternating positive and negative reinforcement.

But Joel may have had another problem on his hands as well. Hedda may have started to believe that Joel was planning to replace her with Lisa.

Once again, the mysterious "emotional tensions" Hedda referred to in her testimony caused her to run away. It was her most farfetched flight of all, and her very last one. This time her imaginary destination was St. Louis, a city she had once visited on business. She used to know an author there and had stayed at the woman's house for a week while she edited her book. Hedda arose early one morning and took four hundred dollars from the drawer where Joel kept his cash and made it all the way to LaGuardia Airport. Even on the way, she must have known she wouldn't really be going anywhere. I'll call Joel so he won't worry, she told herself. As always, the most terrifying thought was that Joel wouldn't worry, that he wouldn't give a damn, that he'd just as soon be left alone with Lisa. So Hedda rushed to a phone as soon as she reached the airport. After she talked to Joel, she went straight home.

Just as he had in 1983, Joel had another of those flashes of compunction and recognition sometime during 1985. Lisa was in danger. He should send Lisa away from him before it was too late. Marilyn was on the road, singing in a club in Boston. He tracked her down and called her there. I want you to take Lisa, he told her. They even talked about him flying up there with the child, although it was a very inconvenient time for Marilyn.

But Joel Steinberg needed Lisa, needed her too much to be able to save her. As his relationship with Hedda approached exhaustion and nullity, Lisa may have become the catalytic element that kept the game moving and changing, the deadly players still engaged. As Jessica Benjamin writes in *The Bonds of Love,* "once the tension between subjugation and resistance dissolves, death or abandonment is the inevitable end of the story . . . for the masochist the intolerable end is abandonment, while for the sadist it is the death (or murder) of the other."

THERE IS a very old but mistaken belief that bringing a new child into the world can provide a solution
to the problems of an adult relationship. Many a woman has re-
sorted to pregnancy to keep a man. Perhaps that was why Hedda
Nussbaum, at the age of forty-three, began trying again to produce a child, consulting with Peter Sarosi, since he was a fertility
specialist. Evidently the doctor found no reason to discourage her
in view of her age, her physical condition, or her state of mental
health. He put her under treatment; Hedda went regularly to his
office for injections. Joel and Hedda had talked to Sarosi about
Joel's lifelong wish to have a son. Why shouldn't a man like Steinberg have a son? Joel was a good father—surely the proof of that
was the delightful Lisa, whom Sarosi sometimes saw as a patient
as a favor to Joel.

Hedda waited and waited for positive results—for the child of
her own and Joel's that would bind Joel to her and perhaps make
Lisa less of a threat.

Joel had meanwhile found a new and terrible way to torment
her, which Nussbaum later described in her testimony: "He
would tell me to put on my shoes, because we always walked
around the house barefoot, and sometimes he would give me
money, tell me to get my coat and get out the door." Life without
Joel was "the worst thing in the world that could happen" to
Hedda. Without Joel, she couldn't survive; if he cast her out she'd
have to kill herself. After Joel went through this same scenario a
number of times, Hedda realized to her great relief, "He didn't
really want me to go, and I would go through the charade of
putting on my shoes and putting on my coat. But whenever
I . . . tried to walk out the door, he would physically stop me from
doing it." Nonetheless, from time to time, Joel continued to order

her to leave him. Clearly, it was an idea he could not get out of his mind.

Perhaps in the end it was Peter Sarosi who helped to prolong their relationship. On June 23, 1986, he called them up excitedly and said to Joel, "I have your son." They had not been planning to adopt another child, but here was an unforeseen opportunity they could not pass up. "Dr. Sarosi explained," Hedda recalled, "that a child of an unwed mother had been delivered at the hospital where he worked and that he would—basically give the child to us." Hedda was "surprised but happy." She listened in on the speaker phone as Joel and Sarosi discussed arrangements to have the baby delivered to them. When Ira London asked her what she was so happy about, Hedda answered blandly, "I was happy to have another child to bring up." She put a pillow inside a dresser drawer, where their new son slept on his first night in their house. Then they borrowed a baby carriage from someone they knew, and he slept in that for a number of months. They named him Mitchell after Peter Sarosi's associate, Dr. Mitchell Essig.

Karen Snyder saw Hedda and Joel carrying the newborn infant into the building. It was a bitter moment for her. For years now she had been making fruitless calls to the police, the Bureau of Child Welfare, and the Battered Women's Hotline. Now she felt completely discouraged: "I thought nothing I'd ever done had made any difference."

With the baby boy in the house, Hedda seems to have had a brief surge of self-confidence. Joel had Lisa, but Mitchell was all hers. It was obvious from her testimony that as far as she was capable of it, Hedda formed a certain bond with Mitchell—the attachment a little girl might feel for a beloved doll. For a while, she even made efforts to revive her career. She sent stories she had written to *Cricket*, a children's magazine. She also sent out some résumés, soliciting free-lance editing, to a number of publishing houses with juvenile departments. Once Hedda answered a blind ad for free-lance work. She had no idea that it was Betty Kraus who saw her résumé and couldn't bring herself to write back.

Marilyn Walton flew into New York at the end of that summer. She spent Labor Day weekend with Joel and Lisa and Greg Malmoulka sailing the waters of Long Island Sound on the *Aqua Viva*. She saw Hedda and the new baby for a little while, when they all set out from the apartment. Joel seemed to be in an unusually benevolent mood. He had bought Lisa a new swimsuit and a T-shirt, and he also bestowed a gift upon Hedda, a pink blouse. But Hedda stayed home with Mitchell that weekend. Having tied her down with a new baby to look after, perhaps Joel felt freer to pursue his separate pleasures.

Lisa was five and about to start kindergarten. To Marilyn, Joel and his daughter seemed to be "great sailing pals." In fact, he was spending almost every weekend on the boat with Lisa. He'd even let Lisa steer a little, although he wouldn't let Marilyn touch the wheel. Marilyn soon realized that Joel was feeling very "tensed out." Nonetheless, he was very proud of how much Lisa had been able to learn, and he seemed that day to be a patient teacher. He and Lisa were always kissing and hugging and being playful with each other. "I observed a great love for each other," Marilyn later testified.

Marilyn had brought along a 35mm camera. She lent it to Lisa, who already knew how to take pictures. Joel said she had her own camera. Lisa had her daddy, Marilyn, and Greg pose for her; when Marilyn later had the snapshots developed, she found Lisa had taken very good ones. Marilyn shot a picture of Lisa, walking toward their table at the yacht club in Patchogue carrying her wet swimsuit.

Marilyn Walton had a low opinion of Greg. "One of Joel's yes-men," she calls him disparagingly. Malmoulka was in and out of the Steinberg apartment almost every day. He was a big, short-legged, barrel-chested man, with thinning blond hair and a mustache. On the trip he made great, strained efforts to be jovial.

At the yacht club, Joel got into a shouting altercation with a waitress, while Marilyn was in the ladies' room. As usual, he had been deliberately boorish. He had ordered a baked potato and had walked over with his plate to the "community sour cream dish." The waitress had caught him dipping his hand into the sour cream, and had loudly expressed her disapproval. Joel wanted Marilyn to complain about her to the manager.

When dessert came, Joel received another scolding, this time from Marilyn, who was horrified to see Lisa and Greg sharing an ice cream. "Don't you let Lisa eat out of Greg's spoon," she told Joel. "Greg is a single man and there ain't no telling where his mouth has been. He could have AIDS or something." Joel was surprised and hurt, and Lisa looked absolutely shocked, as if she could not believe anyone would dare to yell at her father.

I once said to Marilyn Walton, "It's a lucky thing Joel Steinberg never proposed to you."

There was a long silence on the other end of the line, and then Marilyn told me that Joel Steinberg did finally propose to her a couple of times. The first time was over the phone, a month or so before the sailing trip, when again he asked her if she wanted to adopt Lisa. Marilyn told him she was too afraid of his temper to marry him and wrote him a long letter. Another proposal came when they were on the boat together. Joel raised the question and then said he didn't want to get heavy about it while they were out on the water. In Patchogue, they took a walk together, during which Joel promised Marilyn a house in Westchester—the same one he had always promised Hedda. They had been talking about Lisa, who, Marilyn said, should be sent to a private school, and furthermore should not be raised in New York City. Joel was in total agreement about that. Oddly enough, he said nothing whatever about Mitchell. There was something desperate about the way Joel talked. Marilyn thought he was coming to the end of his rope.

She might have married him if he'd asked her in 1978 or 1982, but now it was too late. When she was younger, she'd been attracted to men who seemed stronger than she was, but by now she'd grown very tired of men who tried to dominate her and then folded in a crisis. She thinks now that in a way she did always "dominate" Joel. He seemed to work harder at pleasing her than she worked to please him. If she was in a passive mood, he was ready to take advantage of it. But when she was feeling aggressive, they'd have arguments or he'd suddenly back off.

She still doesn't know what Joel Steinberg really wanted from her: "It was friendship, but it wasn't." Despite the fact that they never became lovers, "the energy with Joel was sexual—there were always these little games and innuendoes." For many years, they had what Marilyn calls for lack of a better term, "a highly charged platonic romance." By 1986, the charge was gone. Her feelings for Joel Steinberg had become essentially maternal.

EVEN AN irregular household can have its routines, its fragile but crucial ties to the outside world, to everydayness and sanity. For about a year, there were two things Lisa Steinberg could count on. In the morning her mother would walk her to kindergarten at P.S. 41, a block and a half away on West Eleventh Street; in the afternoon her daddy would arrive to pick her up. Hedda had not yet stopped taking care of Lisa. She would help her to wash and comb her hair and put out clean clothes for her to wear to school. In her striped Oshkosh overalls and her Health-Tex T-shirts, Lisa looked just as carefully nurtured as the other Greenwich Village five-year-olds in her class.

As for Joel and Hedda, whom teachers and parents knew as "the Steinbergs," they, too, managed to pass muster, although no one really thought to take a careful or skeptical look at them When the principal, Elliott Koreman, interviewed Mr. Steinberg and his daughter during registration, Mr. Steinberg did not inform him that Elizabeth had been adopted. Koreman had an immediate impression of her as an "extremely articulate, very verbal, beautiful kid to look at."

"The Steinbergs" kept a low profile, although many other parents took a passionate interest in the functioning of P.S. 41. In fact, the appointment of Koreman, three years before in defiance of the preference of the district superintendent, had been a decisive victory for the parents and teachers. The Steinbergs did not involve themselves in the politics of the school or the PTA. As one person put it, they "were there and not there," adult figures making walk-on appearances in classroom doorways. Elizabeth Kassowitz, the kindergarten teacher, had the vague sense that Lisa Steinberg and her mother had a "normal parent-child relationship." From her two parent-teacher conferences with Joel, she could later recall nothing unusual. The 1987 PTA president Nancy Stein once caught a glimpse of Hedda with the two children. "I made a mental note," she told Georgia Brown, a P.S. 41 parent, who interviewed her for _7 Days._ "Oh, she's been in an accident and hit the windshield. I looked closely at the kids, thinking, Thank God they weren't with her."

"I'm Jewish," she told Brown, "and somewhere I must have been aware that it was a Jewish home. For _me_ that means nonviolent. _Now_ everyone is thinking abuse, but that's hindsight."

Stein, however, as well as other parents, had felt there was something unsavory about Joel Steinberg that made them want to keep their distance. Perhaps he seemed a bit too eager to strike up instant friendships. He had a boat somewhere that Lisa kept talking about, and he was always looking for families to go sailing with him, issuing his invitations on very short acquaintance.

Even though her father seemed a bit "off," Lisa herself constituted the best proof of "normalcy." Abused children, according to the Board of Education bulletin Mrs. Kassowitz had read and used as a guide on two or three occasions when she had reason to be concerned about one of her students, often cried excessively; behaviorally, they might seem unusually quiet or unusually boisterous. Elizabeth Steinberg did nothing corresponding to any of these signs. She was a cooperative and cheerful little girl, very popular with the other students. Mrs. Kassowitz found her demonstratively affectionate, the kind of child who'd come up to you and wind her arms around your waist.

Rayne Sciarowi, the P.S. 41 music teacher, who saw Lisa once a week, found that she became very involved in singing and dancing and gave her a small lead in the kindergarten musical. She was a good little girl, though a bit on the quiet side, he thought.

In a public school with a more varied population, where the staff might have had much more experience with children from very disturbed homes, perhaps Lisa would have found a teacher astute enough to see that something was wrong. But P.S. 41 prides itself on its sheltered, private-school ambience. In Lisa Steinberg's case, its complacency about itself as a fairly homogeneous community of mostly white children from well-educated, middleclass, professional families led to assumptions that all was well, that every child's home environment measured up to certain standards of decency and normalcy. The passionate desire to hold on to these assumptions amounted to a kind of deliberate blindness. The school's ideas about itself seem to have been embodied by Elliott Koreman, an unselectively broad-minded man admired for the deep personal interest he took in his students. Although a walking advertisement for "caringness," he tended to avoid taking stands on sensitive issues.

One morning in mid-November 1987, I walked into P.S. 41, although the principal and staff had become quite adamant about not giving interviews. I heard the piano playing in the auditorium, and when I looked inside, there were all these little kids, Lisa's age, running around the stage on their toes, flapping their arms up and down to the rhythms of the music. Rayne Sciarowi was the piano player. You wouldn't have known anyone was missing, although the school had just gone through a traumatic period of mourning, anger, and soul-searching. An "expert" had been brought in by Koreman to talk to the kids about death. "Lisa's dead! She's dead!" this woman had insisted loudly to her audience of uncharacteristically subdued first-graders. She wanted to shock them into reality, to make them understand that their classmate's life was over, *finito*, ashes to ashes, dust to dust. It was like one of those truth-telling encounter sessions Joel and Hedda used to find so therapeutic. Elliott Koreman, of course, was from the same generation.

If only I had seen the *other* photos from that same Halloween party, said a former PTA president who agreed to speak with me, Lisa Steinberg would have looked just as normal and happy as all her classmates. No one ever spotted any "patterns of child abuse." Two weeks after Lisa's death, she had the jargon down pat. Even a veteran teacher like Lisa's would have needed the specialized training that the Board of Education, with its one resident expert, could supply to only a small fraction of the sixty-two thousand teachers in the entire system.

At P.S. 41, every student was "special," every teacher was "committed," every day Koreman ate his lunch with the kids. This parent had dealt with her own distress over the Steinberg tragedy by formulating a sociological explanation for it: Lisa had been "a victim of society's stereotyping." "We are a *caring* community," she kept insisting. Look for child abuse in Harlem or Jamaica, in other words, but not here.

All through our interview, I kept thinking of the bitter truth of an observation made two decades ago by George Dennison, a teacher and advocate of children's rights: *Children need justice more than they need love.* Yes, I thought. And also intelligence combined with moral courage. That's what children like Lisa need from adults they encounter outside their homes. Courage seemed to be the crucial factor.

I asked the ex-PTA president a couple of questions about what people around the school could have observed with the naked, untrained eye. What about Lisa coming to school that fall with terribly matted hair? Kids have fine hair and it gets matted, she answered wearily. Did you set eyes on Hedda Nussbaum? I asked her. Sure. Once she had even chatted with Hedda Nussbaum, in the fall of 1986, when she was running for district leader of the school board. They had talked about women's liberation and how important it was to uphold the rights of children. Hedda had impressed her as "a very articulate lady," and had even offered to use her writing and editing skills to further this woman's campaign. There was only one unusual thing that struck her: Hedda's skin "looked as if she'd had a very serious acne problem."

Three weeks before we spoke, however, the ex-PTA president had told the *New York Daily News* that Hedda Nussbaum had resembled a bag lady. Had she only been repeating what others had perceived? Or did she, even now, resist the notion that "one of us" could have been a woman like Hedda?

Although P.S. 41 was an institution that failed Lisa Steinberg, undoubtedly it was the place where she was happiest, perhaps nearly as happy in the hours she spent there as she appeared to be. No wonder she did what she was told so willingly and put her arms around Mrs. Kassowitz, a warm and kindly maternal figure. At P.S. 41, she was safe from the reach of Hedda's anger and jealousy and from the extreme demands for perfect behavior that Joel was beginning to make. She also discovered how good it was to be with other children, a world of equals where no one could boss you around if you stood up for yourself. She became known for her fearlessness in the playground, where it was always Lisa Steinberg who climbed to the very top of the monkey bars. During lunchtime, when the children were let into the schoolyard to release their pent-up energies, Lisa played very hard, tearing around, chasing other kids in games of cowboys and Indians. She could run very fast and still keep her breath. She wasn't one of those little kids who were always falling down and crying.

The waiters and waitresses at Knickerbocker's, a steak house on Ninth Street and University Place, became accustomed in the fall of 1986 to having a certain front table, near the bar, occupied just after three on many afternoons by a big dark man and a disarming little girl. Knickerbocker's had in effect become Joel's office. He would transact business there with his clients or his drug contacts, walking back and forth to the pay phone outside the men's room. Lisa would run around making friends with everybody. Sometimes, to impress a potential client, Joel would feed her leading questions so that she could show off her precocity. It was almost as if Joel Steinberg wore her, this delightful little girl, who softened the abrasive image of her adult male companion. They'd stay at Knickerbocker's quite late, when other five-year-olds were eating their dinners and splashing around in their baths. Some nights they'd go on to still another eating-and-drinking establishment to socialize with Joel's underworld connections. Perhaps when he was with Lisa, Joel Steinberg was able to bask in the illusion that he was good. Certainly his little girl adored her daddy.

Sometimes Joel would let Lisa visit other children, although none of her friends could ever come and play at Lisa's house. There was something about Lisa's house that other children weren't supposed to see, that was none of their business, because then they might say things to their parents or Lisa's teacher. Perhaps Joel had warned Lisa that she could never tell any of them her secrets or even just the many things she knew that no other kids did—how grownups made love, for example, with their penises and vaginas and their mouths. Other children's houses were marvelous places, where kids had rooms with millions of toys arranged on shelves and slept in real beds of their own under quilts that had flowers and animals on them. Perhaps Lisa worked out in her mind that the families who lived in such places were very rich, while she and her daddy and Hedda were poor people. The rich mommies were all dressed up and pretty, with very smooth skin on their faces. "Would you like something to eat, honey?" they'd ask. And she'd find herself saying "Yes, thank you." She couldn't help it even though Daddy would have been mad if he knew, like the time the old man who fixed shoes had given her candy after she said, "Hello, Mr. Traffari," and Daddy had thrown it away and screamed at her in the street. He had rules about eating. Nothing between meals, no sweets. Lisa had to be thin, although when Marilyn was around, Daddy would always let her have ice cream. If Lisa turned into a big fat disgusting pig, Daddy wouldn't love her anymore. Even so, she was always happy to see him, although she wished he didn't have to take her home. "Daddy!" she'd cry and run to him, shinnying up his thighs, covering his face with big kisses, making him catch his breath and laugh.

When Daddy was mad, it must have been like the end of the world was happening. Lisa wasn't ever supposed to do anything that would make him angry or disappointed in her. It was very dangerous because Daddy was so big and strong. When he and she would do wrestling together for fun, he'd throw her down and it would only hurt a little. But once when she was four, he *really* threw her down and she cried and cried. It happened when they were waiting for the elevator. He threw his arm up too, as if he were going to hit her just the way he hit Mommy. Mommy was there when it happened. Lisa looked up and saw her watching Daddy without saying anything.

Lisa forgot to be perfect. The worst thing she did was eating. It was funny about eating. How you knew you shouldn't eat and what would happen to you if you were caught, but even so, you just *had* to. You had to have something and you didn't even know what, so you couldn't help sneaking into the kitchen and eating stuff that you found. Daddy and Mommy called it stealing. "Somebody around here has been stealing food!" Daddy would roar, like Papa Bear, only angrier. "Was it you, Hedda?" No answer from Mommy. "Was it you, Lisa?" "Not me. I didn't do it, Daddy," she'd say because she was so scared. That would make it worse because she had told a lie, and you could never lie to Daddy or to anyone in your own family. Daddy said it was the most terrible thing Lisa could ever do. Even while she was saying the lie, Lisa would remember how terrible it was, but she couldn't stop herself in time.

Daddy never hit her for taking food, but he wouldn't let her have any dinner. She'd go to bed hungry, feeling sick with shame. Sometimes she'd throw up all over herself.

Marilyn Walton had been traveling a great deal, doing road shows of *Ma Rainey's Black Bottom* and *Porgy and Bess.* When she passed through New York in December 1986, she dropped in at Joel's house, deliberately making a surprise visit. There was not even the pretense of a civil welcome from Hedda. She seemed more resentful and afraid of Marilyn than ever. But Joel went into the bedroom and brought Mitchell out, to show him off. He'd been bragging about what a tough little guy he was, how strong his grip was already. Sure enough, when Joel put Mitchell in Marilyn's lap, the baby grabbed one of her fingers. But Mitchell was so dirty that Marilyn was appalled. His clothes, his blanket, his little body, were filthy. Marilyn took off everything the baby had on and asked for a clean bath towel so that she could give him a wash.

Hedda, Marilyn remembers, was furious. She snatched Mitchell away, as if she couldn't stand to see Marilyn touching him. Holding Mitchell in her arms, making a great show of caressing him, she glared at Marilyn and then at her five-year-old daughter.

"You're ugly," Hedda said to Lisa. "You're ugly."

That visit was the last time Marilyn saw Lisa Steinberg.

THERE IS actually a videotape in existence that shows Joel, Lisa, Hedda, and the baby welcoming in 1987 at a New Year's party in Queens given by one of Joel's clients. After Lisa's death, the client sold it to CBS. Mitchell has been cleaned up for the holiday festivities and is wearing a little red-and-white stretch suit; Hedda has heavy makeup on and is wearing a black dress with a big white puritanical collar in which she looks almost demure; Joel, in his dark suit, resembles a criminal lawyer. Joel, Hedda, and Mitchell, in fact, appear to be normal. This time it is Lisa who doesn't look right. The videotape shows her dancing to rock 'n' roll, wearing a floor-length party dress. She is dancing alone and much too frantically; she keeps glancing around with her big eyes and you know she is trying to see whether Joel is watching her. The dance is an offering to Daddy. There is a look on her face of terrible, adult strain.

During Easter of 1987, a friend of Joel's gave Lisa the small brown-and-white rabbit whose rescue from the sealed apartment would later be a matter of such concern for Joel and Hedda. The rabbit was tremendously important to Lisa, her first pet, a living creature much smaller and frailer than either Lisa or her baby brother. It knew her and seemed to love her and depended on her care. She told everyone she had this rabbit—Karen Snyder, the kids in her class, her best friend, Vanessa Wilhelm, who lived in a townhouse just up the block with her mother and father and two older sisters. She wanted Vanessa and fifteen-year-old Amanda Wilhelm to see her rabbit, but she didn't ask them to come upstairs with her, even though the two sisters often walked her home after she and Vanessa had been playing.

The rabbit lived in a cage in the living room, right near the playpen where they kept Mitchell. Hedda made much of it because all her life she had loved animals, almost as much as people. Mitchell was very taken with it, too, even though he was just a baby. Once he started to be able to walk, he would manage to climb over the plastic netting on the sides of the playpen and work his way into the cage, where he would visit the rabbit, sitting with it among its little hard dry turds. Hedda thought some of his exploits were very cute; later after she had lost Mitchell, his visits to the rabbit cage would be among her fondest recollections of him. Most of the time, though, because he was such an active and curious baby, eager to set out on his explorations of the apartment and the whole world, she had to keep him tied down. She had a collection of sashes which she used to attach him to his playpen and keep him from getting into trouble. When he'd pee on his sash and get it wet, Hedda would remove it, if she happened to notice its condition, and put it in the wash and tie him with a new one. Lisa had the rabbit; Hedda had the baby and the tanks of tropical fish.

Joel found the rabbit useful as an educational tool, a kind of object lesson for Lisa. Because he wanted her to understand that her rabbit could die, he took her to an Italian meat market on Bleecker Street so that Lisa could see the slaughtered rabbits, still with their brown fur coats on, hanging down from the hooks. That, he said, was death.

Once Lisa dropped her rabbit by accident and it broke its paw. Joel wouldn't take it to a veterinarian. He felt it was necessary for Lisa to see the rabbit limping. Every time it limped, she'd be reminded of how important it was to take good care of your pets.

Altogether, Lisa was getting away from the apartment and Hedda more and more. There was school and the long hours with Joel at Knickerbocker's and her visits to the Wilhelms and other friends. Mitchell didn't get very much fresh air. There were weeks when he spent day after day cooped up with Hedda. Joel still insisted that Hedda wash Lisa and get her looking nice for school, but now he started taking over the job of walking her to kindergarten in the mornings, even though he would much rather have been sleeping.

"Mommy's sick," Lisa announced to Karen Snyder one morning as she and Joel were going down with her in the elevator, even though Karen had certainly not asked her, "How is your mother?"

Joel, too, felt impelled to say something explanatory to Karen about Hedda. He ran into Karen one night as they were entering the building simultaneously and there was no way she could avoid being buttonholed by him. Hedda indeed, he told her, had become a very sick woman. She kept falling off chairs and hurting herself. Then he told Karen something even more bizarre: Hedda was a member of some cult and had been using Lisa to make pornography.

Despite the calls Karen Snyder had conscientiously made over the years on Hedda's behalf to the police and the Battered Women's Hotline, she had come to have very ambivalent feelings for Hedda Nussbaum. Certainly Hedda was being abused, but when you thought about the children, she was also an abuser. Karen had never seen bruises on the two kids, but she was positive they were being damaged psychologically. Never once in twelve years had Hedda asked to be helped. Once when another neighbor, Joan Bonano, directly confronted her and asked if there was anything wrong (that day Hedda had a face like "steak Tartare"), Hedda went absolutely "batshit."

Karen herself had a weird encounter with Hedda one freezing January night. It was around 1 A.M., the time Hedda usually did her shopping at Food Emporium. She seemed to be coming home from there, wearing her usual costume of tattered jeans and a thin, threadbare black jacket. She was staggering along with two cartons in her arms. When she set them down in the elevator, Karen saw that they were filled with containers of Häagen-Dazs ice cream, far more than could have fitted into a freezer. Hedda took off a glove and put her hand on Karen's face. "It's really cold out, isn't it?" she said. Karen couldn't imagine why she was bringing home so much ice cream. "Hedda," she asked, "are you having a party?" Hedda laughed. "Yeah. Something like that."

The apartment was filling up with stuff, becoming uncleanable and out of control. The living room was like a dumpster for electronic equipment and items Joel compulsively picked up from garbage cans on the street. Computer parts were scattered over the floor, tangled up in the piles of dirty clothes Hedda couldn't get around to washing; there was a bad smell from the garments soiled by the baby. Lisa ran around half-naked. A UPS man who frequently delivered packages for Joel later told the press that the door would always be answered by Lisa: "Almost every time I saw her she was in diapers."

Joel could have cleaned up, of course, but housecleaning and laundry and babycare were women's work. He complained to Hedda about the disorder, but since he contributed to it so much himself, it may have satisfied some need of his. Perhaps the way he and Hedda and the kids were living seemed somehow elemental, if he wanted to get mystical about it. It was as if they were a primitive tribe with their very own culture living smack in the middle of Manhattan. And Joel was both ruler and shaman. He let his hair grow longer and took showers less frequently.

His latest thing was vegetables—instead of being ripped off by the supermarket, you could buy "seconds" and cut off the parts that were brown or rotten; you could even find perfectly edible stuff in what Food Emporium threw away.

Maybe sometimes Joel thought about Charlotte; how shocked his mother would be if she knew the truth about how her son had chosen to live, as if he had become gradually able to discard all the rules she had imposed on him, undo all his upbringing bit by bit, the shirts and ties he'd had to wear to the dinner table, the room that had to be kept immaculate or else. He was still in control, though, perhaps more than ever; he could still do the trick of cleaning up his act for her when he had to present himself in Yonkers as the successful lawyer son. It was like the way he kept his closet despite the state of the rest of the apartment: all his suits, clean and pressed, ready on their hangers in case he needed them.

In May, just as the school year was starting to wind down, Mrs. Kassowitz noticed something about Elizabeth. The child was arriving quite late rather frequently; in the fall she had almost always been punctual. For several months her father had been bringing her to school, but now Mrs. Steinberg had taken over again. Mrs. Kassowitz stopped Hedda one morning when she saw her gray head with its blue bandanna appear in the doorway. She asked her if she could possibly try to bring Lisa in at 8:40; the social time in the first hour of school was very important to the children. Mrs. Steinberg mumbled something about oversleeping.

For a while the situation improved and Mr. Steinberg came every morning. In June, when Mrs. Steinberg again was escorting the child, there was another series of latenesses. The lateness hadn't really become excessive. Still, it troubled Mrs. Kassowitz a little, put her on the alert, although Lisa was still as happy and well-behaved as ever.

Then the term ended and the children and teachers scattered. It was summer.

JOEL HAD given Lisa a special job. She was a big girl now, going into first grade, so she was old enough to do this for him. Besides, she was the person he loved and trusted the most. He wanted her to keep an eye on Hedda, when he himself had to be busy with other important things. He explained to Lisa that her mother could "go off" at times. The way you could tell was when Hedda started staring. Lisa had to remember to avoid Hedda's stare, but she could also bring her back out of it by throwing some cold water in her face, although this might not always work.

This job was scary, but Lisa did her best. She tried not to miss seeing any of the stares. Even when she was on the couch watching "Sesame Street," even when she was very, very tired, she tried to remain vigilant.

Linda Wilhelm knew Lisa Steinberg better and longer than most people. In fact, she had first seen her at the beginning of her life, in the days when Hedda still looked attractive and would walk down Tenth Street with Lisa in her arms. One day Mrs. Wilhelm called out to Hedda from the stoop of her house, "Oh, let me see your baby!" Mrs. Wilhelm was enchanted by infants, and this little girl was special. She never really got to know Hedda, but of course she noticed the sudden alarming changes in her appearance in only a few years. Joel passed by much more frequently, loudly greeting people and locking eyes with them. Usually, he was accompanied by Lisa. Her own youngest daughter needed a playmate and Lisa seemed to need one, too. So one day when Lisa was four and a half, Linda Wilhelm stopped Joel and invited Lisa to play with Vanessa.

Now that it was summer, Lisa spent a great deal of time over at the Wilhelms'. It was the place she wanted most to be, and sometimes she grew tearful when it was time to go home. Mrs. Wilhelm let the two little friends have the run of the whole three-story brownstone. They could play in the basement or even in Mrs. Wilhelm's bedroom, which was the nicest place to watch TV. They drew pictures together, played board games, roller-skated, giggled a lot, and never fought. Lisa's visits kept getting longer. More and more frequently, she'd end up staying for dinner. Her father seemed to have an iron rule about Lisa phoning him just before she was taken home, and Lisa would become upset if she forgot to call him because she was having a good time. Mrs. Wilhelm could see the tremendous anxiety in her.

Linda Wilhelm didn't approve of the way Joel Steinberg treated his daughter, but of course she couldn't very well interfere. She'd noticed the way Lisa, who was certainly never at a loss for words, was beginning to clam up in the presence of her father, afraid to say anything unless he prompted her. Once Joel told Mrs. Wilhelm how the poor kid had dropped her rabbit. Lisa was standing right there, silent and miserable. Joel insisted that she tell Mrs. Wilhelm how she had injured her pet.

Add up these things Mrs. Wilhelm observed over the years, and the picture that begins to form isn't one most people would really want to know more about. If you knew, if you really *knew* unmistakably that your daughter's little friend was having a terrible life, then you'd feel you had to do something. But how could you know for sure? And what could you really do anyway? You couldn't take a kid away from her family.

Mrs. Wilhelm knew Lisa, her daughter's playmate, the way people in offices know each other, or teachers know their students, or neighbors who only meet in the elevator—everyone sealed in their own privacy, knowing and not knowing.

Joel Steinberg's hectic social life had declined considerably as his practice withered. During 1987, he made only four or five brief court appearances. But there were still vestiges of the old gregarious Joel, who enjoyed boisterously impressing others with the position he had arrived at in life. He still sailed the waters of Long Island Sound on the *Aqua Viva,* playing captain on weekends in and around Patchogue and Fire Island. Lisa always accompanied him. Joel also got a kick out of having various acquaintances aboard, totally and nervously dependent on his will and prowess—acquaintances were what he had these days rather than friends.

David Stiffler was one of those people Joel had been saying hello to on Tenth Street for years. He'd struck up his first conversation with Stiffler long ago, when he was walking Sascha. Stiffler was a Scientologist and had tried, unsuccessfully, to involve Joel in Scientology. He was a small man with a thin beard and an uneasy, shifting smile. Sometimes he disappeared from Tenth Street for long periods and went to South America or the Philippines to record traditional tribal music. "Where've you been, Dave?" Joel would ask, and Stiffler would say mysteriously, "Oh, various parts of the world."

One day in the middle of August, Stiffler was standing in front of his building only a few doors west of Joel's, when Joel walked by with Lisa, and out of the blue, invited Stiffler to go sailing with them the following weekend. The following day, Stiffler saw Lisa again when he was parking his car. She was playing out on the street with another little girl. The child walked right up to him and said with the poise of a grownup, "Hi. I'm Lisa, Joel's daughter." He had never even spoken to her before. He thought she was unusually poised, incredibly intelligent. She was also a little beauty.

The three-day boat trip was not an enjoyable experience for Stiffler. Only a year before, Lisa and Joel had seemed to Marilyn Walton "wonderful sailing pals." Stiffler did not find their relationship wonderful in any way. Of course, he didn't know that roughhousing was often the mode of Joel's interaction with Lisa. The roughhousing he saw seemed tinged with cruelty. He didn't like the way Joel ordered Lisa around or think a six-year-old should be required to steer a boat. The steering wheel seemed much too high for her. When something went wrong with a fishing rod she was using, Joel sent her down the hatch for a couple of hours. He kept screaming and yelling at her; once he even warned, "Lisa, I'm going to throw you overboard." Stiffler thought Lisa seemed afraid of her father.

When the boat docked at Fire Island, Joel let Lisa go swimming in rough surf that was high over her head. People on the beach were looking on, astounded. When Lisa came out of the water, Joel said coldly, "Have you had enough?" One of the onlookers remarked to him, "You don't spare the rod." Joel replied scornfully, "You're just a bunch of hippies."

A week later, there was another voyage. This time the passengers included Hedda and Mitchell and a Manhattan attorney. The attorney later told Maury Terry, "It was 'Twilight Zone' out there. I ended that day by saying I never wanted to go sailing

again." He recalled Hedda Nussbaum as "out of it, almost catatonic. Like, she wasn't even there." Lisa was evidently doing her
job that weekend as her mother's caretaker. "She knew that if
necessary she could throw some water in Hedda's face."

One night toward the end of August, a young Puerto Rican
bank secretary named Maria Marty met an enchanting little girl
in The Harlequin, a restaurant on Hudson Street in Greenwich
Village. Marty had come there with her "fiance," Gerard Black,
who was one of Joel Steinberg's few remaining clients. He was
meeting Steinberg and a bail bondsman named Andres Romero
at the restaurant. As the men discussed Black's case, the little
girl came over to keep Maria Marty company. "She was very,
very smart," Maria Marty later testified. "She spoke very well.
She knew everything she was saying about her fishes and the
names of her fishes." Maria Marty wondered how she'd gotten
the bruise on her face "around the cheekbone area going to the
eye."

On the Sunday of Labor Day weekend, Maria Marty saw the
little girl again, because Joel had issued one of his "let's go sailing to Fire Island" invitations to Gerard Black. He and Maria
brought their respective children along, his seven-year-old
daughter and her eleven-year-old son. Joel said Hedda was too
tired to join them; Mitchell had been left behind as well because
he was "hard to deal with." Lisa was wearing dirty shorts and a
sleeveless shirt, although it was cold when they were out on the
water; Maria thought she smelled of urine. No one had bothered
to comb Lisa's hair for a long time; a chunk of it was chopped off
in back. She saw bruises on the fronts of both of the child's legs
and on her upper arms, but the one she had noticed on her
cheek had faded; there was no trace of it in the snapshots taken
that day.

At one point, the child seemed hungry, so Maria Marty offered
her some food. Lisa said she couldn't take it without her father's
permission; she also needed his permission to use the bathroom
on the boat.

As Maria Marty remembered it, the whole day passed without
Lisa having anything to eat. Around eight o'clock that night, Lisa
asked Joel for a sandwich. He made her one, then threw it at her.
She was standing three feet away from him. Maria Marty thought
she looked "like when a kid is scared." Around nine o'clock, they
all drove back to the city together in the rain. Lisa was fast asleep
in the car. Maria Marty advised Joel to carry her into the house
and put a hood over her, but Joel said it wasn't necessary.

Lisa had spent the previous day with Gerard Black and his daughter. Black had taken the two little girls to the Bronx Zoo. Lisa had been better dressed, wearing a pink-and-white jump-suit and brown moccasins, but he, too, had noticed the hacked hair on the right side of her head. "They took hair from the other side of her head to cover it up—so the part was crooked . . . She said her baby brother cut her hair with scissors." Lisa seemed happy that day, excited about starting first grade. As always she played hard, with almost too much intensity, wanting to see all the animals, to gobble hotdogs and cotton candy and ice-cream cones, to try everything. She kept blowing the whistle Black had bought her and his own daughter joined in. Although she barely knew Gerard Black, she kept touching him. "She would run up and grab my hand and lead me to the animals. She wanted me to carry her a lot. I think she was looking for affection." Lisa made an immediate friend of Black's daughter; Black took a photo of them with their arms around each other, their whistles on long cords around their necks. Lisa grinned right at the camera just as little girls are supposed to do when they have their pictures taken, but his own daughter looked rather solemn. "Lisa said a lot of things to my daughter which I don't want to repeat," Black told the *Post*. "I think she was looking for someone to tell these things to."

What were the secrets of Lisa Steinberg's life by the age of six, the things that no one ever really saw? The bruises that began appearing that August carried no fingerprints. They showed up, then faded, because a child heals very quickly. The neighbors who considered themselves watchful never saw them at all. Those who saw them or thought they saw them were reluctant to probe into their origin. If Joel Steinberg threw his daughter a sandwich, he might have been just roughhousing with her; although to an outsider it may have seemed that he was treating her the way you'd treat a dog. Sal Friscia, a man who lived on Tenth Street but never really knew the Steinbergs, remembers seeing Hedda walking down the street wheeling Mitchell and yelling at Lisa, who was in tears. But who hasn't seen such scenes on the streets, mothers provoked to the point where they're out of control, dragging along a shamed, sobbing child? And then perhaps there were things that didn't show, that left no visible marks. Law-enforcement experts, however, will tell you that in households like the Steinbergs', the sexual abuse of children is almost a given.

Lisa must have wondered that summer what it was that she was doing wrong. What was it about her, now that she was six, that made Joel act as if he didn't love her anymore, even though he said he did. She seemed to be losing her specialness in her father's eyes, the favor she'd always been able to count on that protected her from the awful wrath that descended on Hedda. Perhaps it was very confusing that everyone else still thought she was special, the waiters and waitresses in Knickerbocker's, the friends of Daddy's she met who always bought her little presents. She'd cuddle up to her daddy's friends and say to them, "Aren't I your little girl, too?"

School began on September 14. Lisa was very late that day and the student teacher, Stacey Weiss, was surprised when she arrived escorted by her father. Usually the mothers brought the children. She saw Lisa's father for only a moment.

Perhaps the sense that there was something irregular in Lisa Steinberg's situation prompted her to take a good look at the child the following morning during story hour. Sylvia Haron, the homeroom teacher, was reading and the children were seated in a semicircle on the floor. Lisa was directly in front of Stacey Weiss, wearing a very short skirt and shirt that she had obviously outgrown. The shirt crept up on her when she sat down and Stacey Weiss saw a large purple bruise on her lower back; there were many other bruises of various colors on her bare thighs and calves.

Stacey Weiss was in her senior year at Yeshiva University, and this was the first classroom she had worked in. She didn't quite know what to do about Lisa. She consulted her student-teacher adviser that afternoon, and the next day had a word with Mrs. Haron.

From the start, there was friction in Stacey Weiss's relationship with Sylvia Haron. Mrs. Haron, a woman with a rather childlike manner but an excellent reputation, had been teaching for twenty years. She had problems in delegating responsibility, and Stacey Weiss's eagerness to handle more and more by herself seemed to offend her; perhaps she felt a little threatened by the earnest and enthusiastic young woman. Weiss's report to her about Lisa may have smacked of overzealousness. In the past, Haron herself had taken immediate action in instances where she had suspected child abuse. Lisa Steinberg just did not worry her, although after a while, "I watched her, I watched her." As Haron testified in a Board of Education hearing, Lisa's behavior indicated only that she was going to be an outstanding student. "She wanted to be monitor, wanted to read her stories, wanted to write, she was really just the kind of kid you wanted to have in your class."

Oddly enough, Mrs. Haron later could not recall Stacey Weiss's ever saying anything to her about those bruises she had seen on the second day of school. In one early October talk about Lisa, she did find Weiss's observations "helpful," but their topic of conversation was merely Lisa's interactions with other students—the kind of exchange they'd have about any other kid. By then however, Mrs. Haron herself had seen some yellowish gray marks on Lisa's back when Lisa "stretched from her desk to the little boy's desk across from her and her shirt went up in back . . . I asked her what happened? How did you get those? And absolutely true-faced, eye to eye, without a moment's hesitation, the reply was, as well as I can recollect, 'My brother did that.' " Later in the hearing, Mrs. Haron added, "I really thought at the time her brother just took something, a toy or whatever and just like . . ."

"No, there was nothing, there was nothing," she insisted after the UFT attorney asked her whether Lisa had seemed at all hesitant or defensive. "It was open-faced, it was given to me full-faced. It was given to me clear-eyed, there was no hesitation, there was no withdrawal. . . . There was no shame." During the brief conversation she had with Lisa, Mrs. Haron did not think to ask her how old her brother was.

As the weeks of the fall term went by, Lisa Steinberg kept arriving late or missing school. (There were forty schooldays between September 14 and November 2; she was there for only twenty-two of them.) This was something measurable and it did not escape Mrs. Haron's notice, though again, it did not inspire alarm—even coupled with the child's consistently unkempt appearance and those marks on her body.

Finally, in mid-October, Mrs. Haron asked Lisa why she had been absent so frequently, and "her reply was that they woke up too late to come to school." "You come here even if you're late," Mrs. Haron told Lisa, and imparted the same message to Joel when he arrived at three to pick her up. "He kind of scolded her like it was her fault, that was the message that came across to me." About a week later, Hedda Nussbaum sent Mrs. Haron a note, explaining that for the past few weeks they had been rearranging their schedule. That was enough to satisfy the teacher. She saw no need to bring the matter up with the school aide, who might then have talked to the guidance counselor.

Perhaps Hedda had not forgotten the procedures used in public schools, and she could still write a good letter, employing convincing, businesslike language. That part of her, the secretary, the editor, still functioned, the only old persona she hadn't quite abandoned. The word *schedule,* however, was an anachronism, a joke; it hardly described the clockless way they were living that fall with their days and nights running together.

Some time in September, a cocaine-dealer friend of theirs had left a kilo of cocaine with them for "safekeeping." (It remained in their possession until October 31.) Joel, of course, was not a man who lived by the honor system, and Hedda herself could hardly resist her craving for the precious white powder; never had they enjoyed such a seemingly endless supply.

They began freebasing several times a week. By October, they were smoking cocaine nightly, staying up on it together, hardly getting any sleep, though Joel managed to sleep more than Hedda; perhaps that was why he functioned better than she did. And of course the beatings were taking their toll; Hedda wasn't as young and resilient as she used to be. When she wasn't high, the sores on her legs (inflicted, she said later claimed, by Joel's "magic broomstick") were quite painful.

Pleasing Joel Steinberg was growing more difficult all the time. He was even stricter about controlling Hedda's intake of food than he was about Lisa's, and often now, he would not permit Hedda to sleep with him. She would take a pillow and a thin blanket and lie down on the floor next to the bed. When he was angry with her, there would be no blanket, no food.

In contrast, Lisa's relationship with Joel may have seemed enviable. Hedda had stopped bathing her, giving her shampoos, or washing her clothes, and she no longer looked quite so cute and presentable. Still, this did not deter Joel from taking her with him everywhere he went. While Hedda had to stay at home, Lisa would be Joel's little date. Oddly enough, even the way he was punishing her now was something like the way he treated Hedda. Perhaps when Lisa was just a few years older—old enough to be penetrated sexually—Joel would decide he had no further use for Hedda, and his charade of showing her the door would become real. The game of mutual debasement they had been playing for so many years no doubt had immutable rules on both sides. Perhaps for Hedda the most sacred one had been that Joel could do anything to Hedda, as long as she remained in first place.

Ira London asked Hedda how she felt in 1987, when Joel and Lisa were going out together so much.

"I wished that I could go, too," she answered plaintively.

"Did you resent it?"

"No, I didn't resent—well, I—no, I didn't resent it. I just wished that I could come along."

Only a saint or a martyr could have felt such lack of rancor, so Ira London's next question was, "Why didn't you resent it, Miss Nussbaum?"

"Excuse me?"

"Why didn't you resent that you couldn't go?"

"Well, I don't know if it's a matter of definition. I was not happy that I couldn't go."

"Were you angry?"

"No," Hedda said, faltering a little, "I—" Then she recited the response she had been taught to give to questions of that sort: "One of the things I have discovered at Four Winds is that I had a problem getting angry and that's one of the things that Four Winds has taught me to be able to do, is to feel anger."

Perhaps the question of Hedda Nussbaum's capacity for anger had come to occupy a larger and larger place in Joel Steinberg's thoughts. He had reduced her to a ragged shred of her former self, stripped so much away from her, that the anger she had never directed at him might very well be mounting up in her now, ready to break through, to visit some awful retribution upon him. The secret of Hedda's anger was the one thing she had left, the one thing he could not seem to get at—it was their final erotic connection.

Perhaps that was why Hedda's habit of staring came to seem increasingly ominous and threatening. He kept catching her at it all the time now, and it was spreading to the children. Lisa, even Mitchell, had begun to stare at him. Clearly, Steinberg now feared the power of the Greens could no longer be contained. The Greens were still "getting through" to Hedda; through Hedda, they were getting to the kids. Once when Joel was with Hedda in the bedroom and Mitchell was crying in his playpen, the power of Hedda's stare was enough to put Mitchell to sleep even though he was in another part of the house. Hedda had managed to program the baby! As for Lisa—of course she had been affected by the Greens ever since the time she spent with them in 1983; it was only now that he realized to what extent. Lisa's stares upset him tremendously. He would slap her cheeks and tell her to blink to bring her out of her dangerous trances. It was more difficult, of course, to communicate with Mitchell.

Joel tried to keep Lisa separated from Hedda as much as possible. He began letting her spend most of her afternoons after school at the Wilhelms'; by October, she visited them every weekday and ate dinner with them two or three nights a week. Amanda Wilhelm had the feeling her sister's little friend was feeling very scared. Her clothes weren't right anymore—they were the ones she used to wear, but now they were very dirty and much too small, and she had that weird haircut with a big piece of hair just missing.

Penina Spiegel, a free-lance writer who lived in the Village, met Joel Steinberg and Lisa that fall and at first was rather charmed by the father-daughter relationship—the tall, dark, intense man captivated by his delightful little girl. It made Joel Steinberg attractive. She was thinking of having him represent her in a real-estate matter, and they had arranged to meet in Knickerbocker's. All the young waitresses there seemed to be old friends of Lisa's. Penina Speigel was a single woman, and Joel Steinberg was in a flirtatious mood. "I'm getting tired of the editor," he confided to her. That day, as he often did, he put Lisa through her paces. To show off her knowledge of art, he had the child tell Penina Spiegel about Van Gogh's suicide. Then he made Lisa talk about Dawn. As Lisa very haltingly related how Dawn had died in the Christmas tree fire, Penina Spiegel began to feel queasy. Joel explained that he had given Lisa a pair of Dawn's gloves.

There was a basket of breadsticks on the table. When they were leaving, Lisa wanted to take some to give to Mitchell. Joel wouldn't let her. As he put it, he didn't want Penina Spiegel thinking they had nothing to eat at home.

The predawn hours of October 6 were sleepless ones for Karen Snyder because of the sounds coming from the Steinberg apartment through the wall that separated her own bedroom from theirs. In recent months, there had been far less noise than there had been ten years ago. But tonight Joel was unmistakably beating Hedda, and Karen worried that the violence might spread to the children. She made what turned out to be her last anonymous call of complaint—this one to the Sixth Precinct. For years she'd been operating on the assumption that somewhere—perhaps in some giant central computer—there was a file on the Steinbergs, a cumulative record of all the calls she and others had made to the police and Special Services for Children and reports on the observations of the various BCW investigators who had visited apartment 3W over the years. Someday all this information might prove useful, enabling the authorities to remove the two children from the Steinbergs' care. In fact, there was no Steinberg file, just as there was no cumulative record of any household in New York State where child abuse was suspected but never proven over a long period of time. If an allegation was deemed unfounded, it was automatically stricken from the records of the state's central register. Each subsequent complaint was treated like the first one that had ever been made.

On this occasion, the Sixth Precinct sent over Police Officer Glen Iannato and his partner, whom Karen Snyder let into the building around 8 A.M., directing them to the door of apartment 3W. When Iannato knocked, a woman's voice called out that everything was okay; there was no need for any assistance from the police. "So please go away!" The man in there gave him the same message. After some more insistent knocking, the door opened about four inches, and the woman again stated that everything was okay and shut the door in Iannato's face. He resumed his knocking because he wanted to get a look at her. When the door opened a little, he put his foot in the crack. "Okay, just give me time to get dressed," the woman said, disappearing as Iannato and his partner entered the apartment.

When Iannato heard a metallic click, his hand went to the holster of his revolver. But then he saw a cigarette glowing in the dark. "Did you just light that?" he asked Steinberg. Steinberg showed him a gold Zippo lighter. He was on his high horse, he knew his rights, he was a criminal lawyer. He told them they'd better leave, but Iannato still had to see the woman. He called to her to come out and show herself.

It was very cluttered in the living room. Books and broken objects seemed to be piled up, and there was the smell of dust and urine. A young girl was huddled on a couch; a little boy was in a playpen.

"You've overstepped your bounds," Joel Steinberg said indignantly.

It was about fifteen minutes before Mrs. Steinberg came out of the bedroom wearing a housecoat and explained that she and her

husband had just been having an argument. Iannato and his partner saw a broken nose, swollen lips. The woman didn't want any
medical treatment, and she certainly didn't want to press charges
against her husband, so they handed her some pamphlets on
battered women and left.

When he returned to the precinct, Iannato filled out the standard forms, including one that indicated there had been a need
for medical attention. Oddly enough, despite the condition of the
apartment, despite the condition of the woman, Iannato made no
attempt to examine the two children. Certainly he did not find it
necessary to file a report with the SSC, since there was no established coordination between city agencies in cases where child
abuse was suspected.

Lisa had a classmate whom she called "my boyfriend." She had
a more ambivalent relationship with a little girl named Jamie,
which culminated in a schoolyard fight one day in October. "I het
her. She het me," Lisa wrote in a little story for Mrs. Haron,
illustrated with stick figures of round-faced girls hitting each
other. Other girls she drew in school invariably held out their
arms and smiled; they had freckles on their faces just like Lisa.
They were the kinds of pictures an expert might say had been
drawn by a happy, "normal" child.

Mrs. Haron had her first-graders do a lot of writing. She never
assigned them topics. They could make up stories or write about
things that had really happened to them, whatever they wished.
In one of Lisa's stories, a girl named Elizabeth was in a ballet
show. Lisa told Mrs. Haron that this was only make-believe. Other
stories were more true to life: Elizabeth sailed with Daddy to Fire
Island, Elizabeth's mother wrote books. One story was particularly memorable: "It was a wonderful story about my brother is
a mess, there is one that I could remember," Mrs. Haron said at
the Board of Education hearing. The brother climbed into the
rabbit cage and woke up his sister by pulling her hair. The messy
brother was clearly and incontrovertibly a baby; Lisa had even
drawn Mitchell's tether. But somehow the implications of all this
did not register with Mrs. Haron, even though she read the story
on October 16, only a week or so after Lisa had told her how she'd
gotten her bruises.

A ten-year-old fifth-grader was more perceptive than the P.S. 41
teachers. She did not think Elizabeth Steinberg was so happy.

She had first become acquainted with her at Greenwich House, where she, too, had studied ballet. Now, whenever she saw Lisa in the schoolyard, she had the feeling something had changed. Lisa looked frightened. Maybe she was just a little scared of the rowdy older kids. The fifth-grader made it her business to look out for Lisa; she tried to take her under her wing a little during recess.

THE CLOTHES Lisa wore to school the last weeks of her life were overalls and long-sleeved cotton-knit shirts that covered up her thin arms and legs. Hedda testified that Joel had ruled that Lisa wear such clothing even on hot days. Joel had also taught her to blame Mitchell.

One mark could not be covered up—the black eye Lisa came to school with on Tuesday, October 20, the black eye Mrs. Haron later claimed she never saw at all.

Stacey Weiss remembered it differently. At the Steinberg trial, she testified that when she and Mrs. Haron walked into the room that morning, "she saw it as much as I did." In fact, according to Stacey Weiss, Mrs. Haron said something out loud, "not to me, but to the students"—perhaps to the effect that Elizabeth must have hurt herself. Or was this her brother's doing also?

Later that day, Stacey Weiss says, she told Mrs. Haron that Mitchell was one and a half. Mrs. Haron apparently wasn't listening. Subsequently, when she decided to have a little chat with Lisa about cleanliness and neatness, because these days she "did not appear like the best kept girl in town," Mrs. Haron felt no skepticism when Lisa said that Mitchell Steinberg had cut the big clump out of her hair. How could a one-and-a-half-year-old boy have managed to use a pair of scissors?

The black eye had faded a bit but was still quite noticeable on Thursday when two strangers visited the class—Stuart Gross, a free-lance photographer, and a woman who was editing a brochure for Scholastic Books that would be illustrated with photos of P.S. 41 children. As Stuart Gross walked in with his camera, he took a few quick shots of the back of the room. Three of the kids turned around immediately and stared at him. One of them was Lisa, who raised herself in her seat with an expression of incandescent excitement, as if a light had gone on inside her flashing a signal to Gross: "Notice *me!*"

She was a wonderful-looking little girl, just the kind of child Gross would normally have selected as one of his models. But she looked terribly rumpled up and dirty, compared to the other kids; a big clump of hair was sticking up stiffly in the back of her head. It was an unseasonably warm day, so she had rolled up the sleeves of her turtleneck; even from across the room, Gross could see the bruises on her arms; the worst mark, though, was the red welt under one eye. Both Gross and his editor were convinced they were looking at a battered child. Obviously her teacher must have known all about the child's situation—anyone could see what it was—so Gross and the editor felt no need to bring their observations to Mrs. Haron's attention. The child's mother had actually sent her to school in that condition with a release allowing her to be photographed.

Gross picked out two more acceptable-looking first-graders and started working with them. The battered child sat herself near them, off to one side, intently watching the whole process. It seemed terribly important to her to make Gross choose her; of course she couldn't have understood why he wasn't asking her to pose. "Take me," she called out to him. "Take my picture. Take a picture of me and my boyfriend."

Finally, the little girl appointed herself his assistant. In a surprisingly mature way, she told the other children what to do, as if she had had a lot of previous experience before the camera.

Gross could no longer say no to her. Despite his misgivings, he asked her to sit next to a black classmate and shot the two of them studying reading materials together. Lisa is appropriately serious in these pictures, pointing out something on the page like a little teacher. Gross flooded both kids with light so her bruises wouldn't show, had Lisa turn a little to minimize the red welt. He used some black-and-white film that didn't pick up red.

Ten days later, though, when he heard a child had died, he knew which one it was right away.

A new client had fallen Joel's way that week. Charles Scannapieco had phoned him on October 20 from Clearwater, Florida, on the recommendation of a friend whom Joel had represented in a divorce and a suit resulting from a yachting accident. Scannapieco's problems were graver; he had been summoned back to New York for a hearing in Albany that week; he was being charged with one count of conspiracy; and fifteen counts of possession and intent to distribute cocaine.

In upstate New York, the fall foliage was at its peak. That weekend Joel was going to give Lisa a chance to see it. The Albany trip was also going to provide her with another educational opportunity—a rare chance to see Daddy perform in court before a judge.

When he picked her up at P.S. 41 on Friday afternoon, they went immediately to a bank on University Place and waited for Scannapieco outside it. Joel had told his new client it would be easy to recognize him because he would be with a little girl. When Scannapieco showed up, the three of them went across the street to Knickerbocker's, where Joel ate a steak. He also ordered soup, pouring some into a wineglass for Lisa, who also ate a bit of bread. Then they went on to another café, where Joel told Scannapieco to wait while he and his daughter went back to his "office." He had to pick up clothes for the two of them, and some law books. They were going to need lots of books, he said. Scannapieco cooled his heels in the café for three hours, calling Steinberg's office from time to time to find out what was taking him so long. When Joel and the child returned around seven thirty, they all went uptown to rent a car. A number of people stood on line at Hertz, but Joel flashed a card and pushed them out of the way. Scannapieco had arrived a day later than expected, so Joel had had to reschedule his arraignment for the following morning, a Saturday. They were going to spend the night at Scannapieco's house in Lake Katrine, just outside Kingston.

It was a tense two-hour drive. Scannapieco didn't care much for the way Joel handled the car. He insisted on keeping the windows open. Lisa was wearing only a thin windbreaker. She curled up in the backseat, her arms wrapped around herself. Scannapieco kept telling Steinberg to put on the heat, but Steinberg liked fresh air. Finally, Scannapieco pulled Lisa onto the front seat and sat her in his lap. She put her head against his chest, and he wrapped his jacket around her. Joel was talking to his six-year-old daughter about oil wells of all things, some oil wells he owned in Texas. It wasn't long before she dozed off.

When Steinberg noticed that the child had fallen asleep, he did something "just out of a clear blue sky" that shocked Scannapieco. Steinberg reached over and struck her with the back of his hand on the right side of the forehead. When he described the blow at the trial, Scannapieco hit the judge's desk, the heavy ring on his finger making a sharp sound that rang out in the courtroom like the report of a gun. It was one of the most dramatic moments in the trial. You could see the jurors start in their seats. "The blow was pretty forceful," Scannapieco said. "It would bring tears to your eyes on anyone here. She didn't cry—it was amazing. She didn't make any reaction whatsoever."

The child, of course, was wide awake after that. Joel didn't check to see if he had hurt her. In fact, he didn't even seem angry. "Lisa, what's causing this?" he asked her. She said she didn't know. Joel told her she had to stop staring. "Blink and smile, Lisa," he commanded her. "Blink and smile."

"She did it very well," Scannapieco remembered. "She had done it before."

He had asked Steinberg, "What's all this about?" and was told, "I'll explain it to you later."

"I think you'd better tell it to me now."

Steinberg's daughter had a weird medical problem. Since Lisa was awake, she, too, must have listened as her daddy told her new friend what was wrong with her. Lisa had a way of scaring herself—she had the ability to put herself into another world. When this happened, her breathing and heartbeat would slow down and her legs would turn blue from lack of circulation. She would enter a state resembling a coma and refuse to wake up. Several years ago he had to hospitalize her in Middletown. That was why he wanted Lisa to stay awake for the rest of the ride, to keep blinking.

When Lisa first climbed into his lap, Scannapieco had not noticed any staring, although she did seem to be gazing out of the window, looking at the reflections. Not knowing whether to believe Steinberg or not, Scannapieco said he would keep Lisa awake by telling her stories. For the rest of the ride, he told her stories and she told him some.

It was ten fifteen by the time they arrived at Scannapieco's scantily furnished house. The only bed was Scannapieco's king-size waterbed, which he offered to Joel. Lisa jumped up and down on it as if it were a trampoline. Scannapieco was going to sleep on the couch in the living room. Steinberg said, "Lisa can sleep on the floor there with you." Scannapieco made her a makeshift bed of quilts and pillows on the wall-to-wall carpeting ("I've slept on worse," he told the court) and presented her with two Cabbage Patch dolls. He gave her one of his T-shirts to wear as a nightgown. Although Steinberg had brought along a whole garment bag of clothing for himself, the child didn't even have her own toothbrush or a comb.

When the three of them woke up the next morning, Scannapieco and Steinberg took showers, but Lisa did not. She was wearing a pair of dirty-looking cotton shorts and long wool leg warmers.

Scannapieco was a loser—he even looked the part, a ferret-faced young man with a thin black mustache and oily black hair. At the time that he testified, he was out on bail pending his trial; a letter on his behalf to the effect that he had cooperated with the Manhattan district attorney's office had been promised him. In other words, his testimony was not an entirely altruistic act, although he said he had come to court for Lisa: "She spent time with me. As a good citizen, I seen what I seen. That's why I'm here." One did have the feeling, though, that there was some truth to these protestations. Despite Scannapieco's history as a drug addict, despite his alleged activities as a dealer, despite the fact that he owed his mother and sister thousands of dollars—what did come through was that the man had some real protective feeling for children. He realized that Lisa Steinberg was suffering; he treated her kindly. In that sense, he seemed "normal"—he had a basic kind of sanity, lacking in Joel Steinberg or Hedda Nussbaum.

Two years earlier, in better times, Charles Scannapieco had been able to purchase a 40 percent share of the Catskill Diner, which he had recently transferred over to his sister Deborah Koncelik. She ran the place, supervising the waitresses and the kitchen staff and keeping the books. She was a hard-headed, competent young woman, far better able to deal with the world than were her brother or her husband, Glen, a rather spaced-out, hippyish man who worked for a sheet-metal company owned by Scannapieco's partners in the diner.

Deborah Koncelik seemed to be in charge of her brother's affairs. She herself had talked to Steinberg on the phone, first going through Hedda, who made her feel "I didn't reach a lawyer's office . . . She dragged her words like I just woke her up."

Around nine thirty on Saturday morning, she met Steinberg in person. He was wearing a jacket that she considered shabby and not very neat. She felt great disapproval of the way Lisa was dressed because the temperature was forty-five degrees. She didn't look as though anyone took care of her, and she was such a nice, smart little girl. Deborah Koncelik sat Lisa down in a booth and served her some cereal. During the ride to the Albany courthouse she tackled Lisa's matted hair with the pick she used on her own long black frizzy locks. She noticed a purplish bruise above one eye. How did you get that? she asked Lisa. My brother did it, was the immediate answer. From the passenger seat in front, Joel made a comment about what a tough little guy Mitchell was; Mitchell was always doing things like that.

After they reached the courthouse, it was a couple of hours before Steinberg and Scannapieco stood before the judge. "Gee, what a small courtroom," Lisa said to Deborah Koncelik. Joel had arranged for Scannapieco to surrender to the authorities that day, and was confident he would be immediately signed out on his personal recognizance. But the fact that Scannapieco was supposed to have shown up in court the day before did not go down well with the judge. Nor did Steinberg's rambling, ineffectual arguments. Suddenly Lisa, who had sat beside Deborah Koncelik very quietly and patiently, only once whispering that she would like to sit in her lap, saw the nice man who had given her the Cabbage Patch doll she was holding led away by court officers. The judge set Scannapieco's bail at one hundred thousand dollars.

After the hearing, Lisa walked with a furious Deborah Koncelik and her father to a building two blocks away, where Scannapieco had been taken for processing. They waited in a small anteroom for forty-five minutes. For a while, Lisa played with her new doll. Then she climbed up on a shelf just below a high window and stared at the secretaries. After a few minutes she wanted to get down from there. Deborah stood up to help her, but Joel said, "Don't do that. She's a big girl." The shelf was a little too high for Lisa to manage; when she jumped from it, she fell on her knees.

The three of them went back to the Catskill Diner for lunch, then drove to Deborah Koncelik's, where they relaxed for a couple of hours. Joel had bought some pretzels and potato chips. Once he threw some pretzels over to Lisa.

Both Deborah and her husband Glen found Joel Steinberg very "hyper" that day. He kept stopping halfway through sentences and switching to new topics; all a listener could do was periodically say yes or uh. He seemed unable to sit down for more than a few minutes.

Glen took Joel and Lisa for a walk around his acreage. She was very impressed that he and Deborah seemed to have so many cats; she wanted to know exactly how many there were. Then she asked to see Glen's three Dobermans, which he allowed her to pet.

Joel asked Glen if Lisa could take an abandoned wasp's nest back to New York with her for her nature class. When Lisa wanted to climb up on a fieldstone wall, Joel tested it with his foot and said it wasn't secure enough. Shortly after that, Lisa said, "Pick me up, Daddy!" When Joel did so, he held her at arm's length about three feet above the ground. He took a few steps, then, without warning her, just opened his hands and let her drop. The child's feet buckled under her and she fell on her back. Joel walked away.

"Daddy, why did you do that?" she called after him. "Daddy, why did you do that?" Another child would have been crying.

"You were too heavy," Joel Steinberg said, and kept on walking.

On Saturday night, a heavyset, plain-faced woman named Sharon Listing was collecting tolls in a southbound lane of the Woodbury Toll Plaza on the New York State Thruway. Sharon Listing enlivened the hours in her four-by-ten, fluorescent-lit booth by making rapid-fire assessments of the travelers she saw through her small window, taking mental snapshots of them, trying to imagine their lives as she handed them their tickets and change. Most of her transactions were conducted in silence. She was a woman who, in an embarrassed and humble way, believed in the power of her intuition—she had a mind that was much less empirical than, say, Sylvia Haron's, and a willingness to take chances.

Around eight twenty, Joel Steinberg's rented red car drove into her lane. "Since it was a slow night," Sharon Listing later explained in court, "you get to looking around." Joel Steinberg handed her the ticket he'd gotten in Albany and asked how much he had to pay. When she told him, he said, "Just a second," and stuck his hand in his pocket. His dark, disquieting eyes passed over her face. Suddenly, he undid his seat belt, opened the car door, and got out. He stood there in the lane, his eyes darting around as he searched his pockets for his wallet. Cars were lining up behind him.

Since the interior light was on in his car, Sharon Listing made it her business to peer inside it. "I'm nosy," she told the court candidly. "I saw a small child sitting on the front seat. I looked to her face. I looked to her eyes. She looked like she had just got done crying. I glanced up to her forehead and saw a small bruise the size of a quarter." The child made what Sharon Listing thought was a "little sobbing motion as if she was trying to catch her breath."

After Steinberg handed Sharon Listing the toll and started getting back into the car, she took another look at the child and wrote down the number on the license plate.

Of all the people whose lives had crossed Lisa Steinberg's, Sharon Listing was one of the remarkably few who took on any real responsibility for her. She tried to do more for the child she saw for only three or four minutes than William and Emma Nussbaum, Judy Leibman, the P.S. 41 teachers, or the mothers of the playmates Lisa visited.

Something in Steinberg's manner that even later she couldn't quite articulate had alerted Sharon Listing. "Weird," was what she called Joel Steinberg. He seemed far too nervous for someone who was just looking for his money. Didn't most businessmen know where their wallets were? she said in the courtroom rather naïvely. "It could be woman's intuition. The whole thing—it gave me an uncomfortable feeling." Mistakenly, she thought she was seeing a kidnapping. "The colors of the child and the man didn't match. She was fair-skinned and he was darker." Hardly a sound basis for the judgment she made. Actually, though, Lisa Steinberg had been kidnapped—six and a half years before Sharon Listing set eyes on her.

As soon as Joel Steinberg's car pulled away, Sharon Listing closed up her booth and made a call to Mary Jane Litz, her supervisor at the tollhouse. She was shaking all over as she told Litz she had just seen a car going through with a guy acting weird. There was a little girl in the car, sobbing, with welts on her face. Mary Jane Litz and another toll worker, Dana Trapoto, ran over to Listing's booth, then walked her back to the tollhouse. There Dana Trapoto called State Trooper Louis Romano, a police dispatcher in Tarrytown, and reported the possible abduction of a little girl. When she heard Trapoto say *abduction,* Sharon Listing cried, "Oh my God! That's dramatic!" already a little worried that she had exaggerated what she had seen.

Later that night, Sharon Listing learned that she had been all wrong and was made to feel just the kind of mortification that those who consider reporting the suspected abuse of a child often fear they risk. The "hysteria" that she had communicated to the other two women did not reflect well on any of them. They had put Trooper Romano to a great deal of trouble for no reason. All Listing had seen was just a guy driving home with his daughter; she should never have had the temerity to act upon what was nothing more than an "inner feeling." All she and Litz and Trapoto could do was write a collective letter of apology to Trooper Romano; Listing took most of the flak and signed her name first.

*

It's possible that when Joel Steinberg suddenly climbed out of his car in the Woodbury Toll Plaza, he was indeed feeling unnerved. When he got home that night, he told Hedda that Lisa had thought the toll collector at Woodbury looked just like Shayna Green. In fact, there is some resemblance between the two women, with their broad faces, small eyes, and thin lips. Perhaps it was Joel who thought he was seeing Shayna, when he first saw Listing through her window. But what would Shayna Green be doing in a tollbooth on the Thruway? Perhaps he stepped out of the car in order to reassure himself, to recover a little from the first jolt of fear.

That night he may also have been feeling shaken by his poor performance in court and by the low opinion of his efforts that Deborah Koncelik may have expressed. Perhaps he had been treating Lisa particularly harshly because she had witnessed his humiliation. In a conversation with his attorney Adrian DiLuzio months later, he admitted that Lisa actually had been crying just as they reached the tollbooth. Lisa had been misbehaving and carrying on in the car. Finally, he asked her, "Lisa, what am I supposed to do with you?"

The answer Steinberg claimed the child gave him is totally chilling. "You're supposed to hit me," is what she allegedly said. It has the ring of truth, blasting much of the hope one may have had that Lisa would have proved resilient had she lived. Her response to Joel indicates how much she had incorporated his notions of reality, and how already she was learning to do what Hedda did—split parts of herself off.

If Joel Steinberg was feeling persecuted as he drove back to New York, all his worst fears must have been confirmed when Trooper Thomas Dooley stopped him as he reached the toll barrier at the end of the Tappan Zee Bridge. Dooley walked up to Steinberg's car and asked him to identify himself by showing his license and registration. The first thing Steinberg handed Dooley was his attorney's pass for New York State prisons. He told the trooper he was coming from an arraignment before a magistrate in Albany, and that he had more documentation in the trunk. Dooley informed him that he was suspected of having abducted and beaten the child who was sitting next to him. Joel must have felt terror. The charges were uncomfortably close to the truth, and the informant had had Shayna Green's face.

"I'm traveling with my daughter," he told Dooley, not blustering indignantly the way he had when the officers from the Sixth Precinct gained admittance to his apartment on October 6. When he was really frightened, Joel Steinberg always became as mild as a lamb. His ability to manufacture alibis did not desert him on this occasion. He gave Dooley a stripped-down version of the story he had told Scannapieco, omitting the trance and coma angles. His daughter had muscle problems, and had had a fall. At times her jaw and face would lock up. Just as they reached Woodbury, he had been massaging her neck and back to calm her down.

Lisa sat very still in the front seat with the seat belt around her. Perhaps she believed all these stories her father was telling people about her; something was very wrong with her, something that made her terribly different from other children. *Abduct* was probably beyond her vocabulary, but certainly she knew what a policeman was. For the second time in two weeks she was seeing her daddy interrogated by the police. Her daddy had always warned her that if she didn't follow his rules, people might take her away from him. Now this policeman wanted to put him in jail because the fat woman had seen her crying.

Two other troopers and a sergeant also gathered around Steinberg's car. Dooley conferred with Sergeant Caulfield and they decided to take Steinberg and his alleged daughter to the toll-house for further questioning. Caulfield also heard from Steinberg about his child's "nervous disorder." He decided to walk with her and talk with her himself. "Is everything all right, little girl?" "Fine," Lisa assured him. "Okay."

Caulfield examined her under the fluorescent lights in the toll-house. The kid had badly matted hair, but that was about it. He saw no bruises on her face; he didn't ask her to pull down the leg warmers she wore. Meanwhile Mr. Steinberg continued to be most cooperative. Caulfield took some Polaroid shots of the rumpled little girl just for purposes of identification. Over a year later, when he was shown the photos in court, he did notice, for the first time, a discoloration on the left side of her forehead. So did Trooper Noel Nelson.

Trooper Nelson thought the little girl seemed happy that night; "in a festive mood" as he put it in court. Certainly it did not occur to him to wonder why a six-year-old would appear to be feeling festive when it may have seemed to her that her father was under arrest. Lisa was acting that night, performing well, as flawlessly as she ever had. When Nelson told her why she and her father were being detained, she recited Joel's alibi almost verbatim. She had this nerve problem in her back and neck. It had hurt a lot, so she had cried. Her daddy had to massage her to calm her down.

The final proof that Sharon Listing had been totally out of line came when Joel was asked for his phone number so that Lisa could call her mother, and Joel said she could dial it herself. She spoke to Hedda for a moment or two, then Dooley got on the phone to explain the situation. Hedda sounded quite calm, he thought. When he told Hedda what Joel had said about Lisa's muscle problem, Hedda said, "That's correct."

Despite Hedda's even tone, she may have spent the day feeling bitterly slighted because Joel was once again away for the weekend with Lisa. When Dooley said, "I have your daughter," she felt very scared. Had something happened to Joel? She felt vastly relieved when Dooley said Lisa's father was with her.

On the way home, Joel stopped in Yonkers for a brief visit with Charlotte. The desire to see his mother seems to have come over him while he was being questioned in the tollhouse. Perhaps he still felt the old childish impulse to run to her when he was in trouble, not that she had ever given him much comfort. But even in her eighties she was formidable, stronger and tougher than he was.

Evidently he didn't tell Charlotte what had happened on the Thruway. As always, she was delighted to see Lisa. Later she said she didn't see one mark on the child.

ON MONDAY morning, neither Mrs. Haron nor Stacey Weiss noticed that Elizabeth Steinberg had walked to school alone. At three, Joel Steinberg arrived as usual to collect her. In fact, he made it his business to chat with Mrs. Haron about the wonderful time he and his daughter had in Albany over the weekend. He had tried a case in court on Saturday and introduced Lisa to a judge, and afterward they'd been driven around in a limousine and he'd show her the court building. Lisa, he said, had been very, very happy, and certainly, as Mrs. Haron could now see for herself, "Elizabeth was there beaming at him and he was beaming."

Lisa had been writing more stories that weekend. One she wrote just for herself in a notebook later found under the living-room couch went like this: "The Adventures of Lisa. I went to Albany with Daddy. I slept in a water bed. It was soft." Who could blame her for fictionalizing just a little? Improving on reality?

Another story, written for Mrs. Haron's eyes, was rather dark. It was one that Mrs. Haron later studied for a long time, when she took it out of her "permanent folder" after Lisa's death. "The last story is almost ironic," she said at the Board of Education hearing, "because I took it in the vein of Halloween about there was a ghost and she was scared and she tried to wake up her mother and her mother was asleep, she tried to wake up her father and her father was asleep."

During those final days of her life, try as Lisa always did to obey her daddy, she could not make herself fall asleep, even to please him. Like the little girl in her ghost story, she may have stayed wide awake, listening to the sounds in the house, feeling something awful hanging over her—a presence that was trying to tell her very scary things that would happen to her if she fell asleep. Children could die. Daddy had taught her that. Lisa could be dead someday just like the rabbits hanging in the butcher shop or like poor little Dawn. Lisa could be dead any minute, especially if she fell asleep and wasn't watching the shadows in the room and listening. She could even make herself dead if she didn't watch out by putting herself into a trance if the Greens, unseen and faraway, happened to be saying certain magic words.

She didn't tell Daddy what she was thinking because he was very upset at her all the time for the dangerous way she always seemed to be staring into space, even sometimes when she thought she was just looking at him. "Lisa, what are you doing?" he would say, and she'd have to tell the truth, "Staring, Daddy." When he'd come into the living room at night and find her lying on the couch with her wide-open eyes staring at the ceiling, he'd really start yelling. Then he'd go back into the bedroom and she'd hear him talking to Hedda, trying to figure out what to do.

Hedda was very upset herself because Joel was so upset, but she never asked Lisa what was wrong, since that wasn't part of her job. She'd basically given up on Lisa. The only one she wanted to take care of now, besides Joel, was Mitchell. And even that was too much for her, what with the pains in her legs and the way the freebasing kept her up all night for those long talks with Joel that were about all she had left of what was meaningful in life. So more and more now, Mitchell would have to learn to wait, wailing and wailing, until Hedda could manage to attend to him, not that the crying did him any harm and she was still his favorite person. But Joel couldn't stand the shrill, repetitive sounds; he'd stand over Mitchell and *order* him to be quiet, scaring him half to death. Often now, though, when Mitchell was quiet, Joel would go in and watch him to see if he was staring too much. Of course, Joel blamed everything on Hedda and on Shayna and Michael Green and her mother and Judy.

She was quite willing to talk with Joel about ways to try to help Lisa go to sleep. One night they played soft music for her, but that didn't do any good. "Joel said that there were vibrations in the room that were probably keeping her awake and that maybe they came from . . . the fish tanks, you know, the equipment in there, and then one night he was walking around, he said there were vibrations. And there were vibrations coming out of the wall." He was sure Karen Snyder had put an electric mousetrap in the wall. But of course he never could find it.

*

In the mornings when it was time for Lisa to go to school, Joel would still be sleeping and Hedda wouldn't do anything for her. She'd say Lisa could wear whatever she wanted—it was entirely up to her. Lisa would run out of the house, go down by herself to the elevator, and walk all the way to P.S. 41. It was scary to cross the Avenue of the Americas, which was so wide and filled with buses and trucks, but she always remembered to wait for green, and once she got to school, she didn't feel as scared as she did at home. The sun came through the big windows in the classroom, and they were making construction-paper cutouts that week of witches and pumpkins and the class was having a costume party on Friday. Lisa was going to be Roadrunner in the costume Daddy had bought her. Daddy's favorite holiday was Halloween. He had promised to take her to the big parade on Saturday night.

One day, when she was having the scared feeling, she saw Mrs. Kassowitz walking down the hall in P.S. 41. "Mrs. Kassowitz! Mrs. Kassowitz!" she cried and ran up to her and hugged her around the waist and leaned her head for a moment against her belly, and Mrs. Kassowitz hugged her back.

That fall David Stiffler was doing some construction work for his landlord on the façade of his building. He was often outside in the mornings at the time when Joel would walk by with Lisa. "Hey, Dave, want to go sailing!" Joel would call out jovially. Thanks but no thanks, Stiffler would think to himself.

One very cold morning that week, he saw Lisa pass by, walking by herself with her head down. She was wearing a thin chartreuse nylon top with no coat over it. "I knew something was wrong," Stiffler later told the court. "That day she was different. I asked if there was something wrong . . ." Being a Scientologist, he observed that "she didn't make strong eye contact." Concerned as he later professed to be, he didn't think to offer to walk her the rest of the way to school.

On Friday, Lisa Steinberg didn't put on her Roadrunner costume, even though she knew all the other kids would be wearing their costumes to school. Maybe there was so much on her mind that she forgot what day it was. Or maybe she wanted to wear it very badly, but was afraid to wake Hedda to ask where it was. Or maybe Hedda refused to let her have it. So she just went to school in her old dirty overalls and T-shirt.

The party wasn't a very happy one for Lisa. She just took her Halloween candies and sat at her desk, moving the little yellow and orange pieces around with her fingers. A mother was there taking pictures of all the children. When it was Lisa's turn, she forgot to look up and smile.

She couldn't even play with Vanessa that afternoon because Shaughnessy Wilhelm, Amanda's ten-year-old sister, was having a birthday party and didn't want little kids there. When Lisa told Hedda that the Wilhelms had asked her to go home, Hedda for once seemed to be on her side. Maybe she could identify with Lisa a little when Lisa was put into the position of being rejected. Hedda testified that she actually called Mrs. Wilhelm and reproached her for not letting Lisa attend the party.

It was October 30. That day Assistant Principal Barbara Boriotti happened to see Lisa and noticed she was looking a little more untidy than usual, although she did not see any bruises on her, at least not from a distance of two feet. Mrs. Kassowitz also ran into her and later remembered thinking she saw something that looked like a bruise. Elliott Koreman himself had been noticing that for "the last couple of weeks, Lisa looked a little more disheveled than perhaps other children might look, but not to the degree that would cause an alarm to ring or that would make it obvious that there was something that needed to be done."

At any rate, during Lisa Steinberg's last day at P.S. 41, Mr. Koreman and Miss Boriotti discussed speaking to the guidance counselor the following Monday, "concerning the deterioration of Lisa's appearance."

Perhaps the discussion with the guidance counselor would have led to further investigation. Koreman and the counselor might have asked Joel Steinberg to come in and have a talk with them about his daughter. During the talk, Steinberg's behavior and language might finally have raised some alarms about Lisa. Perhaps the police department and Special Services for Children would have been pressed to go through their files to see if there was anything in them about a family called the Steinbergs. . . .

But even then, the "system" might have worked too slowly to save Lisa Steinberg's tormented, broken life.

Fifteen-year-old Amanda Wilhelm was the last friend of Lisa's who saw her alive, standing in the enormous crowd that had gathered on Avenue of the Americas and Tenth Street to watch the Halloween parade. It was bigger and better than ever that year. Everyone was delighted by a cleverly dressed group of people who had gotten themselves up as Dancing Tombstones.

Amanda waved to Lisa. "I noticed," she later testified, "that her personality was very drawn back. Mr. Steinberg had his hands on her shoulders and was holding her back. She said hello to me, and that's all she said."

"Lisa would have wanted to talk to me," Amanda insisted. "She was a very outgoing person."

LIES AND VERDICTS

EVEN AFTER the twelve-week Steinberg trial and a long parade of witnesses, including Hedda Nussbaum, the story of what really happened to Lisa remains as mysterious and inconclusive as Henry James's *The Turn of the Screw*, which is also about children at the mercy of evil surrogate parents, who use them in their games with each other. The Steinberg case, too, remains open to endless interpretation, another classic in the making. Years from now, people may still be writing books about it.

"The truth will set you free," Hedda wrote to Joel from Elmhurst Hospital in November 1987. Or was it Joel Steinberg who wrote that to Hedda from Rikers Island? as Hedda's lawyer Barry Scheck immediately claimed. Like much of the other "information" surrounding the case, the question of which one of them actually put that quote in the mail has yet to be definitively settled. And what was the truth anyway? And why should either of them—collaborators in the destruction of a child, a piece of the future—have been set free? As for "sources close to the case," which could really be trusted? Ira London and Adrian DiLuzio? Or Barry Scheck? And how could the lawyers on either side trust the information extracted from their clients, both of whom were lifelong, compulsive dissimulators? Information from liars used by ambitious attorneys to defend their clients cannot exactly be viewed as fact.

For attorneys, this very problem comes with the territory. They are after all neither detectives nor judges. It is not their business to produce the truth—only a credible and winning prosecution or defense. It is the right of the most hardened criminal, even a Joel Steinberg, to be competently defended. Thus a trial becomes a game, calling for great skill among the players on the opposing teams. A verdict may prove to be a legal triumph for one side or the other but not necessarily a moral triumph.

Barry Scheck's strategy was to act as if the Hedda Nussbaum side of the case had a corner on Morality. He demanded that you love Hedda, Archvictim. Ira London, who had the difficult task of defending an established Monster, did not demand that anyone find it in his heart to love Joel Steinberg. When asked, as he very often was, why he had taken on Steinberg (in fact, London suggested himself to Robert Kalina, after Kalina had decided not to continue working on the case), he would invariably answer that quite honestly, it was the challenge, as well as the sizable fee. Then he, too, would mount a soapbox: Joel Steinberg was being "vilified in every public statement." If he could get a fair trial in the United States of America, "anyone can get a fair trial."

The prosecution attorneys' motives were crystal clear. Nothing would have been more humiliating to the Manhattan district attorney's office than to lose this case, which was the focus of an almost unprecedented outpouring of public sentiment. The problem was, that although millions were out for Joel Steinberg's blood and a verdict of murder in the second degree, the case against him was hardly open and shut. Most of the evidence was circumstantial. There were no incriminating fingerprints, no "smoking gun," no murder weapon other than the human fist— but whose fist had struck the deadly blows? There was a metal exercise bar stained with Hedda Nussbaum's blood, and certain other objects, books, and writings found in the apartment clearly indicated a deviant life-style—but that life-style had been shared by both Nussbaum and Steinberg. Even the bruises that had been observed on Lisa in the weeks prior to her death did not add up to anything definitive. On any given day, some people who had come into contact with the child had seen them; but others swore they hadn't. And either parent could have been beating her—or perhaps the bruises had been inflicted by both. Adding to the puzzle was the question of Lisa's "happy" demeanor, especially the happiness she exhibited when she was out in public with Joel Steinberg; hardly anyone, on the other hand, had had the opportunity to observe the child with Hedda.

If there was public sympathy for either of the two people charged with Lisa's murder it flowed quite naturally in Hedda Nussbaum's direction. Her shockingly battered condition— graphically shown over and over again to millions of television viewers, almost guaranteed her a passport to forgiveness and exoneration. What jurors would want to convict a middle-class white woman with those bruises, that face? Over and over again, in cases where mothers as well as fathers were implicated in child abuse or child murder, juries had a tendency to acquit women.

Nonetheless, Barry Scheck did not wish Hedda to stand trial, even though a Hedda Nussbaum trial would have substantially advanced his own career. Indeed Barry Scheck's adroit handling of Nussbaum's interests, and the arguments he advanced that kept her from being judged by a jury, established what other lawyers soon seized upon as the Hedda Nussbaum Defense. For the district attorney's office to have ruthlessly examined the role Nussbaum as well as Steinberg played in Lisa's death would have been seen as the cruel persecution of a woman who had already suffered enough. A no-win situation, in other words. The only route to victory was to work to convict Steinberg, all by himself, using any means necessary. Nothing would be more helpful, of course, than getting Nussbaum to testify against the man whom she had described to Bellevue psychiatrist Michael Allen as "the giver of love."

Like novelists, attorneys play with the chaotic flotsam and jetsam of human life, weighing all the bits and pieces that attract their attention, not only accounts of large dramatic actions but small telling details; without shame, they grab at whatever seems useful, frequently exaggerating its importance, and of course they edit out whatever seems to run counter to their arguments; when the other side insists on bringing in this contradictory material, they loudly object. Each side creates its work of fiction, using the same events to tell stories with very different themes. Each side can be as fallible in its judgments as any human being—as fallible as Mrs. Haron or Sharon Listing. To complicate everything for the juror (the reader the attorney/novelist wishes to convince), the two stories do not necessarily come out in chronological order; order in the parade of witnesses is often a matter of such expediency, that it is very difficult for twelve people, forbidden to take notes, to track a chain of events or a development in character or motive. Of course this prevents the attorney/novelist from exerting too much control over his creation; randomness and formlessness ultimately destroy the courtroom novel and may or may not contribute to justice, depending upon the case.

The Steinberg trial—relying so heavily on the testimony of Hedda Nussbaum and totally lacking an account of the events of the night of November 1 to the morning of November 2 from Joel Steinberg—merely presented a fragment, and most probably a distortion, of the true story of Lisa. What Lisa knew will never be known.

ALTHOUGH HE had often spoken with her on the phone, Charlotte Steinberg had not set eyes upon her son since that Saturday night in October 1987, when he stopped off at her house with Lisa on their way home from Albany. Since then eight months had passed, during which all Joel's requests to be released on bail had been denied as he awaited trial in the Rikers Island hospital wing, where he could be protected from other inmates. In the prison population, child killers and abusers were marked men, the lowest of the low in the pecking order. Although he phoned her nearly every day, Joel Steinberg never asked his mother to visit him at Rikers.

On June 13, 1988, on his thirty-minute bus trip to the Criminal Court Building on Centre Street in lower Manhattan, Steinberg was harassed by his fellow passengers (on subsequent trips, he would sit behind a plastic shield so that the other Rikers inmates would be unable to urinate on him). He came in to make his final plea for bail before Judge Harold J. Rothwax, a brilliant, exacting, and irascible man with high ethical standards, who would be presiding over his trial in the fall. Rothwax was known for his ability to demolish defense lawyers (he had been one himself for about twenty years and was well versed in all their ploys); no doubt he particularly despised the kind of corrupt, slipshod lawyer Steinberg had been before his recent disbarment. Although it was very unlikely that Judge Rothwax would let Joel Steinberg out on bail in the custody of his mother, Charlotte Steinberg's apartment on Cascade Avenue in Yonkers was going to be offered as security that day, since most of Steinberg's assets were tied up, pending investigation by the IRS and lawsuits against him by Michelle Launders and Nicole Smiegel.

"What would I do with him?" I heard Charlotte Steinberg remark dryly that afternoon at one point during the proceedings, turning to Maury Terry, who had driven her from Yonkers.

Charlotte Steinberg did not look formidable. She was a short, stoutish, neatly dressed senior citizen in a spotless white outfit, squinting at the world through round, thick spectacles. She had walked into the courtroom, taking slow, careful steps, leaning on the arm of a young woman in a miniskirt, who was Maury Terry's assistant.

Under the circumstances, I had expected to see a woman bowed down with grief, for tragedy had certainly struck Mrs. Steinberg like a bolt of lightning. Even if he were to be eventually acquitted, which seemed doubtful, her only son was a ruined man; her granddaughter had died a terrible death; her grandson was lost to her. However, she seemed quite chipper. Mrs. Steinberg was excited to recognize a few of the many TV newspeople gathered in the courtroom. "I've seen *you,*" she said to Mary Murphy of CBS News. "I watch your show all the time, dear," she told Rosanna Scotto of ABC. Of course, one had to remember that Joel Steinberg's mother was eighty-one. Was she showing remarkable feistiness or was it what psychiatrists used to call "la belle indifference"?

Charlotte Steinberg and I had a brief exchange. I was sitting next to her, and she leaned over and joked with me, "You know, my senior citizens group is putting on a courtroom drama, and I'm going to play a court psychiatrist. Think I'll get any good pointers here today?"

When Joel was led into the courtroom, I heard her say to Maury Terry's assistant, "Oh, look, he's got a good haircut," and then, "I think I'll burst out crying." But she didn't, although she did wave to her son when he turned around in his seat and looked for his mother in the crowd.

For most of the time, as Charlotte Steinberg sat there while Judge Rothwax stonewalled each of Ira London's arguments on behalf of Joel, there was no identifiable emotion on her face. Like the rest of us, she seemed to be a member of the audience—a fascinated spectator at this real-life courtroom drama.

She heard Assistant District Attorney John McCusker describe her son as a man who had no close family ties, no profession, no dwelling place, "no life in New York," no place to return—nothing, in other words, not even his aged mother, that would deter him from fleeing the country, as he had once allegedly advised a couple of his clients to do.

"We will rule out," declared McCusker, "that Lisa Steinberg died any kind of accidental death. We intend to prove Joel Steinberg beat Elizabeth Steinberg to death."

There seemed indications that summer afternoon, three and a half months before the trial, that Judge Rothwax had already tried the case in his mind and knew where he stood on the question of Joel Steinberg, even though, as he was the first to admit, he had not heard the evidence that would later be presented by the defense. As he denied Steinberg bail, Rothwax said firmly, "My judgment, based on the facts now known to me, leads me to believe this defendant is probably guilty, will probably be found guilty, and therefore will probably be sentenced to life in prison."

There was a shocked silence in the courtroom, broken by Joel Steinberg's mother. "He's not guilty. I know that," she upbraided Judge Rothwax from her seat.

About fifteen minutes later, after a shouting match between Rothwax and Ira London, who was demanding a mistrial, and after Charlotte Steinberg had had a few private words with her son, reporters gathered around her. "How do you feel about Lisa?" one of them asked her.

The answer came with ease and was uttered brightly, "Oh, she was *darling*. She was *adorable*."

Hedda Nussbaum never had to ask to be released on bail. Her move from the criminal wing of Elmhurst Hospital on November 12, 1987, to a private room in the psychiatric wing there was an early indication of the strategy that was being worked out for her by Barry Scheck and the Manhattan district attorney's office. Dr. Azariah Eschkenazi, chief of the psychiatric prison health services for women, examined her to see if she would be able to stand trial. During their forty-five-minute interview, Hedda Nussbaum made Dr. Eschkenazi aware that she did not wish to discuss her childhood. She felt sadness about her predicament, which seemed appropriate, and expressed concern for Steinberg and Mitchell. She did not speak at all about Lisa. She appeared to have a high IQ. Dr. Eschkenazi did not find "any mental disorder that required hospitalization" and therefore prescribed no medication. Later, when he testified for the defense, he said Hedda had stayed on in the psychiatric unit, "purely for security reasons." Although she had indeed been injured, there was no need to keep her on the medical ward.

What Eschkenazi observed about Hedda Nussbaum was very

similar to what Dr. Michael Allen had noted the day after her arrest, when he had a psychiatric interview with her in the emergency room at Bellevue Hospital. She had been "superficially cooperative" at that time, although he also wrote on his records the word *defiant.* Hedda Nussbaum was logical and coherent. When he asked her questions, she tended to answer them "literally," which was exactly the way she later dealt with questions from Ira London. She seemed to be "considering her responses and the implications of them." Hedda Nussbaum said relatively little to Dr. Michael Allen about her life prior to meeting Steinberg—"the best attorney in the world, literally." She evinced reverence for him and for his powers as a healer, and she rather aggressively refused to discuss the possibility that he was responsible for her injuries. Hedda told Dr. Allen she had always believed in ESP, even long before she met Joel.

Dr. Eschkenazi noted that she suffered from "encapsulated delusions"; Dr. Allen hypothesized that Hedda Nussbaum had a multiple personality: "I felt it was possible some of her experiences had been split off and kept separate from her larger personality." This, he said when he, too, testified for the defense, was common to people who had been "systematically abused in childhood." Whereas battered women were very common, this kind of disorder was uncommon.

"The other possibility I considered," Dr. Allen told the court, "was that she was lying."

Five days after Dr. Eschkenazi's interview with Hedda Nussbaum, Barry Scheck arranged to have her transferred to the psychiatric wing of Columbia-Presbyterian, a private New York hospital, where she was carefully guarded from the burning curiosity of the outside world for the next four and a half months. Some of her most serious facial injuries were repaired by plastic surgery during her stay. Much more surgery of a cosmetic nature was obviously needed, but it had not been performed by the time Nussbaum testified.

Hedda Nussbaum's status was mysterious. She was a prisoner, yet not a prisoner. Unknown to the public, the district attorney's office soon gave permission for Columbia-Presbyterian to issue Nussbaum a pass, enabling her to leave the building to take walks with a suitable escort or even to go farther afield upon occasion.

Reports were leaked to the press by her sizable legal team that Hedda had extensive brain damage due to the beatings she had suffered over the years. In December 1988, when asked by Ira

London about the nature of her brain damage, Hedda replied that she had "difficulty pinpointing to words." Still, her alleged difficulty with words was not preventing her from actively seeking a contract for a book. It would be written Nussbaum said, "to help other battered women," as well as to defray her legal expenses.

Throughout 1988, Barry Scheck had mobilized an extraordinary amount of support for his client. A team of eighteen law students from the criminal law clinic at Cardozo Law School investigated all aspects of the case, conducting interviews and sorting out the contents of several black plastic garbage bags filled with drawings, tapes, photographs, and writings that Scheck had removed from the apartment two weeks after Lisa's death. Some students were assigned to monitor Nussbaum's mail. Others— "the Hedda Psychological Task Force"—took turns working with Hedda directly, bolstering her self-esteem, trying to persuade her to testify against Steinberg. The socially conscious NYU Law Clinic also became involved in Nussbaum's defense.

A coalition of advocacy groups for battered women, including Sister Mary Nerney's STEPS to End Family Violence, stood firmly behind Scheck's client. Leading New York feminists, such as Ronnie Eldridge, Gloria Steinem, and Lois Gould, also took up her cause. Barbara Walters begged Barry Scheck to let her interview Hedda on national TV; so did Phil Donahue and Geraldo Rivera. A woman who had waited twelve hours to summon medical aid for a comatose six-year-old (for we do know *that much* about Hedda Nussbaum) had become the most famous Victim in America. A woman who risked her life to save her child from a brutal father would have gotten a fraction of the attention. A woman who had discovered a cure for cancer no doubt would have been far less fascinating to the American public.

Barry Scheck kept the tone of Hedda's press coverage sympathetic by holding out the hope to various reporters that they would someday be granted an "exclusive" with Hedda. Nothing could have been more bankable than such an interview. The New York daily *Newsday*, which was trying to build up its circulation in Manhattan, believed that it would be Barry Scheck's chosen organ. Even before Nussbaum took the stand, the paper went all out with its Hedda headlines. In the end, however, the Hedda "exclusive" was granted to *People* for the article written by Hedda's old friend Naomi Weiss, for which Weiss received thirty thousand dollars. It ran on February 13, 1989, after Steinberg had been found guilty of first degree manslaughter; according to agreement, it had been carefully vetted by Barry Scheck. A previously scheduled article on the Steinberg trial that would have been far more critical of Nussbaum was apparently scrapped.

The Hedda Nussbaum story Scheck had astutely constructed was the one most people needed to believe. It was as if Scheck knew he could absolutely count on the extraordinary reluctance Americans have these days to pass judgment, especially in cases requiring the making of fine moral distinctions. The word *evil* has been disappearing from our vocabulary. Even *monster* does not have the connotation of evil, for it implies a kind of predestination, a mutant state. A victim, of course, utterly lacks will and choice. It is in the capacity to choose the good act and then do otherwise that evil resides. Along with the notion of evil, the notion of the noble, unselfish, and courageous act also seems to be disappearing from our culture. It was difficult for a great many people to imagine a scenario in which Hedda Nussbaum might have redeemed herself by defying Joel and even risking her life in an attempt to save Lisa by having her rushed to a hospital.

Working to Hedda Nussbaum's advantage, of course, was society's deep-seated "idealization of mother love," which, as Alice Miller wrote in *The Drama of the Gifted Child*, "is the one taboo that has withstood all the recent efforts at demystification."

Jessica Benjamin's definition of domination as "a two-way process, a system involving the participation of those who submit to power as well as those who exercise it," is, as Benjamin acknowledges, a highly controversial one, particularly coming from a feminist. Yet she insists that we must criticize not only our society's "idealization of the masculine side, but also the reactive valorization of femininity." Benjamin finds the tendency to "idealize the oppressed" a major "weakness of radical politics," pointing out that "Even the more sophisticated feminist thinkers frequently shy away from the analysis of submission, for fear that in admitting woman's participation in the relationship of domination, the onus of responsibility will appear to shift from men to women, and the moral victory from women to men."

Benjamin wrote *The Bonds of Love* before the Steinberg case, when the slogan "Don't blame the victim!" became the rallying cry of Hedda Nussbaum's supporters. Those four increasingly loosely applied words are emblazoned on the banner of the Battered Women's movement. For me, they have come to mean, "Don't think! Don't judge! Don't differentiate!" Does even a far more "typical" battered woman than Hedda bear *no* responsibility for the course of her life or the lives of her children?

As the Lisa Steinberg case turned into the Hedda Nussbaum cause, the furor over Hedda's victimization only brought home to me the fact that as a society we care far less about the interests of children, for all the idealization of parenthood that has become so prevalent in the 1980s, than we care about the interests of adults, even blameworthy ones. Of course, the adults we particularly care about tend to be white and middle class.

In the summer of 1989, Sister Mary Nerney's name and the support of her organization STEPS to End Family Violence, became immediately attached to a new cause célèbre in Manhattan that bore some striking similarities to the Steinberg case, although the abusive parents involved in this one were from the underclass.

Thirty-five-year old Frances McMillan was arrested with her husband, Herman, an ex-convict, and charged as he was with the torture, criminal neglect, and sexual abuse of their children. There were nine altogether—the youngest an infant of four months, the oldest a sixteen-year-old boy. Two other children had died of starvation in infancy; another had been stillborn. The police in the desperately poor Bronx neighborhood, where the McMillans had lived since 1965 in a tiny city-owned apartment, were using dogs to search for the remains of the dead babies on an embankment along the Major Deegan Expressway.

For many years, the McMillans had managed to keep the existence of their large family a secret from the overburdened and not terribly interested city agencies and from their neighbors, although some people had seen Herman McMillan marching some of his children in the snow wearing blankets in the middle of the night, as he cried "Ten *hut!* Ten *hut!*" McMillan took cabs to his eight-dollar-an-hour job on a construction site in Hunts Point. There he talked about his kids all the time and said he couldn't live without them; "I love my wife very much," his fellow workers remembered him saying. Once he told them that Herman "was short for hermaphrodite—half man, half woman. That's the best thing you can be." Like Joel Steinberg, Herman McMillan owed a large amount of back rent—his came to only eight thousand dollars.

Over the years, Mrs. McMillan had watched "helplessly" as her husband beat the children with paddleboards, handcuffed and tied them up, held their heads under water, sodomized the sixteen-year-old boy and raped the eight-year-old and fourteen-year-old girls.

According to the *Daily News,* "Mrs. McMillan's court-appointed lawyer said her client might be the '10th victim in the case.' The lawyer likened Mrs. McMillan's plight to that of Hedda Nussbaum, who was not prosecuted on charges of murdering her illegally adopted daughter because she had been battered into helplessness."

In a televised interview, the lawyer complained that because her client was black, she was being treated like a criminal instead of being accorded the privileges Hedda Nussbaum had enjoyed.

All over the country, where women as well as their male partners were implicated in child-abuse cases, lawyers were invoking the "Hedda Nussbaum Defense," often with success.

In Frances McMillan's case, however, there was no question that she, like Herman McMillan, would stand trial.

To blame Hedda Nussbaum, said Dr. Samuel Klasgbrun in a *Newsday* interview during the last week of the trial, was "a classic example of victimizing the victim in the same way we have seen in rape victims—they must have asked for it." Was Dr. Klagsbrun forgetting that a rape is an isolated, one-time occurrence, in which the victim has no possibility of choice? No one should have known better than Klagsbrun that Hedda Nussbaum's situation was one of repetition, extending over years. She became an addict—of a certain kind of poisoned love as well as of cocaine, and for thirteen years, she did not elect to be cured.

Klagsbrun's hospital, Four Winds, specializes in the treatment of addiction to alcohol and drugs; it has a reputation as a drying-out place for the affluent. It is one of a chain of three small, posh, actively promoted psychiatric hospitals owned by Dr. Klagsbrun. Its facilities are luxurious—fieldstone buildings in a Westchester estate setting in Katonah, New York. On March 18, 1989, Hedda Nussbaum moved there from Columbia-Presbyterian. At Four Winds, she worked with a team of psychiatrists, as well as Klagsbrun himself, whom she saw on an almost daily basis, 150 hours in all by December of that year. Some members of the hospital staff, as well as some of Hedda Nussbaum's fellow patients, were reportedly offended by what seemed to be Nussbaum's distinctly privileged status. In addition, the hospital provided psychodrama and art therapy of various kinds. "I'm talented!" Hedda marveled to Naomi Weiss, showing her some pottery she'd made. In one workshop, she'd printed up little cards with her own illustrations of toys and teddy bears and remembered lines of verse: "Children with their faces up/ Holding wonder like a cup," one of the cards read. And, of course, she once more took up photography.

People wondered who was paying for Nussbaum's intensive care (Four Winds normally charges $870 a day). Was Steinberg going to be presented with the final bill? Hedda's benefactor was Dr. Klagsbrun himself—not a famous man when she entered his establishment, but a celebrity by the time his patient was ready to testify at the trial. Nothing could have been more indicative of Hedda's progress toward recovery than her decision to sue Joel Steinberg for forty million dollars' worth of damages. Had Hedda Nussbaum been reborn as a capitalist? Not even Dr. Freud could have wrought such a transformation in a patient who seemed so far gone at the outset. And in less than a year!

In his *Newsday* interview, Dr. Klagsbrun made the point that he believed in the "code of morality" and had treated Nussbaum accordingly. He had by no means excused her "from accepting her responsibility for staying with Joel Steinberg or her failure to help Lisa." In fact, Klagsbrun told another reporter, from the New York weekly *7 Days*, he would refuse to treat a patient he considered evil, even if that put him "in the Godlike position of defining it." Ten percent of the beds at Four Winds were reserved for those deserving of free treatment. Nussbaum fitted into the category of "people who had been terribly hurt by society or by people"—a definition that would make thousands of totally obscure sufferers equally eligible for Klagsbrun's generosity.

Certainly Klagsbrun has not maintained confidentiality about his famous patient, and for this he has been criticized by some of his professional colleagues, despite his claims to the contrary. In *Newsday* and in *7 Days*, Klagsbrun theorized that even his numerous media appearances on her behalf had ultimately proven very therapeutic for Hedda Nussbaum.

No attention from the media ever advanced the cause of Joel Steinberg in any way. The label *monster* seemed more firmly affixed with every article about him, not to mention three disastrous television interviews in the winter of 1988–89, in which he tried to paint a picture of himself as a loving father. Before his trial was under way, Steinberg had consented to be interviewed by only one person—Maury Terry. Shortly after his incarceration on Rikers Island, Steinberg had sought Terry out after seeing him on a Geraldo Rivera special about satanic cults. Terry had a one-man crusader's obsessive, encyclopedic knowledge of the subject and had just published *The Ultimate Evil,* a book that reexamined the Son of Sam case, claiming that the eleven murders had been perpetrated not only by David Berkowitz but by other members of a satanic cult implicated in killings across the country. Terry was a gifted and fearless sleuth, as well as a reporter. Steinberg was tremendously eager to talk to him about the Greens. What Steinberg so badly wanted to tell some understanding ear was a mixture of undifferentiated truths, lies, and fantasies. The fantasies about the cult were still very operative. When Hedda entered Columbia-Presbyterian, Steinberg was convinced that one of the doctors there was a cult member; no doubt it even crossed his mind that Barry Scheck was an agent of the Greens's. Still, some of Steinberg's stories and allegations were corroborated by other people Maury Terry talked to, and he was able to immediately find the deprogrammers Joel and Hedda had consulted in 1983 and 1984.

By the summer of 1988, Terry even had a potentially crucial witness lined up for the defense—a convict named Michael Hawkrieg, who was serving a sentence on sodomy charges at Down State Prison in Suffolk County, Long Island. Hawkrieg claimed that in 1985, at a party given by a homosexual doctor on Long Island, he had seen a video in which a battered Hedda Nussbaum appeared, looking not much different than she did four years later. The child with her in the video appeared to be Lisa Steinberg. The Suffolk County police were very interested in looking into this further, but the Manhattan district attorney's office, evidently intent on protecting the credibility of their potential star witness against Steinberg, would not allow them to complete their investigation. Finally Hawkrieg's credibility was severely compromised when the Manhattan district attorney's office uncovered an absurd conspiracy on the part of Hawkrieg's two cellmates to sell a blank cassette, represented as the Lisa Steinberg video, to one of the networks for ten thousand dollars. Hawkrieg and his two cellmates were then transferred to different facilities upstate where they would be inaccessible to the press. But Hawkrieg still remained prepared to testify. According to Maury Terry, he was suffering from a terminal disease and perhaps felt he had nothing to lose. On January 12, when Ira London and Adrian DiLuzio petitioned to be allowed to interview Hawkrieg privately before he took the stand, they were warned by the prosecution that they could then be called as witnesses against him. On the advice of his court-appointed counsel, Hawkrieg decided not to testify.

If indeed it does actually exist, the videotape Hawkrieg described to Terry would certainly have been a powerful piece of evidence, showing there was a factual basis to what Hedda Nussbaum claimed were only her fantasies. Nonetheless, the part Steinberg played in the making of such a tape would have remained open to considerable question.

In May 1988, Maury Terry published an article called "Joel Steinberg's Version," based on his months of interviews with Joel Steinberg; my own article on the case appeared in the same issue of *Vanity Fair*. Maury Terry's piece painted a damning picture of Hedda Nussbaum's involvement in a sadomasochistic Long Island cult, from the late 1970s to the mid-1980s. Steinberg "alleged that Hedda Nussbaum had been 'in a state' for a few weeks prior to the night Lisa was fatally injured. He said he suspected her 'trancelike' condition had been triggered by a posthypnotic suggestion she received in a letter" sometime in September.

The gist of all the various stories Steinberg had told Terry by then was that he really had no idea what had happened to Lisa on the night of November 1, between the time he left the apartment to have dinner with Andres Romero in a restaurant in Greenwich Village, and his return from there three or four hours later, when he found the child lying on the bathroom floor and Hedda "off in another world."

Yet, since Hedda had been left alone with Lisa during the hours Steinberg was out of the house, it was not difficult for any intelligent reader to figure out what Joel Steinberg wasn't saying.

Hedda Nussbaum had told Barry Scheck that she would not testify against Steinberg unless he blamed her for Lisa's death. When she read "Joel Steinberg's Version" in *Vanity Fair*, she apparently began to entertain the idea of becoming a witness for the prosecution. That month she had her first discussion with members of the Manhattan district attorney's office.

Would she be punishing Lisa's killer or the lover who had betrayed her? Certainly she had not lost her instinct for self-preservation or her capacity for anger. The tables had turned and now she was the one who had become powerful—she, who had been quoted in the article as saying, "Once you taste the stick, you can't get enough of it." Of course none of her supporters would want to believe that she had ever said such a thing. She was the one whose word would be believed, who had the sympathy and love of so many people. Joel had none. His life would be in her hands. In the deadly game they had always played, this must have seemed the most unforeseen twist of all.

On July 7, as a concrete inducement for Hedda Nussbaum, the prosecution delivered to Four Winds Hospital a preliminary letter of agreement that they had drawn up with assistance of Barry Scheck, in which they agreed to drop the charges against her in return for her full cooperation:

> As of this date the investigation into the death of Elizabeth Steinberg has disclosed no credible evidence that Hedda Nussbaum struck, beat or otherwise affirmatively caused physical injury, leading to the death of Elizabeth Steinberg, or aided or abetted others to do so.
>
> This agreement is premised upon that fact. Should such credible evidence be developed from any source, including the statement of Hedda Nussbaum, it is understood that this agreement will be null and void.

Hedda Nussbaum was to assist the district attorney's office in investigating the circumstances surrounding Lisa's death and would agree to "testify truthfully at any trials or other court proceedings concerning the matters covered in the agreement."

Hedda understood this to mean "That I have agreed to tell the truth and to testify if I am asked to testify." But she evidently still had some doubt on that score, and although she signed the agreement, she vacillated many times before the trial. Even as late as October 1988, she expressed to Dr. Klagsbrun a longing to be with Joel.

For four months the existence of the July 7 agreement was kept secret from the press. It was still a secret on July 8, a week before the jury was selected for the Steinberg trial. That morning someone in the D.A.'s office tipped off the media: In a few hours, in a courtroom on Centre Street, Hedda Nussbaum would be making her first brief appearance in public since her hospitalization.

When I arrived at 100 Centre Street at 10 A.M., camera trucks from every network were lined up outside the building. Upstairs on the ninth floor, the courtroom was filled with reporters. Everyone was speculating in whispers. How would Hedda look after her

plastic surgery? Which door would open to let her into the courtroom? Would she really agree to testify against Steinberg? What
would a rehabilitated Hedda have to say?

The other wooden benches were occupied by far more obscure
defendants and their lawyers. Most of the defendants were young,
black, male, and poor. When they were called to stand before
Judge John Stackhouse, the proceedings would be routine, inaudi-
ble, and very fast; after each hearing, the judge would indiffer-
ently toss the documents into a wire basket with unfaltering aim.
Although Hedda Nussbaum was seated nowhere among the hoi
polloi of the courtroom, Barry Scheck was in the front row. He
was younger than I had imagined him, with an appealingly boyish
quality that went over well with the press—though I doubted he
was as guileless as he looked. He had big, soulful hazel eyes and
an expression of moral superiority that would become even more
pronounced in December when Hedda was on the stand. How
are we doing? those soulful eyes always appeared to be asking. He
seemed to have successfully done for Hedda Nussbaum what he
told his students at Cardozo Law School any lawyer must do for
his client if he hopes to win a case: not only create a credible
fiction but then convince himself that every word of it is true.

I was sitting in a row of other reporters; all of us kept turning
around frequently to make sure we wouldn't be missing Hedda
Nussbaum's grand entrance. Even the court officers couldn't help
turning their heads. By midafternoon, when Scheck had a murmured colloquy with Judge Stackhouse and exchanged some papers with him, Hedda Nussbaum had still not shown up.

Finally we gathered around Scheck and asked him whether we
should stop waiting for Hedda. He smiled mysteriously and said,
"Well, it's her option, you know." I was surprised that she had
been granted such an option. But then, in relation to Hedda
Nussbaum, the word *option* had taken on a special resonance for
me. Because, whenever I thought about her, I would always have
to ask myself, Hadn't Hedda Nussbaum really always had options?

On September 29, Hedda Nussbaum opted not to walk into that
courtroom. But she was elsewhere in the building, closeted with
John McCusker and Peter Casolaro. They would end up knowing
each other very well; the grand total of their meetings—at which
no notes were ever taken—would eventually add up to two hundred hours.

All that day, outside a door of the Criminal Court Building,
some photographers were staked out. One of them managed to

get a shot of Hedda as she was rushed toward a waiting car. A gray-haired, matronly figure, no longer in jeans with a bandanna tied around her head, but in a penitentially severe black suit. Surgery would never completely restore that face. Even as a free woman, Hedda Nussbaum would be marked for the rest of her life.

IF JOEL STEINBERG had not been a criminal lawyer himself, although now a disgraced and disbarred one, perhaps Ira London and Adrian DiLuzio would have been able to build up a somewhat more convincing case for him. But probably even then, it would not have been within Steinberg's character to have relinquished control to his two attorneys. He was said to look upon Ira London as a father figure, at least at the outset, although he had a much closer relationship with Adrian DiLuzio, a former Philadelphia assistant district attorney who was hired to assist London after Steinberg's final application for bail was denied.

London was a man with a stable, long-term marriage and four grown daughters, who had begged him not to take the case. DiLuzio, a forty-two-year-old bachelor, lived closer to the edge. When we talked one day after the trial, he spoke with anger and passion against those who would "legislate risk out of American life." Silver-haired London, at fifty-six, was sleek as a seal in his extensive wardrobe of wide-lapelled, double-breasted gray suits. DiLuzio looked deliberately unconventional with his bow ties and thin drooping mustache and his shoulder-length brown curls. At the end of the trial, during his portion of the summation, he shocked some listeners when he referred to Joel Steinberg as "my client and my friend." London, in contrast, a few days before the defense rested its case, publicly disassociated himself from Steinberg, when he revealed to *Newsday* columnist Dennis Hamill his feeling that his client would be convicted. A rift subsequently developed between London and DiLuzio, who had previously been on very cordial terms.

As if he did not grasp that his life was on the line, Steinberg had immense difficulty in bringing himself to disburse money in order to advance his case. Steinberg was exceedingly upset that London had raised money for part of his fee by selling some of Steinberg's stocks at a discount; for this reason, he kept refusing to finance an investigation. "If I had been Joel Steinberg, I would have used money to work up the case anyway," DiLuzio told me. "I would have been desperately afraid of the consequences of not doing so."

Perhaps guilt and remorse made Joel Steinberg undermine his own defense. He continued to claim that the Greens and the imaginary cult were to blame for almost everything: Hedda's injuries, the sexual abuse of Lisa, the buzzword that had supposedly led to her death. But he may have been afraid of what an intensive investigation would reveal about his own activities in the past. In any case, he refused to set one in motion until the last weeks of the trial.

"The fact that he didn't know what he was doing," DiLuzio told me, "was the strongest evidence" that Joel had committed the crime of which he was accused.

Even an inept criminal lawyer like Steinberg should have known how essential it was to help his attorneys create a story that would stand up before a jury, how essential it was that he give them something that would seem to have a basis of truth. "Bullshit was what he gave us," according to Adrian DiLuzio. "It was hardly a case where a defendant gives you information and you run. He would demand that you see him, and then have nothing to discuss."

"You've got to show that the house wasn't so bad," he'd tell his lawyers, or that "my golf clubs were new," or that the pillowcases and sheets weren't stained—the police had just kept them lying around—"That is a disgrace!"

"After a while," said DiLuzio, "you stopped paying attention. You had to play detective with him, confronting his inconsistencies. He'd keep attributing things to people who couldn't have been involved."

As Adrian DiLuzio saw it, Joel Steinberg wasn't evil because his efforts weren't "susceptible to success. Hedda is the narcissist. Joel is the person who has no self-regard. That's why he has to elevate himself." DiLuzio saw Steinberg as an "absurd person. He's still absurd. If he were an evil person and a sane person—or an innocent and sane person—he would simply say, 'Hedda did it.' "

Without that accusation coming from Steinberg, there never was a coherent story. Instead, Steinberg insisted that his lawyers

try various farfetched arguments, based on Steinberg's own study
of Lisa's medical records. Lisa hadn't died of the result as a homicide at all, London argued in his opening statement. DiLuzio felt
humiliated as he tried to prove that Lisa had died of Reyes Syn-
drome, indicated by elevated amount of ammonia in her blood,
or perhaps of a brain injury that had occurred in the ambulance
or the hospital. Joel suggested to Maury Terry that Hedda had fed
Lisa some leaves from one of her poisonous plants, perhaps as an
experiment. As always, Joel enjoyed playing the doctor. With
each new theory his attorneys lost credibility. As his case frag-
mented, their client furiously scribbled notes to them and to
himself on his unending supply of yellow legal pads—"trying constantly," said DiLuzio, "to provide rationality for everything."
Steinberg was still suffering from drug abuse and what he had
done to his brain. A year after Lisa's death he was "trying to
reconcile sane perception with the facts."

One argument that never washed was that Lisa Steinberg had
not actually been abused at all. Elizabeth Kassowitz and Rayne
Sciarowi of P.S. 41 were brought in to attest to that, to their
obvious embarrassment. For a while London even contemplated
calling Sylvia Haron. Heather McHugh, a paid child-abuse expert,
showed how Lisa did not fit the portrait of the abused child,
pointing to the happy stick figures in her P.S. 41 drawings as proof
of this. It was only in his summation that London argued Lisa had
indeed been abused—not by Steinberg, however, but by Nussbaum.

The most convincing story Steinberg told about what had happened to Lisa was essentially the one he had originally told Maury
Terry: he had not taken Lisa along with him when he went to
meet Romero at MacBell's restaurant near Waverly Place on Avenue of the Americas. The child had already eaten dinner at six,
and Hedda had reminded her there was school the next day (in
the previous couple of weeks, as we know, Hedda had certainly
lost track of such matters). When he left the house at seven,
considerately slipping out "so [Lisa] wouldn't know I was gone"
(here we know that Steinberg did not usually spare Lisa's feelings), there was nothing wrong with the child. At nine, when the
concerned father tried to call home, another patron of the restaurant was tying up the pay phone, so Joel asked the bartender to
let him use the phone at the bar. (In a later variant of the story,
Lisa was feeling sick to her stomach when Joel left and he was
calling because he was worried about her.) It was Hedda who

answered when Joel called. He told her Romero wanted to say hello to Lisa, but Hedda said she had put Lisa to sleep because she had eaten some Chinese vegetables and was ill. (Lisa, then, seemed to have had two dinners in only a couple of hours; she was certainly eating a great deal in a household where her food intake was normally stringently limited.)

That night Steinberg and Romero were discussing the oil wells in Texas, the venture Steinberg had persuaded Dr. Sarosi to invest in. Romero needed more information about them, wanted to see some brochures and photographs, so between eleven thirty and midnight, he walked Steinberg home. (Steinberg's downstairs neighbor, Joan Bonano, however, remembered seeing the two men outside the house around ten thirty, examining some photographs.) Joel recalled that on the way he had looked at some hurricane lamps in the window of an antiques store on Christopher Street.

Joel went upstairs to get the material Romero had asked to see. While Hedda was looking for the file in his attaché case, he saw that Lisa was lying on the bathroom tiles. Hedda said the child had thrown up again "in the bed or something" and that she had made her lie flat on the floor. After a quick look at Lisa, Steinberg decided there was nothing much wrong with her and went downstairs to continue his conversation with Romero, assuming that Hedda was taking care of the sick child. He was so furious when he returned to the apartment and found Lisa still on the bathroom floor, that he yelled at Hedda, "You stupid idiot! You bitch!" (words that the upstairs neighbor, Rita Blum, later remembered hearing, but not until around 2 A.M. Blum thought he had been yelling at Lisa.).

As the months went by, Joel Steinberg filled out this story, adding more and more small touches, depending on whom he was talking to. One was that he found Hedda ironing and whistling to herself cheerfully when he walked into the apartment.

Once he did indicate to Maury Terry that he had "swatted" Lisa a little just before he went out, and that he had beaten up Hedda for not taking care of the child, giving her a kick across the bedroom that was the source of the enormous black-and-blue mark on one of her buttocks.

As for the Chinese vegetables, they were the real thing. He and Lisa had picked them up that Sunday when they went out together to get the paper (which indeed was later found in the apartment). The people at the Chinese takeout place would remember them.

Lisa was still conscious, Joel claimed, when he went upstairs for the second time. She seemed very groggy, but she murmured that she wanted him to put her to bed. First, though, he put her in the tub and bathed her all over very tenderly (although for some reason she was filthy when the EMS arrived the following morning.) As he recalled this bathing scene when he was being interviewed on TV shortly before his sentencing, Steinberg added gratuitously and primly under his breath, "No. I don't do anuses." By then he had a new theory about how Lisa had hurt herself accidentally. She had climbed up on the bathroom sink in order to play with Hedda's makeup and had fallen and hit her head on a wicker laundry hamper.

Even more than the immense difficulties of working with Joel Steinberg, the primary determining force in the Steinberg trial, as Ira London saw it, was the iron will and formidable intellect of Harold Rothwax. The judge was famous among lawyers for getting his own way. He could look down the road and see how he wanted a trial to go, and make sure that it got there. After an article in *Manhattan Lawyer* in the fall of 1988, Rothwax became known on Centre Street as the Prince of Darkness. Members of the courtroom press called him Jehovah.

As the judge prepared for the upcoming trial in the fall—the first one that would ever be televised in New York State—he was perhaps mindful of the flamboyant tactics of Jack Litman, the attorney for Robert Chambers in the notorious Preppie Murder case. If there was going to be a show in Rothwax's courtroom, it would be run by the judge.

Ira London told me that very early on, months before the Steinberg bail hearing, Rothwax had expressed the opinion that even without Nussbaum's testimony there would be a very probable outcome of guilt. The judge had been privy to the long hesitation on the part of the district attorney's office to call her as a witness. Indeed, Barry Scheck had always seemed far more eager to have his client testify than had either Casolaro or McCusker, despite Scheck's contention throughout the winter and spring of 1988 that Nussbaum was psychologically unfit to appear before a grand jury. Understandably, the prosecutors had deep reservations about Hedda Nussbaum. She had told them too many different tales. In that respect, London told me, two weeks after Nussbaum had testified, "Joel and Hedda are like identical twins." For the 1987 grand jury hearing, McCusker and Casolaro had gone with a timetable that sug-

gested Lisa had been beaten sometime between midnight and 4
A.M. Not only was there no testimony at the time from either
Nussbaum or Charles Scannapieco (who allegedly saw Steinberg
strike the child during the Albany trip) but, said London, the
jury heard "no testimony from *anyone* that Joel had ever
touched Lisa or admitted to anyone that he had."

After closely examining the grand jury notes that summer, London went on to explain to me, Judge Rothwax came to the realiza-
tion that minus Hedda, the case against Steinberg was very weak.
But the judge had enough confidence in himself to be able to
admit that he had previously been mistaken.

Meanwhile, however, even with the signed agreement in their
hands, McCusker and Casolaro remained doubtful about the
value of Hedda's testimony. According to London, Rothwax told
the reluctant district attorneys that justice *required* that Hedda
testify, whatever her state of mind. During October 1989, he
"manipulated" them into calling her by promising to admit Nussbaum's beatings as circumstantial evidence. Even though Steinberg had never been charged with beating Nussbaum (a great
mistake on the part of the prosecution in Rothwax's estimation),
the beatings could be used to show her state of mind on the night
of November 1.

"He's called the Prince of Darkness because he co-opts your
mind, he co-opts your thoughts," London said, sounding both
bitter and admiring. He and DiLuzio had also been "co-opted" by
the judge. Rothwax told the two defense lawyers that he had
allowed the prosecution to use Hedda's beatings as circumstantial
evidence in order to create a balance, since he *knew* the defense
was going to ask that she be charged as an accomplice. The defense, London admitted, had never even raised the accomplice
issue with the judge!

On October 24, as all these behind-the-scenes legal maneuver-
ings were about to bear fruit, the Manhattan newspapers carried
the details of the agreement Nussbaum had signed three months
earlier and announced that at last she was ready to testify against
Steinberg.

Nothing could have been more therapeutic than the headline
in *Newsday:*

HEDDA

She Lost
Her Daughter

She 'Lost'
Her Son

She 'Lost'
Her Lover

But Now She's
Finding Herself

Hedda Nussbaum slipped into the Criminal Court Building again on October 26. She stood before Judge John Stackhouse for exactly twenty-two seconds as all her charges were officially dropped. Not only the second-degree murder charge, but the ones having to do with criminal negligence, depraved indifference, and willful endangerment of children. She would, however, forfeit her immunity from future prosecution. A reporter sitting in one of the best press seats in the courtroom distinctly heard her say "Whew!" under her breath.

WITH THE Hedda Nussbaum deal in place, there was little chance that the question of how Lisa Steinberg died—and the even more painful question of how she had lived—would be answered in the courtroom.

The second question in particular preoccupied me. I thought of it all through the trial, every time a witness described Lisa Steinberg as "amazingly mature." Pitifully mature, was more like it. I thought of it each day as Joel Steinberg entered the courtroom, puffing a final cloud of cigarette smoke from his nostrils like a fire-breathing dragon, seating himself and then invariably peering over his right shoulder, those eyes slightly magnified by his glasses, trying to see whom he could draw in, whose gaze he could penetrate with his. I thought of it whenever Hedda Nussbaum claimed she couldn't remember something, screwing up her face, as if she were grotesquely imitating a little kid caught stealing cookies—"Aw, I didn't, really!"; every time she made a point of saying that Lisa had been a very sound sleeper. I wished she could have convinced me of that. I passionately wanted to believe that Lisa had slept through her entire life with the mother and father fate had assigned her. It was like wanting to believe that the victims of a plane crash were unconscious as the plane plummeted to earth. It's the thought of their helpless terror that terrifies you most. But Lisa Steinberg's terror wasn't the issue of the trial or technically even a crime.

The crowd of spectators who turned out to see the Steinberg trial waxed and waned, but there were always a lot of reporters. On days when important witnesses took the stand, courtroom artists showed up with their drawing pads and pastels. "We're the piranhas," one of them said. Around 10 A.M., Ira London and Adrian

DiLuzio would arrive. Each day they looked more like matinee idols in their beautifully tailored Barney's overcoats as they wheeled in leather attaché cases of notes on a luggage cart. "Good morning, press," the affable London would say, smiling.

Although it was his trial, Joel Steinberg was never the real draw. That was made clear during the eight days that Hedda Nussbaum testified. Then attendance mushroomed. Enough spectators lined up to fill several courtrooms. Television and press people arrived at dawn in order to be sure of finding seats. They whiled away the waiting time interviewing spectators: representatives of battered women's groups, Larry Weinberg and Herbert Alpert and other acquaintances of Joel's and Hedda's, teenage girls from Sephardic High School in Long Island—their teacher brought them there to show them what happened to women who allowed themselves to be totally dominated by men. "I know that love is blind, but this is ridiculous," one seventeen-year-old said to me.

The women reporters took to interviewing each other—fierce debates for and against Hedda would be taped. The issues that Hedda Nussbaum brought to the fore broke up friendships among the sisters of the press. "I could have been Hedda Nussbaum," a radical feminist writer proclaimed proudly as she sat at the table at Forlini's Restaurant (one of Steinberg's former hangouts) during a luncheon where the guest of honor was Michelle Launders.

Having made a political decision to stand by Hedda, without full knowledge of the facts surrounding the case, Hedda's supporters were not about to back away from her. Indeed they seemed to prefer not to know too much about Hedda Nussbaum, even though a November 1988 position paper published by a New York Coalition of Battered Women's advocates expressed a commitment in its first paragraph to "reporting all child abuse including knowledge of, or suspicion that a child was abused by a battered woman." Although the paper was eloquent on the plight of the battered wife, it did not deal with the issue of how the abuse of a child by a mother should be addressed, apart from that one brief phrase. What to do if a victim had a victim? Every statement from this coalition implied that a battered woman could not be held responsible for what she did to her children or failed to do for them. Yet, if women were men's equals, were they not equally responsible for their acts? It seemed to me and to a few others, especially Susan Brownmiller, the author of *Against Our Will*, that to make Hedda a heroine would set the cause of women back considerably. Brownmiller's own early investigations into the Steinberg case, combined with her unsparing insights into the dynamics of male control and female submission, had inspired her to write *Waverly Place,* a fictional work that proved eerily prescient as the testimony in the trial accumulated. When we listened to Peter Casolaro speak of Nussbaum's "weakness of mind" in his opening statement, weren't we hearing him express a very old and retrograde view of women? A woman's innate "weakness" was, in fact, the foundation of the prosecution's case. Wasn't that just the kind of view that had been drilled into Hedda Nussbaum during the years when she was growing up? Wasn't it the view Lisa must also have internalized by the time she was six?

One person you could always count on seeing at the Steinberg trial was Michelle Launders, checking in each morning as punctually as if she were reporting to a job. A bodyguard, supplied by Catholic Charities, accompanied her. After months of seclusion and depression, Michelle Launders still felt shaky. She seemed to feel she needed a source of strong male support. It made some people indignant to see her there. They said Michelle Launders was making a spectacle of her grief, probably with a view toward bolstering her image in her future lawsuit against Steinberg, Nussbaum, Virginia Liebrader (Dr. Bergman's former assistant), and several New York City agencies. (In October 1989, it was decided by the Manhattan Supreme Court that Lisa's natural mother could not sue over her wrongful death because she had abandoned Lisa and therefore could not be viewed as her heir.)

Michelle Launders always sat in the same place—in the front row on the left-hand side of the courtroom, in direct line with Joel Steinberg's hunched back. Whenever he turned around to peer at her, she would stare back at him without flinching. Parts of the testimony, though, were terribly hard for her to bear—the relentlessly detailed descriptions of Lisa's injuries, the color blowups of portions of the child's bruised, naked body that were passed around to the jury. (Indeed, it is said that these autopsy photos made even Joel Steinberg weep the first time he had to look at them.) Sometimes Michelle Launders would rise from her seat, her face rigid and flushed, and walk very rapidly in the direction of the outside corridor. Still she'd always walk back in after she'd pulled herself together, and after I got to know her a little, I understood why. She didn't come there each day only because she wanted to see justice done, but because she hungered for every scrap of available information about Lisa Steinberg. Who was this daughter she had buried? Who would Lisa have been had she lived? Lisa's death had tested Michelle Launders's faith. Why had any of this happened when she had tried so hard, at nineteen, to do what she considered right? She could understand, she told me one day, why another young woman in her place might have considered abortion. But that was not Michelle's way, her "option," as she put it. "Of all people in the world," she said bitterly, "why did I have to pick the two of them?"

Each of the eight days in December that Hedda Nussbaum testified, she would enter through a small door on the left-hand side of the courtroom and walk right past Lisa Steinberg's natural mother as she made her way to the witness stand. She was close enough for Michelle Launders to reach out and grab her, whirl her around. But Hedda knew better than to turn her head. She didn't walk so much as march toward the witness stand, swinging her right arm back and forth as the high heels of her sling-back, open-toed shoes made loud clicks on the bare wood floor.

Nussbaum had little to fear. She'd had her two hundred hours of rehearsal with Barry Scheck and the prosecutors and had memorized the script. They had prepared her for every possible contingency, critiqued her affect, which still needed some work. The night before her first appearance on the stand, they had brought her to the courtroom and had her familiarize herself with the set, so to speak. Barry Scheck had strongly advised her not to make eye contact with Joel. In fact, to guard against this possibility, he had reserved seats for himself and Judy Leibman in the center of the right-hand front row, directly facing the witness stand. While on the stand, Hedda was to keep her eyes focused on her sister and her attorney as much as possible. (One juror later told me that she had observed Scheck making hand signals to Hedda at strategic moments.) Just as Joel Steinberg had helped to create the former, allegedly totally abject Hedda, Barry Scheck, with the assistance of Dr. Klagsbrun, had created this new one, who seemed, as Ira London once said to me, to be made of "hard, stainless steel." She did give Joel Steinberg one brief, peripheral look, as she took her seat on the first day and smoothed the folds of her black wool skirt. When Casolaro asked her if she could identify the man sitting at the defendant's table, she had to look at him again. This time she took longer. "That is Joel Steinberg," she said expressionlessly.

Joel's gaze, however, was fixed on Hedda Nussbaum; for once his pen wasn't moving on his yellow pad. He had recently proposed that he cross-examine her himself, but London and DiLuzio had not been at all receptive to the idea. Perhaps Hedda Nussbaum had never seemed more attractive to Joel Steinberg than she did from her seat of power across the courtroom. Taking his eyes off her, he scribbled a note to London, "Find out if she's dating anyone." Steinberg was seriously obsessed with that question.

NOVEMBER 1, 1987, started as just a normal Sunday in the Steinberg household—if you wanted to discount the fact that the parents of two small children had stayed up all through the previous night, smoking freebase together. But of course this had become routine. Joel Steinberg, according to Hedda, had slept till around 3 P.M. Hedda told Casolaro, "I think I had not been able to sleep at all that night. So I didn't get up." When Ira London, pressing her harder, took her over the same territory a week later, she said she may have had only an hour's sleep, "Or I didn't sleep at all. I don't know." After all, she was the one assigned by Joel to take care of the children and answer the phone. She thought she had probably watched the Sunday morning television shows with Lisa, who had been up since eight. Nussbaum told London she had also done some ironing and fed and dressed the two children, but then, in response to his next question, said that actually Lisa had "dressed herself, but I would generally put out her clothes for her."

London was far more critical of her mothering than Casolaro. "You would check them to make sure they were appropriate for the weather?" he said with some irony. "Yes," Hedda answered without hesitation. Scheck had no doubt taught her that the shortest answers were best. And London, despite his intended sarcasm, often played into Hedda's hands by his tendency to prompt her, phrasing his questions so that they could be answered with simple yeses and nos. If a question on a sensitive issue required more of a response, Hedda's favorite reply was, "I don't recall."

In the story Nussbaum told Peter Casolaro during her direct testimony, the first thing Joel did upon awakening was to ask if she and Lisa had drunk any water that day. Joel believed that a large intake of water was necessary for health reasons. He felt that

Hedda didn't drink enough. Lisa, "because she was imitating me," said Nussbaum, had "recently stopped drinking a lot of water." Did she really believe Lisa was imitating her in disobeying Joel? At times, Joel would order Hedda "to fill two liter bottles of water and drink all of it."

That Sunday, Hedda naturally gave Joel a truthful answer— "No, I didn't drink any," although if she were terribly afraid of him, a white lie might have been in order. How would he have known how much water she had drunk while he was asleep? Lisa, according to Hedda, "also said she hadn't had any," and Joel, clearly having awakened in a nasty mood, said they'd both better drink some and he'd ask them about it later.

Yet, in the account Nussbaum gave London during cross-examination, Joel did not seem quite so immediately preoccupied with the water question. Suddenly she remembered that as soon as Joel woke up, she had brought him a cup of coffee. He had also turned on the TV in the bedroom to watch the football games, even though the Giants weren't playing that day. And now she was unable to recall Lisa saying anything to Joel at all.

Hedda told Casolaro that around three thirty she had begun preparing the big Sunday lunch for the family. Hedda's menu differed markedly from the vegetables from the Chinese takeout place on Avenue of the Americas. In fact, she told London the meal had included spareribs, which took about an hour to cook. In describing the preparation of the food to Casolaro, Hedda said, "We, the whole family, went into the kitchen to prepare lunch. Joel was cutting vegetables, he had gotten a large box of all kinds of vegetables at the supermarket the day before. . . . Lisa did some cutting. She had a little knife of her own that wasn't very sharp. She could cut things like potatoes that were soft enough." Mitchell sat outside the kitchen "in his little seat and watched."

I remember being startled by this picture Hedda painted of domestic harmony; in the Steinberg case, any mundane detail seemed amazing. The image of Lisa cutting potatoes with her own little knife was one of the few concrete memories of her, apart from incidents relevant to her death, that Hedda was able to summon up during her testimony.

Around four the family had eaten. Right afterward, Joel asked Hedda and Lisa again whether they had drunk any water. Again they both said no. (Suddenly they were all in the bedroom together.) "Okay, come with me," Joel said and led them into the kitchen, where "he took out a very hot pepper, one of the vegetables he had bought," and gave Lisa a small piece and Hedda a larger one. "And we both ate them. Which made us want to drink a lot of water."

Hedda obediently turned on the cold water. She kept "continually" filling glasses for herself and Lisa, which they both drank—"perhaps four or five glasses."

"Joel was standing in the hallway right outside the kitchen while we were drinking the water, and he said to Lisa, 'If you don't' something—I can't recall what he said, but he said, 'If you don't, I'm not going to take you with me tonight.'" What was it that Joel had demanded of his daughter? On the last day of her testimony, Hedda suddenly remembered that Joel had just wanted her to drink enough water.

"He was planning to take Lisa out to dinner with him that night. And then he went into the bedroom." Hedda knew Joel was planning to go out at seven to meet Andres Romero.

Now the mother and the little daughter—the little rival—were alone in the kitchen. Lisa, Hedda Nussbaum told Casolaro, said her stomach hurt from drinking so much water. (It is not known whether this met with a sympathetic response.) Then Lisa asked Hedda, "Well, do you think Daddy is going to take me with him tonight?" If Lisa did indeed ask this question, it shows that she wasn't so amazingly mature and sophisticated, after all—she didn't understand that she was asking the wrong person.

Hedda was not about to reassure the child. She answered Lisa coldly. "Well, he said if you don't—that whatever. I assume he plans to take you. Unless you [don't] do it."

Lisa, obviously very sensitive to her daddy's bad moods, said timorously, "Will you ask him for me?" It was one of those days when she didn't know where she stood with her father.

"So I said, 'Well, go in and ask him yourself.' So she went out of the kitchen into the bedroom. And I continued standing there drinking more water with the faucet running . . . And when I had my fill I shut the water off and went into the bathroom, sat down on the toilet. The next thing was that Joel came into the bathroom carrying Lisa in his arms."

Hedda Nussbaum, of course, had had far more practice than Lisa in taking Joel Steinberg's mood temperature. Perhaps she knew that Lisa would be asking for trouble if she went into the bedroom. But, with the faucet running, Hedda couldn't hear a thing, even though the bedroom was only a few steps away from the kitchen, across the small hallway. No raised voices—Joel's enraged, top-of-the-lungs one and Lisa's thin pleading one. No loud thud like the sound a body makes when it falls against a hard surface. At least, so she claimed.

If Hedda knew that Joel Steinberg had in fact killed Lisa, either striking her just after she went into the bedroom or much later, this was as far as she was prepared to go in protecting him. (Similarly, Joel Steinberg's insistence that he didn't know what happened to Lisa after he left the house also seems aimed at protecting Hedda.) In other portions of her testimony, when Nussbaum seemed to be offering Steinberg a basis for pleading insanity, her protective gesture—if it was intended as that—may also have been a twist of the knife. No plea could have been more ego-threatening to the man Nussbaum knew so well. Steinberg later not only refused to go for an insanity plea but, from what Adrian DiLuzio told me, even apparently sabotaged an interview with a court-appointed psychiatrist in January 1989. Whatever pride Joel Steinberg has left is based on the requirement that the world accept his fabrications and find perfect rationality in his fantasies.

If he did indeed strike out at Lisa at some point that Sunday, we must consider the possibility that Steinberg was in the grip of his cocaine-exacerbated paranoia at the very moment he was confronted by the child. Lisa's inability to sleep that week had apparently made Steinberg fearful, if we are to believe Hedda. Did she stare at him once too often with her terror-stricken brown eyes?

The scene in the Steinberg bathroom is the least convincing part of the story Hedda Nussbaum told in court.

Hedda is sitting on the toilet, staring at the strange spectacle of Steinberg with his hands stretched out in front of him, palms up, with the limp body of Lisa draped across his arms—the stance of a prophet or a messenger of doom. Lisa is naked, except for underpants, although only minutes have passed since she went into the bedroom fully clothed. (Either Hedda was simply making most of this up, or was unwilling to admit that Lisa was usually kept semi-naked, even in November.) All Hedda says is, "What happened?" Not "My God! What happened?" or anything expressing an emotion stronger than curiosity.

According to her, Joel Steinberg then answers, "What's the difference what happened? This is your child. Hasn't this gone far enough?"

This dialogue has always seemed very questionable to me, coming from a man who has just slugged his daughter into unconsciousness. It has a definite accusatory ring. Of course, Joel may have been alluding to a belief that Lisa had been programmed that day by Hedda in response to a command from the Greens.

Hedda stands up, and Joel hands Lisa to her (Hedda is not too weak to support her weight of forty-three pounds) and says, "Flush the toilet." He helps Hedda put Lisa facedown on the bathroom floor, at which point Hedda obediently flushes. All this seems to be happening in slow motion, like a dream.

"And then I went over to her," Hedda Nussbaum testified, "to— I checked her, lifted her eyelids because they were closed, to see, I don't know what I was looking for. I did that."

Like Steinberg, she has her notions of what constitutes artificial respiration, since she had "a course and a refresher course" in CPR at Random House. "I took her neck pulse and her breath, and then I started to pump her chest." But the child does not move at all. Joel steps back from them and stands just outside the bathroom door. Like a Red Cross coach, he gives Hedda instructions: to put Lisa's hands under her head, to pull her arms back and forth at the elbows.

What Joel Steinberg allegedly says next to Hedda seems generic Steinbergese, language befitting his role as Hedda Nussbaum's guru: "Relax, just go with her. Stay in harmony with her." Joel always wanted Hedda "to be in that kind of harmony with him, to have a feeling together, and he would try to sort of help me to go to that place where we could really relate well on that level."

"And I think I also tried to, you know, revive her and see if she'd wake up, and hit her on the face a little [Lisa was still lying facedown], and I said, 'She's not waking up.' And he said, 'Let her sleep. She hasn't been getting much sleep lately.' " Or so Hedda Nussbaum told Casolaro.

During her cross-examination by London, she couldn't remember what Steinberg had said to her as he stood in the doorway. In fact, she has him just walking back into the bedroom as she goes on trying to perform CPR. A couple of minutes later, he returns to see how Hedda is doing—he keeps walking back and forth, in fact, buttoning his shirt, continuing to change his clothes. Under the circumstances, he is amazingly composed. In a little while, he will meet Romero and the two men will have a business discussion. Steinberg is sane enough to do business that night. Yet why has his devious criminal lawyer's mind shut itself off at this crucial point? Even if he feels little concern for Lisa, wouldn't Joel Steinberg now begin to feel great concern for himself? What on earth prevents him from calling his medical connection and friend, Dr. Peter Sarosi, and asking Sarosi to have a look at Lisa? Sarosi could have quietly had her admitted to Beth Israel Hospital, and perhaps seen to it that few questions would be asked. But then Hedda doesn't suggest this practical idea either, even though she notices that Lisa's breath is raspy and that she keeps bringing up small amounts of undigested food and water. Hedda wonders whether the child "drowned" in all the water she was forced to drink.

"Don't worry," Steinberg says to Nussbaum. "She'll be okay. I'll get her up when I get back," and repeats the "go with her, relax, stay in harmony" instructions. Does he feel Lisa has merely put herself in a trance? He shuts the bathroom window and leaves the apartment, promising to call Hedda in half an hour. It is a little over an hour since Lisa was allegedly carried into the bathroom.

At least three hours will now pass before Joel's return. Hedda Nussbaum is alone in the house with a sixteen-month-old boy and a six-year-old who will not wake up, or move or speak, despite Hedda's ineffectual efforts to revive her—a child whose breathing sounds very, very bad. Hedda Nussbaum has gone to high school and college, even graduate school, has written natural science books for children published by Random House. She has what is known as a trained mind. Absolutely no one is threatening her; no Steinberg is barring the door or blocking off her access to a phone. The worst she can expect from Joel is another beating—she's had years of those. The Steinberg Hedda described in the courtroom did not even sound angry after he asked her that very peculiar question: "Hasn't this gone far enough?" What runs through the mind of Hedda Nussbaum as she stares down at the small limp body on the bathroom floor?

There are phones all over the apartment. There is even one in the bathroom. If she could only bring herself to dial it, she could call 911, or Peter Sarosi, or Dr. Heiss, another pediatrician Lisa used to go to. Dr. Heiss's number is still somewhere in the house. But then, as she admitted in the courtroom, Hedda decided not to. The survival of Lisa was not as important as demonstrating to Joel Steinberg how obedient she was, so that she would not forfeit his love. Of course, she may also have been afraid of the questions doctors might ask her, even Peter Sarosi.

Tears fell from her damaged tear ducts as Hedda Nussbaum described to Peter Casolaro and the jury and millions of television watchers the most important moment in her life, the moment of supreme option, when the life of a six-year-old depended on the movement of one of her fingers.

"And I said, 'No, Joel said he would take care of her, he would get her up when he got back,' and I didn't want to show disloyalty or distrust for him, so I didn't call."

And so she cried in the witness box because it was such a terrible thing about herself to have to tell. But the truth may have been even more terrible than that.

Hedda has to kill time during all the hours that Lisa is lying there, do something to take her mind off things until Joel the healer gets home. For a while she does keep working on the little girl, checking her pulse and breathing. Mitchell has been napping through all of this. Now he wakes up in his playpen, probably with a wail and very wet. Hedda doesn't know what she's doing exactly, so she lifts the baby out and puts him on the floor and he runs right over to his sister. He always likes to see what Lisa's doing; sometimes he pulls her hair to wake her up. Tonight she doesn't seem to want to play with him. Hedda thinks Mitchell could hurt Lisa, although Lisa's quite beyond being hurt by anyone now. She has the feeling that Lisa's unchanging stillness might prove traumatic for Mitchell, so she puts him in his antique feeding chair that used to be Lisa's and pulls down the tray, so he won't be able to move around.

She's making Mitchell some dinner when the telephone rings and she walks into the bathroom to answer it. By now it's seven thirty. Reaching for the receiver and casting her eyes over Lisa lying at her feet does not remind Hedda that she ought to defy Joel and call a doctor. After she informs Steinberg that Lisa's condition is the same, she tells him she's feeding Mitchell. "Do what you have to for yourself also," he says cryptically. Obviously he does not feel impelled to rush home. Hedda is not sure what Joel means. His peculiarly worded sentence could be interpreted to mean, Save yourself. But it turns out he is merely giving her permission to eat something, for which she is grateful.

Hedda puts Mitchell back in the playpen, hooking the end of the rope around his waist to the railing. She tries to communicate the seriousness of the situation to the baby: "Whether he understood the words—he understood something, because I said, 'Your sister is very sick and I am very upset, and I would like you to go back to sleep.'" Mitchell lies down on the filthy mattress and obeys her.

Nervously Hedda walks back into the bathroom. She notices

now that Lisa has soiled her underpants. She pulls them off her and washes them out and hangs them up to dry—construing this as taking care of Lisa. The child is naked as she lies on the cold, dirty tiles, so Hedda finally puts a towel under her and drapes a blanket over the still body. There are mothers who would not stir from the side of an injured child, mothers who would grasp that child's hand or cradle the child's head in their arms as they waited for help. It could be argued that these are useless gestures, and Hedda Nussbaum is no sentimentalist. While she does keep dutifully checking on Lisa, there really isn't much point, because it isn't making any difference whatsoever. "So I didn't need to work with her every minute. And I wanted to keep busy, so I rearranged Joel's files."

It takes about an hour to do all the filing. When Ira London asked Hedda Nussbaum to account for the hour that followed, she said she was unable to recall what she did after that, but she certainly hadn't left the house to drink beer in a parked car on Tenth Street, as Ira London suggested in his questioning.

At ten Joel comes home and asks for his oil investment file to take down to Romero. From where he is standing in the doorway, Joel can look down the little hall into the bathroom and see the top of Lisa's head as it rests on the floor near the toilet, exactly where it was three hours ago. After a few minutes with Romero, he lets himself into the apartment again. At which point, "I said to him something like, 'Okay, you said you would get her up. Get her up.' And he said, 'No, we have to be relating when she wakes up.' " Joel is calm; presumably Hedda had sounded anxious. Still, she, too, feels it is very important for them, as it has always been, to get right on the same wavelength.

Joel naturally suggests that they smoke freebase together. Just the day before, their coke dealer friend had removed most of what was left of his kilo of cocaine from the apartment; in fact, he may have expressed in very threatening terms his anger and dismay at being ripped off. Thriftily, Hedda put away a little private stash Joel doesn't know about. She is as greedy as any street junkie; she does not want to share it even with Joel. First, she says slyly, We don't have any more coke. But Joel is on to her. "Well, see if you can find any around the house," he says. Needless to say, Hedda comes up with it. "Because I never lied to him. I trusted him."

After Hedda processes the freebase in the kitchen, she and Joel go into the bedroom to smoke. Hedda gets on the bed, but Joel paces back and forth and talks and talks, though he is not as fascinating to Hedda as he normally is: "I don't think my mind was really with him. I was thinking about Lisa and I was also during the evening getting very, very sleepy and nodding off."

At one point, Joel tries to explain to Hedda what happened to Lisa at six o'clock: "I knocked her down and she didn't want to get up again." He seems to still be thinking that Lisa has put herself into one of her supposed trances. "For the last week of her life, Lisa did nothing but stare," Hedda Nussbaum told Ira London. "This staring business has gotten to be too much for her," says Joel. Lisa was breaking the rules by "talking negatives." Joel has been trying to teach her the power of positive thinking, so she should have known better than to expect him to talk positively when she was talking negatively herself. Perhaps the little girl made the fatal mistake of saying, "Daddy, why *can't* I go with you?" when Hedda sent her into the bedroom, and got hurled against the wall for just for using *can't*.

Around four in the morning Hedda tells Joel she hopes he is feeling they're relating well enough by now to be able to help Lisa. Then all of a sudden her faith in him wavers. "This is ridiculous," she says.

And she is quite right about that. It is absurd. As absurd as Hedda Nussbaum's not being able to dial 911, as absurd as being jealous of a six-year-old, as absurd as bringing a child into their lives in the first place.

Following this statement, Hedda Nussbaum becomes a take-charge kind of person. She can be one if she wants to. Don't forget that Joel is really a little boy, and while he is rough with his Hedda-bear and his Lisa-bear, he collapses meekly if you give him an order. Hedda knows that as well as Marilyn Walton, although to keep things exciting she lets him believe he's the stern daddy instead.

When Hedda Nussbaum gets herself off the bed and walks decisively into the bathroom, Joel Steinberg obediently follows. He announces he's really going to do something now, and tells Hedda to get the bed ready, clear everything off it. When the child is laid down there, Joel gives Hedda a demonstration of his faith-healing powers. Sitting next to Lisa, he rests his arm upon her chest. A little of Hedda's faith immediately returns. Now she can no longer hear Lisa's raspy breathing.

Nonetheless, she now feels the necessity to figure out what's wrong with Lisa. Actually, *she* begins thinking very much like a

lawyer; it's Joel who acts like someone "off in another world."
Hedda wants to check the "legal definitions" of *unconscious* and
trauma, so she doesn't consult a medical dictionary but one of
Joel's lawbooks "So I could have an explanation, an understanding, so he could do something for her."

"Did you come across the word *coma*?" Ira London asked her.
"Yes."

"Did you skip by that?"

"Yes, I remember thinking that that's not what's wrong with
Lisa. That's like too permanent a condition."

Joel eventually dozes off, but Hedda stays up. At six she wakes
Joel and tells him Lisa has stopped breathing.

The jury listened to this story twice—once when Hedda was questioned by Casolaro and once when Ira London cross-examined
her. London asked her who her tears were for.

"Hedda," she answered in her dead, flat voice. "And Lisa."

O N DECEMBER 8, 1988, while Nussbaum was still testifying, Thomas Joseph Andry and Leo Greis, two young police officers from the Sixth Precinct, were subpoenaed to appear as witnesses. They were not called to the stand on that date, but they did spend some time in the witness room. When they walked in there, they saw the same woman they were sure Andry had questioned on the night of November 1, between 8:40 and 9:50 P.M. Her hairstyle was different, she was conservatively dressed and had gained some weight, and the condition of her nose had improved. Nonetheless, the sight of her only confirmed their original convictions—convictions that had probably made them unpopular with William Lackenmeyer and other fellow officers. It had cost Andry and Greis something to stick to a story that could have blown a hole in the prosecution's case.

The two young men were what Greis called "brothers on the job." Around 8:40 on that Sunday night, in November 1987, a call had come in on their patrol car radio; a woman had broken into a brown sedan, parked on the corner of Tenth Street and Fifth Avenue (a few hundred feet away from the Steinberg building). Greis drove right over there and backed the car up as Andry walked over to the vehicle. The woman was sitting in the front seat on the passenger side, with her head back, her feet outstretched. She looked like a homeless person, he thought, in her jeans and black jacket, with a blue bandanna tied over her gray hair. She had a prizefighter's nose and a dazed expression in her eyes.

Andry opened the door and said, "Is this your car?"

The woman answered, "I just wanted to sleep in it."

When Andry told her to get out, she slowly walked away from him toward the steps of a church, carrying a can of Budweiser.

She sat herself on one of the steps, put down the beer, and stared out into space without moving.

As Andry checked the car, he smelled smoke—a kind of smoke he couldn't identify. He walked back to the woman and said, "I'm not mad at you. But don't go back in there. Remember what I said."

There was something about this woman that stayed with him—"A look in the eyes," the dazed way she acted, the flatness of her voice. But he did think she was intelligent. Although she appeared to be battered, Andry saw no fresh cuts or bruises on her and therefore did not try to provide her with medical attention. Neither he nor Greis saw the limp or the two black eyes that police officers noticed the following day. Greis, too, got a look at her—from a distance of ten feet. Neither felt it was necessary to charge the woman with attempted car theft. They had discretion in such matters. Therefore, they did not bother to take her I.D.

Andry and Greis were not on duty together the following few days. On November 3, they both saw Hedda Nussbaum on TV. Even that look in the eyes was the same, Andry thought. He didn't see Greis again until the morning of November 6, when the two men were walking into the stationhouse. They stared at each other and exchanged silent nods. "It was like we already knew what we were going to say to each other," Greis told the court.

The jury later discounted the testimony of the two officers. "The young one [Andry] seemed dense," Allen Jared, an actor and waiter, told me. "His grammar seemed so bad that I had a hard time listening. They didn't see Hedda's black eyes, split lip, her limp. Even if it had been her," Jared said, "it didn't seem to make much difference."

But it did make a difference if one was open to considering it. And not even John McCusker's hard questioning, often implying that the two men had been slipshod in their duties, could shake them from their certainty that they had seen Hedda Nussbaum that night on Tenth Street, during the very period when she was supposed to be at home tending to Lisa.

Could it have been fear that made her run out of the house? Fear of the consequences of something that had just happened in the apartment? Fear of what Joel would do to her when he got back? Or of the deep trouble they both would be in if Lisa didn't wake up?

The strange smoke Andry smelled could have been freebase. Hedda might have smoked a little in the car to cool herself down. Had she gone out on the street to wait for a drug connection?

When Ira London asked her about it, Hedda denied that Joel Steinberg had beaten her after he returned from dinner. Yet a beating between 1 and 4 A.M. might have caused the black eyes and the limp that were observed later. Some of the injuries on her face looked very recent, according to Michael Allen and Neil Spiegel, the Bellevue doctors who examined her on November 3.

Rita Blum, the upstairs neighbor, was home the night of November 1. For years she had heard more from the Steinberg apartment than other tenants in the building. Sounds traveled to Mrs. Blum not only through the airshaft, but through the radiator pipe that ran up from the bedroom of apartment 3W. Mrs. Blum told the police that between 1 and 4 A.M., she heard a lot of banging and noises of furniture being moved.

When I interviewed Karen Snyder in 1987, she told me that Rita Blum had thought Hedda was being beaten and that the beating had been followed by sex—which Mrs. Blum, over the years, had found to be the usual pattern. Rita Blum and her husband Peter also talked to the ground-floor neighbor, Joan Bonano, about the sounds that had been heard that night.

Originally the police believed that Lisa had been attacked by Steinberg after midnight. When they first questioned Rita Blum, they did not ask her if she had heard anything a few hours earlier; nor was she asked about that when she testified before the grand jury.

Notes from the district attorney's office, however, indicate that Blum heard voices coming from apartment 3W around eight thirty—she thought she was hearing a male and female conversing with each other. Then there was a sound of an apartment door opening and closing.

It could have been Hedda Nussbaum leaving the house. Blum could have overheard her talking to Joel on the speaker phone, or perhaps to a male caller or visitor. Or perhaps Hedda's low, husky voice had seemed like the "masculine" one and the thinner "female" voice had been Lisa's.

Obviously Blum could have been a crucial witness. But she was out of the country during the period of the trial. The district attorney's office seemed unable to find a way to effect her return from Switzerland.

In December 1988, Judy Cochran, Executive Director of Children's Rights of Pennsylvania, was doing law-enforcement liaison work with the police, district attorneys' offices in the state, and the FBI. Judy Cochran is a frequently consulted expert on crimes where children are the victims: sexual abuse, torture, murder, interstate abductions. She was on the staff of the Attorney General's Task Force on Domestic Violence during the early 1980s.

On Thursday, December 1, the first day of Hedda Nussbaum's testimony, Judy Cochran received a file on a suspected child molestation case in Sunbury, Pennsylvania, that had come to the attention of the state police just after Thanksgiving. A severely traumatized four-year-old girl, enrolled at a local daycare center, had been taken to a doctor by her distraught mother. When the doctor examined the child, he found definite physical evidence that she had been penetrated with some object. From what she was able to tell them, the abuse had been going on undetected for several months. The child named names: someone called Shaynie, who apparently worked at the center, as well as a much younger woman, one of two aides who happened to have the same first name. The aide had a boyfriend. On various occasions the little girl had been taken for a ride in a blue truck to a place she thought might have been a "store." The interior walls of the "store" were painted blue. The little girl and the aide's boyfriend would lie down together and take a "nap," while someone took photographs of them. The walls of Dr. Michael Green's new office, a short ride from the daycare center, happened to be painted blue, as Judy Cochran and the police subsequently found out.

The doctor who did the forensic examination of the four-year-old reported his findings to the Child Protection Service, who then, as required by law, immediately notified the director of the daycare center about the allegations that had been made against members of the staff. (The state law requiring immediate notification has since been changed.)

The director told Child Protection that it must have been the parents who were abusing the child. After that, the agency took no further action, as far as the daycare center was concerned.

The investigation might have ended right there, but as it happened the child's uncle was a state trooper and he put pressure on the local police to look into the matter thoroughly.

Although the child's allegations were not made public, her mother spoke to other parents, who began pulling their children out of the center over the next two or three days. Do you know anything about a Shaynie? people were asking their kids. Judy Cochran strongly suspects that the daycare director alerted the Greens that Shayna's name had come up in the statements the little girl had made. "That's how we lose so many cases," she told me. The police would have proceeded to mount a quiet investigation without directly contacting the daycare center, as Child Protection had done.

The agency is feared in Pennsylvania because it has the power to remove children from their families. But in Cochran's estimation, it is something of a paper tiger, because its real mandate is to keep families together at all costs. Arrests of heads of households create welfare families, which cost the state money. Child Protection will investigate a suspected abuse, but will frequently call the allegation unfounded, even though law enforcement may continue to work on the case. Agencies throughout the country have similar policies, as well as low-paid, minimally trained staffs, competent to fill out forms but not necessarily adequately equipped to make sensitive determinations involving the lives of endangered children. Certainly this was demonstrated by the New York City BCW investigators, who from time to time, while Lisa was alive, followed up Karen Snyder's complaints by visiting the Steinberg household and went away believing they had seen a happy child. In Pennsylvania, workers have a six week training period and earn around fifteen thousand dollars a year. Most look for better-paying jobs within nine months. The work they do does not have high priority as far as the state is concerned. In New York City, the BCW and SSC were also poorly staffed and funded. There seems to be a widespread institutional apathy about the welfare and safety of children.

The Sunbury mother was very young and easily intimidated. She became petrified with fear that Child Protection would take her daughter away from her, after the director of the daycare center warned her that she and her husband had been reported as the suspected abusers. The director also threatened the mother with a lawsuit because of what she had been telling the other parents about the harm that had been done to her child. As a matter of fact, the director threatened to sue any parent who cooperated with a police investigation, and none of them ever did.

Then, on Tuesday, December 6, Hedda Nussbaum testified on TV about the October 1983 encounter group at the Steinberg apartment and Michael Green's alleged revelation that Lisa had been sexually abused by Shayna Green. When that news hit Sunbury, the rest of the parents pulled their children out of daycare. By that time, Judy Cochran had heard reports of the sexual-harassment complaint made against Green in 1985 before he took up residency in Pennsylvania.

"We needed forty-eight hours," Judy Cochran told me. But now that Hedda Nussbaum had talked about the Greens, everything was moving too fast. A writer for the Sunbury *Daily Item* turned up on the Greens' doorstep on Wednesday morning. A number of New York reporters also showed up in town. Dr. Green told the press that "a good percentage" of Nussbaum's statements were untrue. He specifically denied that his wife had ever abused Lisa. "I'm going to take a little rest," he told the *Daily Item* reporter as he put some suitcases into a car. "I've been working pretty hard."

The next day, Cochran and two detectives arrived at the Greens' house for some preliminary questioning, but found that it had been emptied of all its furnishings—not the usual preparation for a holiday. The doctor and his wife and their nine-year-old son had moved out lock, stock, and barrel. Perhaps they had begun to pack when Nussbaum first took the stand. But Judy Cochran doubts that their flight had been inspired merely by the embarrassing publicity of her testimony or anxiety about what else she might divulge. The Greens would have been quite correct in fearing they wouldn't stand a chance in a morally upright, old-world working-class community like Sunbury if they had to face accusations of child molestation, even if those accusations proved to be unfounded. Without having the Greens available for questioning, however, the police investigation was short-circuited.

A week later a notice appeared in the *Daily Item*. Dr. Green had taken a leave of absence for "personal reasons." He suggested that his patients ask their doctors for referrals to other specialists in the area. He had placed the ad in person and paid for it in cash. Green left no forwarding address in Sunbury, even for his accounts receivable. Nor did he use his credit cards during the three months that the Pennsylvania State Police continued to look for the couple.

By July, when Green returned to the area and opened his new medical center, fitted out with the latest and most expensive equipment, the police investigation was no longer pending. By then the mother of the four-year-old had gone to live in another community and given up. She felt she was only hurt by reporting what she charged was abuse, that nobody cared about her daughter. By December, the Sunbury daycare case was expunged from the records of the Child Protection Agency.

*

For years Judy Cochran has studied and indefatigably tracked down people who sexually abuse children. There are two main types, she explained to me—preferential and situational. You tend to find the preferential perpetrators involved in daycare cases where they have access to very young, nonverbal children. Some are introverts who do not use force, but there are also sadistic sociopaths, motivated by the need to inflict pain and to be in control. Not all perpetrators are male, by any means, even though the stranger we warn our children about is invariably a man. In many cases, Cochran has found that female perpetrators are protected from detection and punishment by societal attitudes.

Within the situational group, there are the morally and sexually indiscriminate—people who may experiment if a child happens to be available. They, too, have their listings in a chart Judy Cochran showed me in a handbook for investigators published by the National Center for Missing and Exploited Children. To my initial surprise, the motivations attributed to those perpetrators were merely "Why not?" (for the morally indiscriminate) and "Boredom" (for the sexually indiscriminate). Was that really all? Out of boredom, someone would victimize a child? But after months of studying the Steinberg case, it seemed to make perfect sense.

Sex crimes against children are on the rise in this country. In twenty-nine states, reports of sexual abuse increased 57.4 percent between 1983 and 1984, and 23.6 percent between 1984 and 1985. It is in fact the fastest-growing category of abuse. No doubt the increase has some connection to the spreading use of crack and cocaine. In February 1989, Manhattan District Attorney Robert Morgenthau revealed that during the preceding two years in New York City, there had been a 161-percent rise in drug-related child-abuse cases overall.

Judy Cochran does not find the Steinberg case particularly unusual—not even from a socioeconomic standpoint. She does find it surprising, though, that Steinberg and Nussbaum did not dispose of Lisa's body. What had stopped them from doing that? When she compares the Steinberg case with those she has worked on herself, she sees patterns of affectless behavior that seem all too familiar—from the lack of appropriate concern over Lisa's alleged sexual abuse by the Greens to the absence of what professionals call the "grief mechanism" following the child's death.

As I talked with Judy Cochran over many months in 1989, I came to think of her as the repository of America's worst, most shameful secrets. Like other professionals who deal with horror on a daily basis, her manner is quite blunt and matter-of-fact. "I'm surprised there isn't a baby buried in every cornfield," she said to me one day over the phone.

Hedda Nussbaum's injuries did not shock Judy Cochran "I've seen much worse," she told me, and dispassionately outlined the progressive course of the average sadomasochistic relationship. A couple like Joel and Hedda, Cochran said, would not be able to see they were doing anything wrong. "They think other people are all crazy. That's what *we* do to have sex." In such a relationship, if the male partner is sexually abusing a child, the female partner will very likely let him do as he pleases, but not necessarily out of fear; she may derive sexual excitement from her knowledge of what is going on.

Judy Cochran is particularly interested in Joel Steinberg's ease in obtaining kids: "That needs to be investigated much more fully. For pedophiles, access is the key thing. Often people with this kind of deviation don't use their own kids to a high degree. Joel may have been a provider," said Cochran. "Sometimes he might have been paid off in drugs."

Steinberg's doctor contacts also seem to fit the profile of the well-to-do pedophile. People like Steinberg like to provide themselves with good references, Judy Cochran told me. "You'll find a high percentage of professionals and big-business types" involved in child pornography. It's a very expensive and dangerous hobby. "A doctor can quietly take care of injuries that can't be made public."

Like Maury Terry, Judy Cochran is convinced that there are existing videotapes of Lisa Steinberg. Even twenty years from now, they may come to light, because collectors of child pornography never destroy their valuable collections. Some of Steinberg's millions, she speculates, may have come from the sale of such tapes.

Photography has become an increasingly important component in the sexual abuse of children; since it has become so easy for amateur filmmakers to produce videotapes, a veritable cottage industry has been created. The activities of sex rings often include filmmaking. Some movies are shot for blackmail purposes.

When a child reaches Lisa's age, said Judy Cochran, "she has been taught every trick in the book. Anything you've seen in adult pornography will be duplicated." But this is also the time when molestation starts becoming dangerous for the perpetrator.

Restrictions have to be placed on the child's contacts outside the home. "Kids of five, six, or seven can be coerced and threatened with punishment. You go from bribery to threat to physical force."

"The Steinbergs," Judy Cochran said to me one day with cold fury, "were keeping *animals.*"

The videotapes are still missing.

The Greens are a mystery.

Gregory Malmoulka disappeared during the week of November 1, 1987, and has not surfaced since.

Hedda Nussbaum is *not* a battered woman, Nussbaum's civil attorney Betty Levinson said cryptically on the "CBS Sunday Morning News" after the jury's verdict on Joel Steinberg came in.

"What is this Satanic crap?" Joel Steinberg wrote Marilyn Walton in the summer of 1989, from Dannemora State Prison where he was serving a term of eight and a half to twenty-five years. "My soul reflected goodness and religiosity . . . If you recall, I was educated by the Jesuits and was always philosophically devoted to loving concepts."

L ISA STEINBERG weighed forty-three pounds. Joel Steinberg was six feet tall and weighed 180 pounds.

Hedda Nussbaum was five foot six and weighed 125 pounds.

In the end, after much agony, that was what it all came down to for the jurors. Most of them didn't believe Hedda Nussbaum, didn't believe Charles Scannapieco or Marilyn Walton or Ira London's closing argument—presented only at the very last minute during his summation, as if pulled out of a magician's top hat: that Hedda Nussbaum had struck the blows that killed Lisa Steinberg. Weights and measurements, at least, were knowable, unlike intent, which Judge Rothwax told them was "the silent, secret operation of the mind." They all had tremendous difficulty entering the mind of a Joel Steinberg or a Hedda Nussbaum.

In "Where's Hedda?" an article Ivan Fisher wrote for *7 Days* a month before Nussbaum testified, Fisher prophesied that proving Steinberg's guilt would be "far more complex than connecting what appear to be evidentiary dots.

"Look at it this way: the case appears to follow the pattern of a general negligence case. Say General Motors makes a car with faulty brakes and someone dies as a result. In such a case, the manufacturer is responsible *res ipsa loquitur,* a legal term that means 'the thing that speaks for itself.' But *res ipsa loquitur* doesn't apply to murder cases. It's not enough to convict a father who is at home when his daughter dies, apparently because she was beaten."

In Fisher's estimation, "Steinberg's villainy" would very likely prove to be "the deciding factor in the jury's mind. . . . This is, finally, a case in which the viscera surrounding the events may have more bearing on the verdict than the evidence presented."

(Fisher neglected to mention that he had ever personally known Steinberg or Nussbaum.)

There were four charges for the jury to consider. For three of them there was no necessity to prove intent: second degree murder, showing depraved indifference and recklessness (fifteen years to life); second degree manslaughter, reckless behavior causing death (five to fifteen years); and criminally negligent homicide, the lightest of all the charges (one-third to four years). Then there was first degree manslaughter, in which the intent to inflict serious physical injury resulted in death (eight and a half to twenty-five years).

Allen Jared had thought it would only take them four days at the very most to convict Joel Steinberg on second degree manslaughter. Two jurors, however, believed that Steinberg had intended to kill Lisa, which Jared himself couldn't go along with. "I couldn't have lived with the murder charge," he told me. "I don't think he meant to kill her. When she was dying, they did call 911."

But what really stunned Jared and some of the others was the discovery that "a whole lot of people thought he was innocent." Three for sure, Jared told me. Three were iffy. Except for a woman with a master's degree, who wanted to convict Steinberg on second degree murder, but felt Nussbaum should have been on trial as well, "the black element thought Joel was innocent overall. They figured Joel had been railroaded by the press, that everyone was prejudiced against him." The black jurors were not shocked by certain details about the Steinbergs' life-style, such as the fact that the two children did not have proper beds. They were also able to conceive of the possibility that a white, middle-class woman might be capable of beating a little girl—that there could be such a thing as an abusive mother. It was much harder for the white jurors to entertain that idea, especially the men.

Allen Jared found himself very moved by Hedda. "For some strange reason, I can understand the way she thought. I've never seen anyone put themselves through anything like that. You could sense it in her eyes."

Jeremiah Cole, an insurance executive, who was acting as foreman, described himself as "a little bit old-fashioned. If I see a woman being struck by a bigger man, I would feel I had to intervene. If I had to kill him to stop him, I would have done it. But we could not consider that in any way."

While controversy raged in the jury about which parent had

struck the blows, there was no question that both Steinberg and Nussbaum were guilty of an act of omission in failing to provide Lisa with medical assistance. In each of the four possible charges against Steinberg, the acts of omission and commission were joined, which some legal experts believed was an advantage for the defense. Did omission on Steinberg's part constitute conscious disregard or depraved indifference to human life? Had he been intoxicated on the night of November 1 or influenced by his illusions about his healing powers? Or was he simply trying to save his own skin?

On the afternoon of January 23, the first day of deliberation, the jury sent Judge Rothwax a note, asking him to what extent intent could be excluded from a charge of second degree murder. "What's wrong with them?" a reporter grumbled in the courtroom. "I'd have been out of there in five minutes with murder two." So would Hedda Nussbaum have been, according to an interview in that day's *Newsday* with Dr. Klagsbrun. Were Joel to be acquitted, he said, Hedda would feel "betrayed, misunderstood and hurt," because she would interpret it to mean that the jury had not believed her. If Joel was to be convicted on the most serious charge, "then she's vindicated—not that she walks away, as much as she feels she walks away much more clearly understood." "She won't even go out to dinner," added Judy Liebman. "She's just too uncomfortable."

By the following day, the jury sent a note indicating that they were deeply divided on murder two. They asked when they would be able to consider a charge of first degree manslaughter. The judge replied that first they would have to acquit Joel Steinberg of murder. Because the intent to cause physical injury resulting in death was the basis of the manslaughter one charge, not even the prosecutors felt it was really applicable to Joel Steinberg.

The jury would, in fact, deliberate for eight days, which to Allen Jared felt "like being in prison. We would sit there, looking out the window, looking at the free world." As three black jurors held out for acquittal and those who desired second degree murder refused to settle for a lesser charge, it began to seem impossible that they would ever reach an agreement.

Those who waited for news in the courtroom began to have a strong sense of impending anticlimax. After four long months, the trial had produced no clear answers. Now there was a strange kind of emptiness even among those who called out for vengeance—for the monster to be "boiled in oil," as Mayor Koch suggested, in an indiscreet comment that had made headlines during the trial and nearly compromised the jury. The jurors, of course, weren't reading the papers, but as one of them put it, "we felt the pressure of the society in which we were living." Later they would hear that eighty percent of that society had expected and desired a verdict of second degree murder.

The twelve New Yorkers who had come together as randomly as strangers on a subway car included an immigration inspector, an engineer, a woman with a Ph.D. in philosophy, a senior bank assistant, a Postal Service employee, a physical therapist, a retired office manager, a bus driver. There were six blacks, five whites, and one Oriental; six men, six women; six who were over fifty. They fought and wept and kidded around with each other and let off steam every night in the hotel near Kennedy Airport, where they were sequestered. They sent twelve notes to Judge Rothwax on yellow lined paper, three of which had to do with that vexing question of Joel Steinberg's intent.

Shirley Unger, a retired city agency administrator, became an important peacemaker. "I used the middle ground," she told me. "Mostly for leverage." The people who believed Steinberg was not guilty "felt a certain resentment that they were being called upon to defend their position." The resentment became more pronounced when the middle ground dissolved and the lineup in favor of convicting Joel became nine to three.

As Shirley Unger saw it, Joel thought Lisa was trying to hypnotize him. He struck out at her angrily and she hit her head against something. "He was protecting himself. I really think he loved the child." On the other hand, "Joel's thought that he would be giving up everything . . . was sufficient to make him put off getting help. Freebasing was a method of warding off reasonable activity."

The jurors tried very hard to be organized, businesslike. They devised a scheme of making lists: evidence that Joel was guilty; evidence that Hedda was. "As we discussed each item, it would lead to our talking."

Shirley Unger thought the prosecution had missed the boat. As it turned out, the jury did not use Hedda's evidence to convict Steinberg. Nussbaum's testimony was used only to corroborate that Joan Bonano had seen Joel on the stoop at ten o'clock. "They certainly should have both been tried," Shirley Unger said. "The court regarded her as an accomplice." She considered not trying Hedda "a great error."

"A lot of the jury felt Hedda should have been tried for something," Allen Jared told me. "The fact that she was able to walk out scot free aggravated them a lot. I wouldn't go out of my way to prosecute her, but it wouldn't particularly bother me if she were prosecuted on some lesser charge . . ." But then, feeling a wave of sympathy, he changed his mind: "The woman has suffered enough. Just look at her, for Christ's sake."

By the fifth day, the jury began focusing on the forensic evidence, which had been interpreted in very different ways by Dr. Douglas Miller, a New York City medical examiner testifying for the prosecution, and by Dr. John Plunkett, a forensic pathologist and assistant medical examiner from the Minneapolis–St. Paul area, whom the defense had flown in as an expert witness. They were distrustful of Plunkett, who practiced in a very small rural county and was being paid by the defense; Miller was a New York official and had gone to better schools.

Dr. Miller believed that Lisa Steinberg had died of a subdural hematoma, specifically caused by a blow to her right temple. But there had also been two other significant blows—one to her jaw and one to the back of her head, neither of them causing fractures. Miller contended that all three blows had been struck with enormous force, which he dramatically compared to the impact of an automobile collision or a fall from a third-story window. There was no question in his mind that the killer had to be a large, strong person.

Dr. Plunkett believed that Lisa's death had resulted from a swelling in her brain caused by the injury to the back of her head. Most of the bruises on the child's body—on her jaw and forehead, the left and right sides of her chest, her upper back, her left shoulder blade, were approximately the same age and could have been caused by a single episode. The injury to the back of her head suggested to him that Lisa had been shaken and then "propelled into a solid surface." When this occurred, the movement of her brain inside her skull had had a sufficient momentum to cause the fatal swelling. In the scenario Plunkett had suggested, Lisa had tried to ward off her attacker. "She was in a fight," Plunkett said with great conviction. Certain superficial bruises and fingernail scratches on her skin indicated that to him. (There were fingernail scratches on Hedda Nussbaum's skin as well.)

Lisa's killer, Plunkett said, could have been an adult of any size, not necessarily a six-foot-tall, 180-pound man. At one point, in his testimony, though, Dr. Plunkett wearied and uttered some words that would prove very costly to Joel Steinberg. Lisa Steinberg, he said, could have been killed by any adult capable of "picking up and throwing" forty-three pounds. The words "picking up" made a strong impression on the jury. For how could a debilitated woman with broken ribs pick up forty-three pounds?

The jury also relied heavily on the testimony of Dr. Neil C. Speigel of Bellevue Hospital. Spiegel had made reference to Hedda Nussbaum's generally wasted condition and her numerous broken ribs. The jury forgot Spiegel said these were old fractures.

The videotape of Hedda, filmed at the Sixth Precinct on the night of her arrest, undoubtedly also influenced their thinking on the question of whether Hedda could have lifted forty-three pounds. Judge Rothwax gave the jury permission to use it to judge her physical capabilities on November 1, despite his previous admonition that it could be viewed only as evidence of Hedda's state of mind. Although Nussbaum is a rather broad-shouldered woman of above medium height, on the videotape, where she is photographed standing alone against a white background, she looks much smaller than she does in real life and there is no opportunity to see her in motion. Hedda Nussbaum was small when the jurors first saw images of her, then larger than they had probably imagined when she appeared before them in the courtroom, then diminished again in their minds by the final showing of the tape during their deliberations (they saw it three times in all)

On Hedda's supporters, of course, the tape had an even stronger impact. Right after the trial, Naomi Weiss and other women would say that Hedda Nussbaum had been "near death" on the night of November 1. But no medical findings ever really supported this opinion. Even the infection on her right leg had been described by Spiegel as only "potentially fatal." Nonetheless, to the very end, one picture of Hedda Nussbaum was worth a thousand words.

On Friday, January 27, Peter Casolaro walked into the courtroom with a copy of *Crime and Punishment;* perhaps he was carrying it for good luck. Judge Rothwax had become increasingly grim and testy. "I'm not the fucking prince of fucking darkness," he told a reporter from *Newsday,* and admitted that the Steinberg case was as much a mystery to him as it was to everybody else. There were speculations by now about the possibility of a hung jury. Ira London was tense but ebullient.

For five days the jurors had been sitting in the same seats as

Jeremiah Cole went around the room clockwise, trying to give those who were less aggressive a chance to speak. Since people had grouped themselves together according to their factions, Shirley Unger suggested that everyone now change places. This seemed to break up the deadlock. That night everyone finally decided to agree that the blows had been struck by Steinberg. But should the verdict be second degree murder or a lesser charge?

Juror 12, the bus driver, who had believed most strongly that Steinberg should be acquitted, was now agitating for criminally negligent homicide. Jeremiah Cole was equally determined to bring in a verdict of murder in the second degree.

Cole was a zealous foreman with years of corporate experience. He viewed the deep divisions in the jury as a management problem, susceptible to being solved by management techniques. He'd even studied up on them during the weeks of the trial. Shirley Unger and Allen Jared found Cole "strong, articulate, and fair-minded." Others, particularly Juror 12, came to resent the control their foreman exerted.

On Saturday morning, the jurors received permission to relax a little by taking a walk near their hotel. They arrived in the courtroom an hour and a half later than usual. Shortly afterward, they sent Judge Rothwax a note asking for his instructions on manslaughter in the first degree—especially the meaning of intent and serious injury. "Intent," the judge told them, speaking slowly so they could all take notes, was "the mental operation that can be determined by all circumstances surrounding a case" as well as "events leading up to it and following it." Rothwax admitted that it was not easy to establish that a person intended "the natural and necessary and probable consequences of his acts." In manslaughter one, intoxication by drugs was not a defense, unless it could be argued that drugs had made someone incapable of forming a particular intent.

As the jurors left the courtroom, one of them, Helen Barthell, seemed to make a point of smiling very broadly at Ira London. He took this to mean that things were going well for Steinberg, since he was unaware that Mrs. Barthell was one of the leading proponents of murder two.

All that day, the jurors found their foreman terribly lethargic and depressed. "I give up," Cole finally told them despairingly. "Do what you want to do." Instead of partying back at the hotel on Saturday night, he went straight to his room.

This behavior was only a performance. Earlier that week Cole had conferred with Allen Jared, asking for acting pointers on how to behave like a man whose will had suddenly collapsed. Only Jared knew Cole was faking: "I told him, 'This is a very dangerous ploy. Either everyone is going to hate you, or it's going to work.' Jerry thought he'd just get everyone mad at him," thereby creating unity, "and then they'd work together." It was a "daring thing," but it brought about the desired result. Once Cole withdrew, people broke into small groups and starting negotiating with each other. Cole waited until late Sunday afternoon to recover from his apparent breakdown.

Intermittently, all through Sunday afternoon, those seated in the courtroom heard loud, muffled voices coming from the jury room. Things were really coming apart in there, Allen Jared told me, people were crying. Although everyone felt "it would be a cop-out not to come to a verdict, a motion was put on the table to go out and say, 'We can't do it.'"

Intent was still the problem as well as continued resistance by the hardliners to anything but murder two. Juror 12 could not be moved from demanding negligent homicide. He had still not convinced himself that Joel intended to cause Lisa serious physical injury.

For Juror 12's benefit, Cole drafted a tenth note to Rothwax at 5:10:

> If there was no intent, but acts resulted in injury nonetheless, would that be grounds to conclude intent as spelled out by law?
> What is the least amount of injury that would be classified as serious injury under the law?

After it was read aloud, London stood up and demanded that Rothwax answer the first question in the negative with a simple no. Rothwax refused. *No,* he said, would not adequately answer that question. Angrily, London argued that the more the judge fed into the jury, the less they'd be likely to understand. "I intend to carry out my obligation to clarify the confusion," Rothwax responded coldly, his mouth tightening into a straight line.

If there was no intent, could one say there was intent anyway? That was the gist of Juror 12's dilemma. In part it stemmed from semantic confusion; in part, perhaps, from something Juror 12 understood about Joel Steinberg's nature that he couldn't find the right words to express to the others. Neither of the two charges the jury was considering seemed to adequately relate to death by child abuse—to a killing that did not seem to be a deliberate act but rather a convergence of so many circumstances. One could look at such a killing as the result of an individual's entire history, going back to the earliest experiences in his lifetime—as if forty years ago the child Joel Steinberg and the child Hedda Nussbaum already carried within them the seeds of the death of an as yet unborn child whom they would not encounter until they became parents themselves.

For Shirley Unger, the judge's answer to Note 10 finally made everything clear: "The judge extended the meaning of intent." And indeed he had. According to Shirley Unger's understanding of the way Rothwax interpreted the legal term, "you had the right to assume from the result that this was the intent." Even in an act of omission, you "had the right to infer intent." By that standard, of course, "Hedda was as guilty of omission" as Steinberg.

By Monday afternoon, everyone but Juror 12 had agreed to settle for manslaughter one. "We couldn't go downward," said Shirley Unger, "because the people who wanted murder two felt they had compromised as much as they could." But Juror 12 was back to arguing that Steinberg hadn't struck the blow. He kept citing some of Dr. Miller's wording to support his position: Miller had said only that you "had to have" enormous force, "he didn't say, 'you *got* to.' "

Jeremiah Cole had reached the limits of his patience. He and Juror 12, according to Allen Jared, "got into this big to-do." People took refuge in the bathrooms, went to the windows and stared down at the traffic on Centre Street.

Cole was feeling totally defeated—this time it wasn't an act. Shirley Unger went over to him and suggested that his chair be rotated to Jared. Then she and Allen Jared managed to calm down Juror 12. "You have to go with reason and logic," Shirley Unger told him gently, "not emotion."

"When we made him understand," said Allen Jared, Juror 12 said, " 'Oh, I see. You've shown me something. You've shown me a new light.' "

Allen Jared took over as foreman. Fifteen minutes later, they had a verdict.

BY LATE afternoon, on Monday, January 30, the courtroom was full of restless reporters starved for news—the Joel Steinberg reading society, trying to keep their minds on their books: everything from *Pride and Prejudice* to *Trump on Trump*. Outside in the smoky, airless, poorly lit corridor where even the tepid drinking water always tasted criminal, TV camera crews were camped out on plastic milk cartons amid huge tangles of cable. Ira London had gone downstairs to play poker in the press room. Michelle Launders had left the floor and gone to a private lounge outside the district attorney's office, where she kept vigil with Graceanne Smigiel. The two women were still praying for a verdict of murder two. Only then, said Michelle Launders, would Lisa be able to rest in peace.

Mrs. Smigiel had been showing up more and more frequently at the trial—partly, perhaps, to win sympathy for her suit against Steinberg, Nussbaum, and Peter Saroci on behalf of Travis Christian Smigiel, a.k.a. Mitchell Steinberg, partly because she wanted Steinberg's blood. But there seemed to be another reason as well. It was clear that she had formed a strong maternal bond with Michelle. Often if you looked over at the two of them during difficult parts of the testimony, you would see Graceanne Smigiel's arm around Michelle Launders, her left hand with its extraordinarily long maroon fingernails resting on Michelle's shoulder. The testimony that had the most powerful effect on Mrs. Smigiel's emotions was a statement Hedda made to the effect that Joel Steinberg had never bought clothes or toys for Lisa or Mitchell. She was a woman who seemed to derive great emotional satisfaction from material possessions, and the thought of that kind of deprivation struck her to the heart. Afterward she stood with Michelle in the corridor, shaking from head to foot.

She always had the latest snapshots of her grandson in her pocketbook and would show them to anyone who asked to see them. Travis Christian Smigiel was doing fine. Nicole had gotten him a punk haircut. He was talking a lot now, picking up expressions from all the teenagers in the house. "I wiped out," he'd say when he fell down. But he still was having nightmares. She couldn't stand the thought that "those people" had ever even seen her grandson, or touched him.

Michelle Launders was still in tremendous pain and as shy as ever about facing the public and the press. Nonetheless, she had agreed to appear one December night at a candlelight vigil in Washington Square, organized by the Lisa Organization to Stop Child Abuse, a group that attorney Seth Friedland and a Greenwich Village dentist named Charles Reich had formed with disaffected P.S. 41 parents and concerned professionals. The Lisa Organization was lobbying to make child abuse a felony in New York State and to amend New York's felony murder statute by having it include a new category of crime: homicide by child abuse. It was also seeking reforms in the Social Services laws to prevent unfounded reports of abuse and neglect from being expunged from state records and demanding the establishment of special mandatory training programs for teachers, police, social workers and medical personnel.

Michelle Launders said she couldn't make a speech, but she did stand up as Lisa Steinberg's mother on the platform in the park where her daughter had played. With the end of the trial in sight, there was the sense that her hardest, loneliest days were still ahead of her. She hadn't figured out what to do with her life. All she knew was that she'd never go back to working for an insurance company. Maybe she'd go for a cruise for a week or two—alone.

The jury had sent its last note to Rothwax at four o'clock that Monday: "What is reasonable doubt?"

It was a doubt, said Judge Rothwax, "based on logic which you conscientiously have after the use of your powers of reason, which arises out of the credible evidence or lack of credible evidence. A doubt which arises out of reason. Benefit of that doubt must be given to the defendant and your verdict must be not guilty."

Six of the jurors wrote this on their pads.

After the jury exited, the judge had declared a recess, but suggested that everyone stick around for the next fifteen or twenty minutes. In the Bess Myerson trial, one reporter told me, the jury had asked the same question and then come right out with a verdict.

But it was not until six thirty that a buzzer again sounded in the courtroom. A court officer went into the jury room and came out with another piece of folded yellow paper. He carried it over to three other court officers, and you could see by the tension and gravity on the faces of those uniformed men that something important had happened. All whispering and bantering stopped. The verdict was in.

Michelle Launders and Graceanne Smigiel walked swiftly to their seats just before Judge Rothwax sealed the courtroom. Joel Steinberg took his place at the defendant's table; his teeth were clenched, every muscle in his face seemed on the verge of snapping. When the verdict was read aloud by Jeremiah Cole, Steinberg bit his lip and repeated to himself, "Man one. Man one."

Juror 12 was weeping.

"WHAT'S THE POINT?" asked Hedda Nussbaum, walking away from Lisa's grave with Naomi Weiss a year after Lisa's death. It was the first time she had seen the small stone marker in Michelle Launders's family plot. She reportedly had Naomi Weiss drive her there, and brought along offerings of dolls of Lisa's two favorite television characters, Ernie and ALF, hoping the plastic would last through the winter. Before Weiss's eyes, she knelt down and addressed the dead child, although Weiss did not hear what she said. The obligatory scene was later incorporated into the *People* article Weiss may already have been thinking about writing. "What's the point?" asked Hedda Nussbaum, sobbing in Weiss's arms. "Lisa's not here."

Even after months of therapy with Dr. Klagsbrun, Hedda Nussbaum did not seem to grasp the point of mourning. Perhaps her tears were for her own numbness—not a passing state, but a permanent condition.

A few months later, when Nussbaum was searching for an established writer to collaborate with her on her intended memoir, she dismayed two leading women novelists by her insistence that she had been a good mother. Her main proofs to support this contention were that Lisa used to have an extensive wardrobe and that for a long time Hedda had kept her looking nice. It seems that one of the greatest humiliations for Hedda Nussbaum was the revelation that she had been such a terrible housekeeper.

Now she lives in a small cottage in Westchester County, where once again, according to Romany Kramoris who has visited her there, there is a place for everything and everything is in its place. In October 1989, when Romany Kramoris told Hedda she had met me and that I was writing this book, Hedda Nussbaum quickly reread the *Vanity Fair* article I wrote in the spring of

1988. The article suggested that the relationship Hedda had with Joel was a sadomasochistic one and that there might have been a strong component of sexual jealousy in Hedda's feelings for Lisa. Nussbaum told Romany Kramoris that now she didn't think the article was so bad. But there were a couple of important errors she wanted to call to my attention. She and Joel Steinberg had unscrewed only *one* light bulb, that was one of the items. The other was that the UPS delivery man, who talked about seeing Lisa in diapers a number of times, had been mistaken. What Lisa had been wearing when she came to the door was "a little play outfit." (Yet the EMS technicians and the police remembered trying to resuscitate Lisa in total darkness, and the UPS man recalled Lisa's outfit as a diaper.)

But that was all Hedda Nussbaum had to say—as if these two points exonerated her from the role she played in Lisa Steinberg's life and death. Clearly she has no understanding of what she did that was so wrong—of how she sinned, if one dares to use such an old-fashioned term.

What is the meaning of Hedda Nussbaum's rehabilitation if she still cannot recognize what she did?

Joel Steinberg sat through his twelve-week trial in silence, but he was at no loss for words on March 24, 1989. Just before Judge Rothwax sentenced him to serve eight and a half to twenty-five years at Dannemora State prison, with a recommendation against parole, Steinberg asked to address the court. He rose with a loud squeak of his chair and spoke far too long. It was like watching a standup comedian running out of control, lip-synching words to an endless, senseless tape, woodenly making the gesticulations that the script called for.

First we heard Steinberg the doctor parading his medical expertise after looking over the radiology reports, as if the dead child were a "case" he had been asked to give his opinion on, a corpse he was examining in the autopsy lab of his mind. The child was "extremely well-nourished," he observed to the court. Mitchell had not so much as a diaper rash, he threw in challengingly. And as for the victim's bruises—obviously Steinberg was a man who knew a bruise when he saw one—they were merely "echymoses" to "the surface of the skin, not going any deeper than fatty tissue"—other than an arachnoid hematoma, which he did acknowledge, reminding the court that there had been no injuries to the external scalp.

At that point Steinberg's eyes swiveled toward the judge. Noticing a peculiar expression on Rothwax's face, he asked him whether he was laughing.

"I'm not laughing," Rothwax answered. "I'm just astonished by this."

Shortly after that, the doctor ran out of steam and was abruptly replaced by Steinberg the loving father: "At no point did I ever neglect them. At no point did I ever strike them. I do not hit or use any form of discipline on those children. She had a wardrobe, dolls, and everything she would need. Every teacher wanted her. . . . I took Lisa with me—I had a superior, playful, delightful relationship with her. I doted on her, went running with her, rollerskating, bike-riding, with her. . . . Scannapieco's eyes were quite dilated."

Just as he had demanded that Lisa charm the world while she was alive, Joel Steinberg fell back now on the memory of her superb facsimile of a "consistently . . . delightful, happy, outgoing" little girl as his best plea for clemency: "Children reflect what happens to them. It has to be constant."

Naturally, he felt remorse as well as paternal pride. He had been asked about remorse on "Inside Edition" a few weeks before, and he felt no embarrassment about uttering much the same words again: "I understand what you mean by remorse. I have remorse about losing my life."

His greatest regret (not to mention his costliest mistake, since it was the only incontrovertibly provable part of his crime) was "not making the judgment to seek medical attention the moment I came home. . . . I did not call Heiss or Sarosi. What bothers me the most is whether had I done that, she would have lived."

Toward the very end of Steinberg's speech, he was suddenly reminded of that old idea of his about investing in relationships: "I invested my life in those children. There's not one report that doesn't say those were beautiful children. . . . Everyone is the source of positive words describing that child. It could not be an accident. . . . I feel that pain every day. That's my loss."

"You're beginning to repeat yourself somewhat," Judge Rothwax finally interrupted him. His tone was uncharacteristically merciful, for he was not a man who had much patience with repetition.

"Thank you, your honor," Steinberg said, sitting down immediately. "I have nothing more."

ONCE MAURY TERRY played back for me one of his interviews with Steinberg: "Lisa was a little reporter," I heard Steinberg say in his raspy, feverish whine. "She was a little reporter."

But all Lisa Steinberg has left us in the way of a report are some drawings she did during the last week of her life on the sketch pad that was later found beneath the beige couch.

With a black crayon, Lisa labeled one of her pictures MOMMY. In this picture, Hedda Nussbaum has a face with no features; orange hair flames out from around a blank circle. A large portion of this drawing has dense crayon scribbles over it. Maybe after Lisa finished, she was afraid she'd revealed too much. Still, you can see one of Hedda's arms thrusting forward very plainly. A large, thick, forceful arm. The hand at the end of it bristles with sharply pointed fingers.

The drawing marked DADDY on the facing page has even heavier crayoning over it. Nothing is left of Joel Steinberg except two enormous, obliquely slanted, ovoid black eyes.

Elsewhere, usually in the very lightest pencil, Lisa Steinberg drew herself. A tiny, freckle-faced ghost, a girl without arms.

On the first two pages of the pad is a story about a little animal. It was lost in a dark wood. "It krad and krad."

Lisa Steinberg was a child lost in a dark wood.